Dan and Jimmy have been great sources of wisdom in my life. I love that they wrote *Daily Wisdom for Men* to share incredible words of wisdom from the Word of God with you. Now you can benefit from their guidance as I have. I highly recommend you read this book.

Jon Gordon, author of fifteen bestsellers, including *The One Truth* and *Energy Bus*

Daily Wisdom for Men is truly a great, daily reminder for men to live their best and bring the kingdom of God here and now. Use this devotional to get your heart and mind set on the things that matter most.

Trent Dilfer, Super Bowl XXXV champion quarterback and the head coach at the University of Alabama at Birmingham

Men are under constant attack today. Their integrity, marriage, fatherhood, and manhood are being challenged nonstop. They need help! This daily devotional offers bucketloads of practical encouragement.

Richard Blackaby, author of *Experiencing God* and *The Ways of God*

If you need a daily spiritual challenge to help you step up and step into life, this book is for you. Every day, you'll receive a short, powerful, inspiring, practical jolt of spiritual adrenaline that will help you be the man you long to be.

Chip Ingram, founder and CEO of Living on the Edge and author of *True Spirituality* and *The Real God*

Some boys never grow up to become men. Mature men have a daily habit of looking in the mirror to assess who they are and who they need to be. Dan and Jimmy have created this daily devotional to be that mirror for us. Every page challenges men to reflect and live that day in a God-honoring way. If you want to mature as a man, read and apply each page one day at a time.

Dan Webster, founder of Authentic Leadership Inc.

Practical and gritty! Dan and Jimmy have written a devotional that is by men and for men. Their words echo the never-changing truth of God's Word to challenge and encourage men in an ever-changing world.

David Meyers, president of Christian Business Men's Connection

Jimmy and Dan are the real deal. They are authentic men of God seeking to love, live, and lead like Jesus while encouraging other men to do the same. In a world where the hurricane winds of an anti-God culture seek to blow men off course, we need tools like *Daily Wisdom for Men* to help us navigate back to the narrow road that leads to true life, freedom, joy, and purpose—to find God's kingdom way and finish this life well.

Dan Anderson, president and CEO of Kingdom Way Ministries and the national ministry director of Fellowship of Companies for Christ International

BroadStreet Publishing® Group, LLC
Savage, Minnesota, USA
BroadStreetPublishing.com

Daily Wisdom for Men: A 365-Day Devotional
Copyright © 2024 Dan Britton and Jimmy Page

9781424565603 (faux leather)
9781424565610 (ebook)

Cover and interior by Garborg Design Works | garborgdesign.com

Printed in China

24 25 26 27 28 5 4 3 2 1

DAILY
WISDOM
for MEN

A 365-DAY DEVOTIONAL

DAN BRITTON & JIMMY PAGE

BroadStreet
PUBLISHING

We dedicate this book to the most important men in our lives—
our grandfathers, fathers, brothers, and sons.
They have lived out Proverbs 27:17:
"Iron sharpens iron, and one man sharpens another" (ESV).

Pop, Edward T. Britton II

Dad, Edward T. Britton III

Brothers, Steve Britton and Dave Britton

Sons, Elijah Britton, Austin Muck, and Garrett Shondelmyer

Grandson, Jesse Daniel

Grandpa, Howard L. Page

Dad, Raymond Page

Brother, John Page

Sons, Jimmy, Jake, and John

JANUARY

VISION EYES

Where there is no vision,
the people perish.
PROVERBS 29:18 KJV

Craig MacFarlane is blind, but he has great vision. At age two, a tragic accident left him completely blind, but he turned his defeat into victory by becoming a world-class athlete who won over one hundred gold medals in sports like wrestling, track and field, and downhill skiing. Craig has a powerful inner vision that fuels his drive to overcome. He has motivated millions with his vision to be the world's greatest blind athlete. Craig may be blind, but he can see.

It has been said, "One person with vision in their eyes can multiply and change the world." Since the beginning of time, men who have eyes with vision have shaped and changed history. They saw things differently. There was a vision that was born deep in their soul, and it changed the way they lived—and the way others lived too. They had vision eyes.

A vision without action is a daydream, but action without vision is a nightmare. There are some great ways we could define *vision*. John Maxwell defined *vision* as "a desired future; a picture of something that I don't possess right now, but it is something I want to see and experience, and something I want the people I am leading to experience."[1]

Vision is not simply a goal, an objective, or an item on your to-do list. Vision is both seeing and doing. It makes the impossible become possible. As blind and deaf writer Hellen Keller is credited with saying, "It is a terrible thing to see and have no vision." Vision is a dream God has put on your heart that is bigger than yourself and, if accomplished, will bring glory to God and change people's lives.

Father, give me vision eyes so You can use me to impact the world. Amen.

---

1   John C. Maxwell, "Turning Vision into Reality," interview by Ron F. McManus, *Enrichment* (Winter 2000): 21, https://enrichmentjournal.ag.org.

SEEK DISCOMFORT

As servants of God we commend ourselves in every way:
in great endurance; in troubles, hardships and distresses.

2 CORINTHIANS 6:4

Life is good, but it can be hard too.

Resilience is the ability to go through a lot of really hard stuff and bounce back. It's a mix of grit, toughness, and confidence. It's one of the most important qualities we can develop. Resilience isn't a one-time thing but an all-the-time thing. We're wired to desire comfort, pursue the easy path, and avoid pain. But resilience requires that we seek out discomfort. We see adversity as an opportunity to grow and get better.

As you take on greater challenges, you will increase your capacity to face trials and to handle, get through, and use failures. They will make you stronger and help you overcome even bigger obstacles.

Paul knew discomfort and hardship very well, and he didn't see them as things to be avoided. Paul saw discomfort as refiner's fire: a way of becoming everything he was made to be.

Spartan Racing, which involves challenging obstacles, has become a perfect way for me to develop resilience. It drives me outside my comfort zone and forces me to prepare for the pain and suffering of the race. The more I avoid discomfort, the less discomfort I can tolerate. The exact opposite is true too. To be your best, seek discomfort. Get comfortable being uncomfortable. Do hard things and use those challenges to get ready for and capable of growing despite every storm.

Father, help me seek discomfort on the way to becoming a resilient man of God, able to weather all storms of life. Amen.

NEVER GET GOOD AT

*"People look at you and think you're saints,
but beneath the skin you're total frauds."*
MATTHEW 23:27–28 MSG

We have witnessed the exposure of the moral failures of key Christian leaders and pastors. Every time I learn about what was happening behind the scenes, my heart breaks for the leader, their family, their organization, and the body of Christ. We all suffer when someone falls.

Brennan Manning said it best: "The temptation of the age is to look good without being good."[2] When we value behavior over being, we're driven to look good without being good. This is plain old hypocrisy.

There is wisdom in creating a never-get-good-at list. If we get good at these things, we will fail at living in Christ. So never get good at

- learning without transformation,
- repenting without brokenness,
- leading without humility,
- giving without sacrifice,
- speaking without blessing,
- praying without listening,
- worshiping without passion,
- loving without commitment,
- dreaming without action, or
- living without Jesus.

Let's commit to being walking, talking, living examples of what God can do in and through us. As men of God, let's be the real deal.

Father, no more faking it. No more hiding sin. Reveal to me where I need to stop looking good without being good. Amen.

---

2   Brennan Manning, *The Ragamuffin Gospel* (Colorado Springs, CO: Multnomah, 2005), 126.

HARD VERSUS IMPOSSIBLE

"What is impossible with man is possible with God."
LUKE 18:27 CSB

There's a difference between hard and impossible. What we think is impossible is usually just hard. The Navy SEALs say when you feel like quitting, you're only 40 percent of the way there. Having gone through leadership training with SEALs and my leadership team, I experienced this firsthand. Now their 40-percent rule rattles around in my head whenever I work out.

Many times in life, we feel like we have nothing left only to discover we had more than we thought. It may be with a difficult relationship, a challenging health issue, or a deep financial crisis. When we are in the middle of it, it often seems impossible to fix or get through. We may feel like quitting or giving up. But almost everything we face in life is just hard, not impossible, even when it doesn't work out the way we hope.

We have the power of the Holy Spirit living in us, the same power that raised Jesus from the dead. And while there are no promises that life will be easy, we know nothing is impossible with God. Our greatest limitation is often in our head. We don't think we can do it or that things will change. We often give up before a breakthrough. Next time you're facing something that seems impossible, remind yourself it's probably just hard. And then rely on Jesus to get you through it—no matter how the story ends.

Father, remind me that no matter how impossible it seems, with You it's just hard. Amen.

STOP THE ME MONSTER

Each one of us is to please his neighbor for his good, to build him up.
ROMANS 15:2 CSB

My favorite comedian is Brian Regan. In one of his routines, he talks about running into a "Me Monster," a guy who talks for everyone else and tries to top everyone's story. Identifying Me Monsters is easy because they're completely consumed with themselves. Me Monsters lurk in sport teams, schools, businesses, communities, and families.

The first full-blown Me Monster I encountered was a teammate in college who was excited after a tough loss just because he scored his goals. Despite the team's performance, his excitement about how well he played and what he did on the field was vividly evident. What bothered me the most was I realized I had the same selfish tendencies, but they were hidden in my heart. I was consumed with my own play, not wanting to celebrate other players' successes or join with the team to mourn our loss.

We need to kill the Me Monster daily. We need to crucify our old self so Christ can live in and through us. When we become a living sacrifice, we crucify the Me Monster.

Do you have too much pride and not enough humility? Too much selfishness and not enough servant attitude? Too much self-promotion and not enough celebration of others? Commit to celebrating the successes of others regardless of your own success. Stop the Me Monster in you.

Father, reveal my pride and selfishness. Heal me of my pursuit of self and teach me how to die to myself every day. Amen.

GREAT POWER, GREAT RESPONSIBILITY

As a prisoner for the Lord, then, I urge you to live a life worthy of the
calling you have received.

EPHESIANS 4:1

In the *Spider-Man* comics and movies, Uncle Ben delivered an iconic line
when he reminded his nephew, Peter Parker, that "with great power comes
great responsibility." He knew power could be used for good or bad, for
selfish pursuits or the greater good. Power must be tied to a sense of moral
responsibility.

Too often we get confused about the essence of true power. We think
power is in our position of leadership, our bank account balance, or the people
we know. But that's not true power. True power is in the inner man. It's in the
strength of our character and our surrender to the Spirit. Power is strength
under the direction of God. All other power is called force. Someone can force
someone else to do something, but that's motivated by control, not love. Force
produces anger, resentment, and rebellion. Power attracts. Force destroys
relationships, but power brings love and unity.

Ephesians 3 says true power comes when you are rooted in the love of
Christ (vv. 17–18). When you are rooted in love, you don't worry about what
other people think. You don't try to impress. Instead, you are free to love fully
and to leverage everything you have for the blessing and benefit of others and
the glory of God.

When Paul encouraged us to "live a life worthy of the calling," he was telling
us to surrender to God, follow the leading of the Holy Spirit, and love others.

Father, make me into a man of love and power for the good of others. Amen.

DON'T BE STUPID

As iron sharpens iron,
so one person sharpens another.
PROVERBS 27:17

Something in us as men says we can stand alone; we don't need others. We are self-disciplined and independent. I once heard an athlete say, "We would have a great team except for all my teammates." Yes, we talk team, but we value self.

This also happens in our spiritual lives. We fall into a trap of isolation. But the Christian life is a team sport. There is a great African proverb that states, "If you want to go fast, go alone. If you want to go far, go together." Isolation is the Christian's silent enemy. There is pride in isolation. We begin to think we can live our faith through our own power. Once we distance ourselves from those who know us best, the absence of accountability can bring many unhealthy changes.

Accountability needs to be a nonnegotiable in your life. It stops the sin of isolation. So many leaders have gone down in flames because they did not have someone to hold them accountable. Jesus and His disciples modeled accountability, and numerous verses reveal its value. Jesus even sent out His disciples in pairs. Accountability allows men to live for Christ with greater purity and passion. Don't be stupid and think you can live for Christ without being connected. Let's sharpen each other. Live the Christian life as it is intended to be lived: as a team sport.

Father, help me be open and transparent with at least one other man and welcome accountability. I don't want to isolate myself. Amen.

PERFECTION:
THE ENEMY OF PROGRESS

"My grace is sufficient for you,
for my power is made perfect in weakness."

2 CORINTHIANS 12:9 ESV

Perfection has prevented plenty of great ideas from coming to fruition. In fact, perfectionism almost always leads to procrastination (at best) and complete paralysis (at worst). No great project or calling can be completed without progress, but too often, God gives us an idea or asks us to do something, and we fail to follow through because we're afraid the results won't be perfect.

How many times have you been compelled to do something only to let the idea grow cold with procrastination? How many times have you put an idea on your to-do list with your best intentions to do it only for you to never do it? Unfortunately, this is a pretty common occurrence for men. Many of your ideas are inspired, and if you act on the inspiration, they will probably bless somebody else or even lead to more opportunities. Not acting on them is a sad, unfortunate cost of procrastination.

Intentions without actions are dead. Just like faith without works is dead. We are made to act on our intentions. We are made for action. The worst decision is no decision. The worst action is no action. Progress is the antidote to perfection. One step after the other will move you in the direction of completion. Progress leads to happiness, joy, and deep satisfaction. And when you act out of obedience to a God-inspired idea, you will glorify God in the end. Take a step forward and let progress be your guide.

Father, help me turn my intentions into actions that lead to progress for Your glory. Amen.

ONE PRAYER FOR LIFE CHANGE

"Lord, teach us to pray."
LUKE 11:1 ESV

I believe one prayer has the power to transform lives. I usually utter it dozens of times throughout the day—most of the time out loud. It is a two-word starting point. This prayer has helped me, as a man of God, to understand both the simplicity of prayer and the power of God. What is the prayer?

Yes, Lord!

When we pray these two words, we acknowledge God is in charge, and we are not. We give up control and place all our trust in Him. When we simply pray, *Yes, Lord!* we are responding to His leading and direction. We are placing Him in charge of our lives.

Yes, Lord! is a prayer of

- surrender,
- obedience, and
- confession.

This prayer places God first in our lives. We reboot our hearts and return to what is most important: God as our Savior and source. When we say yes to God, we are saying no to everything else. It places the Lord Jesus Christ at the center of our lives.

Pray the prayer that can change your life and the lives of others. *Yes, Lord!* is a breakthrough prayer that can be used to revitalize your prayer life. The Lord is pleased when He hears you speak these two words. Pray them aloud. Pray them silently. Whatever you do, just pray them. Then you'll experience His power and presence in your life.

Father, I give You my life. I need Your power and presence. Guide me to improve my prayer life. Teach me to pray. Amen.

BUILD A BOAT

When everything was ready, the LORD said to Noah, "Go into the boat with all your family, for among all the people of the earth, I can see that you alone are righteous."

GENESIS 7:1 NLT

Noah was a righteous man living in unrighteous times. He built an ark at God's instruction to preserve life amid a world drowning in wickedness. Just as Noah built the ark, we, too, are called to construct a "boat" of righteousness to preserve our culture for Christ.

God gave Noah the blueprint for the ark, and it took him and his sons about 120 years to complete. Just as Noah followed God's ark blueprint, we must follow God's Word as our blueprint for righteousness. Hebrews 11:7 tells us, "By faith Noah, when warned about things not yet seen, in holy fear built an ark to save his family." Noah's ark served as a refuge for his family and any who would join them. In the same way, our lives should be a refuge of love, faith, and virtue for our families and communities. Ephesians 5:25 reminds us, "Husbands, love your wives, just as Christ loved the church and gave himself up for her." We have a duty to protect our family members' minds, bodies, and spirits and to be a shelter for everyone we encounter.

Noah faced ridicule and doubt from his society, but he remained steadfast. We may face challenges, but our boats of righteousness will withstand the flood of worldly temptations. After the flood, Noah's family helped rebuild civilization. We have the privilege of rebuilding and renewing our culture for Christ. Men, let's start today.

Father, help me build an ark of righteousness that protects everyone I influence. Amen.

OPEN KITCHEN

We loved you so much that we shared with you
not only God's Good News but our own lives, too.

1 Thessalonians 2:8 nlt

In an open-kitchen restaurant, you can watch cooks prepare the food as opposed to a typical restaurant where food is prepared behind closed doors. A friend of mine from Asia uses this concept when hiring staff and identifying leaders. Before hiring, he looks for open-kitchen people: those willing to do life with him and his team. He gets to know prospective staff members by meeting their family, going to their church, and getting to know their friends.

An open-kitchen philosophy has three key ingredients:

1. Transparency: We should share not only the gospel but also our very lives. Transparency creates a culture of authenticity because everything is on the table—not under the table.
2. Time: In a microwave generation, we don't have time to wait and let something simmer and slow cook. An open-kitchen mindset errs on the side of slowing down and letting time reveal true colors. It takes time to walk with someone and see them at their best—and their worst. But it's worth it.
3. Trust: Trust is the result of transparency and time. Once trust is established, an open kitchen unfolds. Trust means there is freedom to be yourself. Communication goes to a whole new level.

Living with an open-kitchen mindset has incredible benefits: unity, harmony, chemistry, understanding, and connection. It is always easy to impress from a distance, but it's hard to impact up close. Let's pursue an open kitchen in all areas of life. It's worth it.

Father, it is hard to be transparent, slow down, and trust. Help me pursue an open kitchen in all areas of life. Amen.

ONE THING. EVERYTHING.

"Whoever is faithful in very little
is also faithful in much."

LUKE 16:10 CSB

How you do one thing is how you'll do everything.

I can still hear those words ringing in my ears. So much wisdom packed into a simple statement. If you cut corners in one area of life, you'll cut corners in every area. If you don't care about the quality of your work, you won't care about the quality of your relationships or health. The negative effects of compromising on little things and the positive effects of paying attention to little things are obvious. Little things matter. Like making your bed with excellence when you wake up. Or dressing well to present yourself in a professional manner. All these little things add up.

As a dad, convincing my kids that little things mattered was a challenge worth tackling. From making sure they did their morning routines to inspecting the quality of their work, if I accepted half-done work or a half-hearted effort, I got more of it. And I knew it meant I wouldn't be able to count on them to do something with excellence the next time I asked.

Little things matter to God. Those who are faithful with little things are trustworthy. They can be counted on. And God tells us that those who are faithful with the small, insignificant tasks of life will be even more diligent with the important stuff. Being faithful is a matter of consistency, integrity, and trust. Do the little things with excellence today.

Father, help me be faithful with the little things so You can trust me with the big things. Amen.

GOD DAYS

Teach us to number our days carefully
so that we may develop wisdom in our hearts.

PSALM 90:12 CSB

Psalm 90 is the oldest of the 150 psalms in the Bible. Moses wrote it as a prayer, asking God for instruction and revelation: "Teach us to number our days." He asked God how to make every day count, so he even threw in the condition of "carefully," realizing that slowing down is key to seeing every day as a gift from God.

I love the second part of this verse: "So that we may develop wisdom in our hearts." More than ever, we need wisdom. Daily! When we count our days, we make our days count, and we grow in wisdom. A great definition of *wisdom* is "seeing things the way God sees them." When we view every day in this way, there is no waste. Every day counts. When every day counts, we don't have just good days, but we have God days. Not perfect days but God days. God days are days with His fingerprints all over them. He is working and using the good and the bad for His purposes. Each day is filled with mission and meaning. No wasted days, just God days.

Here are three reasons to believe the best is yet to come:

1. God is in control.
2. God is good.
3. God wants the best for you.

When we count our days as men, we make our days count. No more wasted days or even good days. Just God days ahead.

Father, I want more wisdom. Help me see things the way You see them. Make today a God day. Amen.

INTO THE STORM

We are afflicted in every way, but not crushed;
perplexed, but not despairing; persecuted, but not abandoned;
struck down, but not destroyed.

2 CORINTHIANS 4:8–9 NASB

Life is full of storms. Sometimes we anticipate them, and other times we get surprised by them. But rest assured: storms will come.

Because of the Rocky Mountains in the west and the great Kansas plains in the east, Colorado has a unique climate that allows for both cattle and bison to roam freely in close proximity. Cattle and bison are similar in many ways, but one distinction is worth noting: how they react to storms.

Cattle see a storm coming and scatter. They run away in fear, believing they can avoid the storm. In the end, it always overtakes them. Their frantic running scatters the herd, and this keeps them in the storm longer—extending their pain and discomfort.

The bison, on the other hand, see the storm and run into it. They come together as a herd and run straight into the storm. By moving toward the storm, they shorten the time they spend in it, and this reduces the negative impact. By staying together, they defeat fear and remain encouraged. They can and do overcome it together.

The question for today is this: Will you act like the bison or the cattle? Will you confidently face the storm with faith? Or will you run away in fear? Will you come together in unity, or will you scatter? Choose to weather the storm and emerge on the other side better, more united, and stronger.

Father, weather the storms of life with me. Don't let me run away in fear, but help me face them. Amen.

I HAVE A DREAM

The LORD said to Samuel, "Do not look at his appearance or his stature,
because I have rejected him. Man does not see what the LORD sees, for man
sees what is visible, but the LORD sees the heart."

1 SAMUEL 16:7 HCSB

In his "I Have a Dream" speech, Martin Luther King Jr. said, "I have a dream
that my four little children will one day live in a nation where they will not be
judged by the color of their skin but by the content of their character."[3] This is
one of the most powerful and influential speeches ever given in the history of
our nation.

Unfortunately, we judge ourselves based on our best day, and we judge
others based on their worst day. We judge others based on their actions or
appearances, and we judge ourselves based on our intentions. This makes us
feel better about ourselves. If we're honest, we know that even our character
wouldn't be a pretty way to be judged. It is by the grace of God that our
unrighteousness has been replaced by His righteousness.

David wasn't chosen because of what was seen but because of what was
unseen. God didn't choose David because of David's character or because he
would live a perfect life. God chose him because David was "a man after my
own heart; he will do everything I want him to do" (Acts 13:22). David loved
God and pursued Him.

What if you could see what God sees in you—the man He dreams for you
to be? What if we strived to live up to God's dream for our lives? What if we
could see the best potential in others? Even though we will all make mistakes
and fall short, God is not done with us yet.

Father, help me see as You see, not the external but the internal. Amen.

---

3   Martin Luther King Jr., in "Read Martin Luther King Jr.'s 'I Have a Dream' Speech in Its
Entirety," NPR, last updated January 16, 2023, https://www.npr.org.

THE POWER OF YOUR WORDS

Gracious words are a honeycomb,
sweet to the soul and healing to the bones.

PROVERBS 16:24

As men, we are often known for our strength, actions, and leadership. But our words have tremendous power. Our words possess the ability to bring life or death, blessing or destruction, encouragement or despair. We must choose our words wisely because they will shape our relationships, families, and even ourselves—for better or worse.

Let's be honest: the world is a super negative place right now. Just as a single spark can ignite a flame, our encouraging words can ignite the spirits of those who feel defeated, discouraged, or lost. We have the capacity to speak life into tough situations. By choosing to use our words to encourage others, we become catalysts for positive change in the lives of those we encounter.

In contrast, words spoken in anger, criticism, or judgment can wound deeply, leaving lasting scars on others' hearts. Just as fire can consume, our negative words can destroy relationships, erode trust, and hinder personal growth. It is our responsibility to guard our tongues and restrain our impulses, ensuring our words align with the love, grace, and mercy God has shown us.

People are counting on us to speak words of life, to build up rather than tear down, to encourage rather than discourage, and to inspire rather than crush. By doing so, we honor God and reflect His character of love and compassion to those around us. Our words have the power to shape destinies and even turn others toward God.

Father, thank You for the gift of words. Help me speak life and encouragement and be a positive force for good. Amen.

CONSISTENCY IS THE KEY

My dear brothers and sisters, stand firm. Let nothing move you.
Always give yourselves fully to the work of the Lord.

1 CORINTHIANS 15:58

My college coach loved to work over the officials during our games. He used phrases to get under the officials' skin like, "Ref, you are consistent in that you are inconsistent!"

Even though the phrase was not directed toward me, I have often reflected on how that phrase applies to me. Regardless of how consistent we intend to be about what really matters in life, all of us still fall short at times. Inconsistency leads to a breakdown of trust and a delay in growth. But consistency leads to continual forward progress. With consistency, we become steady, reliable, and persistent. Are you consistent or inconsistent?

Consistency is a common ingredient of an uncommon life. When we believe little things can become big things, we understand the power of consistency. When we do the little things right, we will see big life changes.

Paul was always challenging followers of Christ to be consistent and fully committed. In his epistles, he wrote about bone-crushing discipline, eye-popping faith, out-of-bounds generosity, and walk-through-fire consistency. In 1 Corinthians 15:58, Paul encouraged us to do four things to produce consistency:

1. Stand strong.
2. Be immovable.
3. Excel in kingdom work.
4. Trust in God for the results.

A consistent life always leads to an obedient life, and an obedient life always leads to an abundant life. Fruit comes from a consistent life, even when we can't yet see it.

Father, I long to experience the power of consistency. Mark my life with unwavering commitment that will not crumble under changing or difficult times. Amen.

CONTROL YOUR THOUGHTS

We take captive every thought
to make it obedient to Christ.

2 CORINTHIANS 10:5

Throughout the Spartan Beast obstacle race back in 2016, my sons and I faced mental and physical challenges and adversity. Facing 13.1 miles, thirty obstacles, and trips up and down the mountain carrying a sandbag, log, or bucket of rocks brought the internal dialogue of doubts and physical fatigue. Mile thirteen proved to be particularly tough, partly because we thought we would be nearing the finish line, but we suddenly faced the reality that there was a long way to go. My body was failing, and my mental game wasn't fairing much better.

One of the greatest things about sport is that it mirrors life and can develop the internal character we need to be successful. We're faced with opportunities to overcome challenges and obstacles or to shrink back.

As my sons and I faced the physical suffering of the competition and the uncertainty of how much farther we had to go, we had an opportunity to build grit and resilience. The alternative was quitting the race, and that simply wasn't an option. We knew it all started with our thoughts because our thoughts control how we feel and what we do. In the end, we all pushed through and finished.

Here's what we learned: control your thoughts because your thoughts control you. The mental side of life will determine your results. There's no way around it. That's why the Bible focuses so much on our thinking. Real change is only possible if you get hold of your thoughts.

Father, help me control my thoughts by focusing on what's true, positive, right, and encouraging. Amen.

THE LEADER'S PRAYER

Pour out your hearts to him,
for God is our refuge.

<small>PSALM 62:8</small>

Hearing coaches and athletes pray right before a competition is always interesting. Many pregame prayers can sound like a rah-rah talk or a desperate plea for a big win. What is the proper and correct way to pray? Try this leader's prayer:

Lord, I lead for You alone today. In every blessing and every burden I encounter, I celebrate Your goodness and greatness. The way I lead demonstrates my love for You. I stand for the cross and declare my loyalty to You.

When I lead, I feel Your pleasure. My heart longs for Your applause alone. All my abilities are from You. I am under Your authority as my ultimate leader. I will respect and honor all coworkers, employees, clients, and even competitors.

My leadership is my offering to my Savior. I am Your warrior in the heat of battle. I am humble in victory and gracious in defeat. My words bring healing and refreshment that inspire and motivate. I speak words of life.

Legacy isn't a successful career. Instead, I want to see the power of Christ transform the lives of those I lead. Victory is becoming more like You every day. Bless those I lead in great ways and increase their faith and confidence.

In Jesus' name. Amen.

How do we as men pour out our hearts before God so we are spiritually ready for life? We pray.

Father, I admit my prayers are focused on myself. Help me be the leader You want me to be, starting with how I pray. Amen.

SENSE OF URGENCY

Be careful how you live.
Don't live like fools,
but like those who are wise.

EPHESIANS 5:15 NLT

When athletes make the Olympic team, some have the opportunity to relocate to Colorado to train at the US Olympic Training Center (OTC). As they enter the world-class weight room, they are greeted with a sign above the door: "Enter these doors with an unrelenting sense of urgency." Training with a sense of urgency puts them in a position to compete at their best. If they put anything off until tomorrow, they simply will not win.

Athletes who get to train at the OTC understand their opportunity. Every aspect of their life is mapped out. The OTC controls the food they eat, the sleep they get, the training they do, and even the way they think. But it's up to each athlete to bring the sense of urgency—their seize-the-day mentality.

Urgency narrows our focus to things that matter most. Distractions are a direct threat to performance in sport and life. Ordering your priorities is the starting point to living a meaningful life. Keeping the list narrow to the most important people and projects is essential. Urgency also improves time management. If you have all the time in the world, you are likely to waste it. But when now matters, you use your time wisely. Urgency helps you make better decisions, knowing small compromises will take you off course. Today, live with a sense of urgency. Make the most of every opportunity.

Father, help me use my time wisely and live with a sense of urgency so I can bless others and glorify Your name. Amen.

THIS IS A BIBLE

I rise before dawn and cry for help;
I have put my hope in your word.

PSALM 119:147

In 1961, legendary football coach Vince Lombardi, while holding a football in front of him, said to his Green Bay Packers, "This is a football."[4] Could it be any more basic than that?

In the same way, I think Jesus stands in front of us each day and holds up the Word of God, saying, "This is a Bible." He starts with the basics. All it takes is following His direction. So start by taking in the Word of God. Read through the Bible—it will change you. Time after time in my life, I've realized that spiritual victory is directly related to time spent in His Word. Reading the Bible can be a daily battle when we have so much on our to-do lists. Plus, the Enemy doesn't want us in the Word. He knows the Word transforms our lives and others' lives too. He'll do anything to prevent that from happening; he'll throw everything at us to stop us from cracking open the Book of Truth. But don't let him win.

1. Grab a Bible.
2. Open it.
3. Read it.
4. Experience it for yourself.

Get going and dive in. Just you and the Bible. Open it, read it, study it, meditate on it, and linger in it.

Father, give me the desire to read, study, meditate, and linger in Your Word. Amen.

---

4   David Maraniss, *When Pride Still Mattered: A Life of Vince Lombardi* (New York: Simon & Schuster, 1999), 274.

OXYGEN FOR THE SOUL

Encourage one another and build each other up,
just as in fact you are doing.

1 THESSALONIANS 5:11

Just as oxygen nourishes our bodies, encouragement breathes life into our souls. Life is full of challenges, responsibilities, and pressures. At times, we may feel overwhelmed, weary, or uncertain. The antidote is always encouragement. In 1 Thessalonians 5:11, Paul reminded us to "encourage one another and build each other up." These simple words hold profound significance. Encouragement has the power to lift spirits, ignite hope, and renew strength.

Jesus is the ultimate example. He constantly encouraged His disciples and those He encountered. He saw the potential within each person and spoke words of affirmation and inspiration. He looked beyond their failures, weaknesses, and doubts. He focused on their God-given purposes and futures. We, too, can choose to be men who see the best in others and inspire them to reach their full potential.

Most people appreciate encouragement. Most of us are truly thirsty for a positive word, especially from someone we admire and trust. Criticism comes easily, but encouragement takes intentionality. Genuine encouragement requires us to partner with God so we can discern what's going on and give the right words and insight. Encouragement fans the flames of hopes, dreams, and aspirations. An encouraging word from you may be just what someone needs so they don't give up.

Father, help me be a man of encouragement, attentive to others' needs, so I can offer the right word at the right time. Amen.

REAL DEAL

Whoever conceals their sins does not prosper,
but the one who confesses and renounces them finds mercy.

PROVERBS 28:13

Every day, a gorgeous leather Bible with gold-tipped pages sits on my desk as a powerful reminder. It looks nice on the outside, but when you crack open the book, the pages are blank. Yup—not a single word or letter. It appears to be a Bible on the outside, but it actually contains nothing of God's message on the inside. Just blank pages.

A publisher sent me this fake Bible so my team could get an idea for a cover for a future ministry project. But it's now a motivator for me to be the real deal—to be authentic and make sure my life isn't fake like the fake Bible.

As men, we tend to value the external over the internal, the public over the private. We learn to cover up our "stuff"—our hurts, fears, wounds, and gaps—and fake it. We get pulled into the trap of posing—looking good and impressing others. We become experts at covering up our true selves. We've learned how to conveniently tuck our hardships away.

You can't fool the Almighty.

God has a way of slicing through our hearts. His touch grips our souls and exposes our faking. It can be risky to be real, but you can't play it safe when it comes to following Christ. No more faking. God wants you to be a man who is the real deal.

Father, I want to be the real deal. Show me the gaps. No more faking it. I ask for Your touch today. Amen.

PAY ATTENTION TO GOD'S WARNINGS

Listen to advice and accept discipline,
and at the end you will be counted among the wise.

PROVERBS 19:20

God often gives us warnings and guidance to protect us from harm and lead us on the right path. Just as a loving father watches over his children, our heavenly Father desires to guide and instruct us. It is crucial for us, as men of God, to pay attention to these warnings and obey His voice.

God's warnings can come to us in various forms. They may be through His Word, the wise counsel of fellow believers, or the promptings of the Holy Spirit. It's our responsibility to remain attentive and discerning, ensuring we are receptive to His guidance. When we pay attention to God's warnings, we demonstrate humility and a recognition of our need for His wisdom. We acknowledge we don't have all the answers, and His ways are higher than our own.

Ignoring God's warnings, on the other hand, can lead us down a path of destruction and regret. It is easy to become self-reliant, thinking we know what is best for our lives. However, when we neglect to listen to God's voice, we miss out on His protection, guidance, and blessings.

God uses warnings, like rumble strips on the highway, to wake us up, keep us on track, and avoid disaster. He warns us because He loves us. His warnings are not meant to hold us back but to save us from harm and lead us into His perfect will. How is He warning you today?

Father, open up my heart and mind to Your warnings and guidance. Amen.

WHAT'S YOUR WAY?

Preach the word of God. Be prepared, whether the time is favorable or not.
Patiently correct, rebuke, and encourage your people with good teaching.

2 TIMOTHY 4:2 NLT

My dad saw his business as a way to share his faith. Every time he met with people to help them with their investments, he would end each meeting by giving them a favorite devotional, gospel tract, or Bible. He was often invited to speak at churches for their men's breakfasts, and he challenged the men to share their faith in the workplace. Every time he spoke, he set up a resource table in the back with the items he loved to give away when sharing his faith. His favorite resources were gospel tracts. He left one with every tip at a restaurant, and he handed them out at toll booths.

I remember attending one of those men's breakfasts. When my dad ended his talk, he opened it for questions. A young man challenged my dad, saying that he felt tracts weren't an effective way to share the gospel. My dad asked, "What's your way?" He didn't have a way. Then my dad said, "I like my way better than your no way!"

Paul encouraged Timothy to always be prepared to preach, whether the time was favorable or not. *The Message* says today's verse this way: "Proclaim the Message with intensity; keep on your watch. Challenge, warn, and urge your people. Don't ever quit. Just keep it simple."

I can imagine Paul saying what my dad said: "What's your way?" Find your way and proclaim the gospel at all times.

Father, I want to find a way to share my faith with others. Show me how I can share Your good news. Amen.

DO GOOD DEEDS ANONYMOUSLY

"Be careful not to practice your righteousness in front of others to be seen by them. If you do, you will have no reward from your Father in heaven."

MATTHEW 6:1

As followers of Christ, we are made to do good works. In fact, works flow from our faith. Our motivation for doing good deeds is just as important as the deeds themselves. In Matthew 6:1–2, Jesus warned us against seeking recognition or applause when practicing righteousness. Instead, He encouraged us to do good deeds anonymously because the reward from our Father in heaven is far greater than any earthly recognition.

In a world that often glorifies self-promotion and public acknowledgment, Jesus invites us to a different way of living. He teaches us that our acts of kindness and generosity should flow from a genuine desire to serve and bless others rather than seeking personal recognition or validation. Serving and giving with anonymity enables us to help others without expecting anything in return or seeking praise. It is a humble act of selflessness that reflects the heart of Christ.

It's hard to do good things secretly because we want others to think highly of us, but that desire is rooted in pride. Anonymity not only protects our hearts from the snares of pride but also preserves the dignity of those we serve. It allows them to receive help without feeling like they owe us. God sees what we do behind the scenes, and He sees our motives. Let's be on the lookout for ways to meet needs without others knowing it was us. God sees and rewards our acts of kindness done in secret.

Father, teach me to do good deeds with pure motives, seeking to bless others without expecting recognition or reward. Amen.

LIVE WITH INTEGRITY

The integrity of the upright guides them,
but the unfaithful are destroyed by their duplicity.

PROVERBS 11:3

To have integrity means we are committed to Christlike wholeness, both privately and publicly. Proverbs 11:3 says integrity should guide us but that a double life will destroy us. We need to be transparent, authentic, honest, and trustworthy. We should be the same in all situations and not become someone different when circumstances change. *Integrity* means to do what is right even if no one is looking. It is not about being perfect, but as a leader, parent, friend, teammate, or coworker, it's about being a man who is the real deal.

The two key ingredients of integrity are honesty and truth. When these become optional and negotiable standards, gaps in our integrity will develop, and hypocrisy is born. I define *hypocrisy* as "the gap that exists between the public life and the private life." It is the difference between the external life and the internal life. Oswald Chambers nailed it when he wrote, "My worth to God publicly is measured by what I really am in my private life."[5]

There is a constant war in our souls. We do not want others to see us as we really are. We are afraid the gap will be exposed. However, God desires the exact opposite. He wants us to bring the dark things—the things we have buried in our hearts—into the light so He can purify us. He wants every aspect of our lives to be filled with integrity. He wants us to be real, full of integrity.

Father, You want me to live a life of integrity—filled with authenticity, transparency, and honesty. Reveal my gaps so I am the real deal. Amen.

---

5 Oswald Chambers, "The Servant's Primary Goal," My Utmost for His Highest (website), March 17 devotion, https://utmost.org.

AUTHENTIC MASCULINITY

Set an example for the believers in speech,
in conduct, in love, in faith and in purity.

1 TIMOTHY 4:12

Our culture has so distorted the idea of masculinity; we need to reclaim it, rise above the fakes, and demonstrate what a biblical man looks like. This happens through our words, actions, emotions, faith, and purity.

Our words carry weight and influence. That's why we must be men who choose words that build up, encourage, and inspire. And what we say must be marked by truth, integrity, kindness, and wisdom—reflecting the character of Christ.

Our actions should raise the bar and set the standard for others. By demonstrating honor, honesty, and humility, we become trustworthy. We take responsibility for our choices and treat others with respect and dignity.

Love should be the driving force in our relationships. That means we control our emotions and love sacrificially and selflessly, just as Christ loved us. We demonstrate this most clearly in our willingness to serve others while expecting nothing in return.

Faith forms the foundation of our lives. We should be men whose trust in God is evident in how we navigate challenges, make decisions, and pursue our calling as leaders in our families, workplaces, and communities.

Purity is essential in a culture that often glorifies moral filth. We are called to be men who honor God with our bodies, minds, and hearts. That means going against the flow and not conforming. The world needs godly examples of authentic masculinity. Leading by example means living out our faith with boldness and authenticity.

Father, help me embrace authentic masculinity and lead by example in all areas of my life. Amen.

NO LONE RANGERS

Make me truly happy by agreeing wholeheartedly with each other,
loving one another, and working together with one mind and purpose.

PHILIPPIANS 2:2 NLT

Teamwork means that we work together with others and express unity in Christ in all relationships. In Philippians 2:2, Paul encouraged us to be one, united in spirit and purpose. We all need to be on one team—God's team. We need to encourage and equip one another. Do you celebrate and hurt together? We need to be shoulder-to-shoulder with other men, locking arms to accomplish God's work. There are no lone rangers when someone values teamwork.

A lone ranger gets completely lost in his own world and consumed with his own desires. He chooses not to engage. Lone rangers are everywhere. They lurk in every church, in every community, in every organization, and in every family. These men are completely detached and focused on themselves. In fact, they are enemies of true teamwork.

In life, working together is more powerful than working alone, especially when it comes to teamwork. A quote attributed to Mother Teresa highlights the power of teamwork: "I can do things you cannot, and you can do things I cannot; together we can do great things." Many live by the me-rather-than-we philosophy. And unfortunately, life is usually all about "me." As a man, it is hard to die to self every day. But that is the only way we can achieve God's best. Give up the lone-ranger mentality and join a team.

Father, there is only one true team—Team Jesus Christ. Help me lock arms with others and not live as a lone ranger. Amen.

GIVE WHAT YOU HAVE

"I am the vine; you are the branches.
If you remain in me and I in you, you will bear much fruit;
apart from me you can do nothing."

JOHN 15:5

Men are made to serve others. But honestly, we can't give what we don't have. Our ability to make a positive impact in the lives of others stems from our connection to Jesus—the true source of life. In John 15:5, Jesus told us that apart from Him, we can do nothing. Just as a branch remains connected to the vine so it can receive nourishment and bear fruit, we must stay connected to Christ, abiding in Him through prayer, study of His Word, and worship. When we remain in Him, He empowers us with the love, grace, and wisdom we need to make a difference.

Our giving flows out of the overflow of God's love and grace within us. Our actions become an outpouring of His character working through us. If we attempt to serve and give from our own strength or resources, we may quickly find ourselves exhausted, discouraged, or ineffective. When we rely on His truth and the Holy Spirit, our capacity to love, serve, and give multiplies exponentially.

Connecting to Jesus isn't a sometimes thing; it's an all-the-time thing. As we abide in Christ, we receive the abundant resources we need to love, serve, and give. Let us rely on Him, knowing it's through our connection to Him that we find the true source of life and the ability to make a significant impact in the lives of others.

Father, thank You for the privilege of serving and giving to others. Fill me with Your love, grace, and wisdom so I can give. Amen.

360 ACCOUNTABILITY

Refuse good advice and watch your plans fail;
take good counsel and watch them succeed.
PROVERBS 15:22 MSG

For more than thirty years, I have had at least one friend I connect with on a regular basis—someone who asks me tough questions. Accountability has allowed me to live for Christ with greater purity and passion. I need a brother in Christ in my face, making sure I'm doing what I've committed to do (e.g., spending time with the Lord daily, setting aside large amounts of quality time with my family, making wise financial decisions, and training my body). Every aspect of my life is evaluated in 360-degree accountability.

Accountability never works when it's demanding. There can be no judgment or condemnation, only tough love and compassion. It only works when it's voluntary. Then the hidden things can be exposed; God deals with the sin and heals us. Chuck Swindoll said, "Accountability includes opening one's life to a few carefully selected, trusted, loyal confidants who speak the truth—who have the right to examine, to question, to appraise, and to give counsel."[6]

Transparency unlocks authentic accountability and fights isolation. We need other men with whom we can be open, honest, authentic, and vulnerable. When we are willing to confess our sins to at least one trusted friend, we experience healing. God forgives us of our sins, but we experience true healing when confession moves us from the dark into the light. Men, it's time to get 360-degree accountability.

Father, help me be open and transparent with at least one other believer. I don't want to live out my faith alone. Amen.

---

6   Charles R. Swindoll, "Accountability," Insight for Living Ministries, June 20, 2021, https://insight.org.

FEBRUARY

KNOW WHO YOU ARE

If anyone is in Christ, the new creation has come:
The old has gone, the new is here!

2 CORINTHIANS 5:17

The world wants to give us a fake ID based on relatively unimportant characteristics like our race, gender, or even political ideology. But God assigns us our true identity.

When we surrender our lives to Christ, He transforms us from within. The old self, with its sinful patterns and shortcomings, is replaced by a new self empowered by the Holy Spirit. This truth reminds us that our past mistakes and failures do not define us. We are forgiven, redeemed, and given a fresh start.

Ephesians 1:5 declares that God has adopted us into His family through Jesus Christ. As His beloved sons, we have the privilege of belonging to a loving and supportive spiritual family. This truth assures us we are never alone. We have brothers in Christ who can encourage, support, and walk alongside us on this journey.

We are called to reflect the character of Christ in our lives. Galatians 2:20 reminds us that it is no longer we who live, but Christ who lives in us. Through the indwelling Holy Spirit, we are being transformed into the likeness of Christ. His love, compassion, humility, and righteousness become evident in our words, actions, and relationships.

As a new creation, an adopted son, and a recipient of Christ's character, live with confidence, purpose, and a sense of belonging. Embrace these truths and allow them to shape your true identity.

Father, thank You for the truth that I am in Christ. Don't let me accept any other false identity. Amen.

GRANDMA PARKS

May the Master pour on the love so it fills your lives and splashes over on everyone around you, just as it does from us to you.
1 Thessalonians 3:11–13 msg

When you think of undying, unwavering, radical commitment to Christ, who comes to mind? For me, it's a four-foot, nine-inch, sixty-one-year-old grandma named Su-Ja Parks (a.k.a. Grandma Parks). I met her at a sports camp in South Korea during a Fellowship of Christin Athletes (FCA) missions trip. Grandma Parks was serving as a youth pastor in Seoul, South Korea—something she had been doing for thirty-seven years. Talk about undying, unwavering commitment! Each night, I watched her worship God with incredible passion, pray over the kids nonstop, lay hands on the campers, and intercede on their behalf. One night she was on her knees—on the wood floor—for over an hour.

God used Grandma Parks to change my life forever. What gripped me was her commitment to the kids and to the Lord. Year after year, she served the youth in her church. I thought she was just an old lady who volunteered for the camp. Little did I know that she was a spiritual giant. She was anointed by the Holy Spirit to bring life change.

I desire to be found faithful like Grandma Parks. What about you? How can you be radically faithful to the Lord, year after year? I am sure the Lord says to her at the end of each day: "Well done, good and faithful servant!" She taught me what undying, unwavering commitment is all about. Let's commit to being this faithful as we serve the Lord.

Father, I want to be found faithful like Grandma Parks. Teach me what it means to have undying, unwavering commitment to You alone. Amen.

AS A MAN THINKS

As he thinks in his heart, so is he.

PROVERBS 23:7 NKJV

As a man thinks, so he is. Our thoughts have the incredible ability to influence our actions, attitudes, and, ultimately, our destinies. In a world that often defines success solely by material wealth and achievements, we must recognize that true success starts from the inside out. It begins with our minds—where thoughts take root and beliefs get formed. As we cultivate a mindset of strength and resilience, we lay the foundation for a life of accomplishment and fulfillment.

To truly embody success, we must first believe we are who God says we are. Embrace this truth: you are fearfully and wonderfully made, equipped with unique gifts and talents. Choose thoughts that empower, uplift, and inspire you to become everything you were made to be. Guard your mind against negative influences that seek to undermine confidence and derail dreams. Surround yourself with positive, like-minded individuals who challenge you to grow and strive for greatness. Fill your mind with wisdom, truth, and inspiration through reading, learning, and counsel from successful mentors.

Remember: success is not a destination but a journey. Along the way, setbacks and challenges will inevitably arise. Instead of dwelling on failures or defeats, choose to see them as opportunities for internal transformation. Every setback is a stepping stone to building greater character. Do you think that?

Commit to renew your mind daily. Embrace empowering thoughts and align yourself with the limitless possibilities of a God-empowered life. Rise above challenges, inspire others, and leave a lasting legacy of success for generations to come.

Father, guide my thoughts and renew my mind. Help me embrace empowering thoughts and align myself with Your truth and power. Amen.

PRIDE BOMBS

Let someone else praise you, not your own mouth—
a stranger, not your own lips.

PROVERBS 27:2 NLT

While on the phone with a friend having a great conversation, I felt the need to slip in how I knew someone important. I said it to make myself look good—bragging. I had dropped a pride bomb. As soon as I said it, my friend responded, "Why did you have to say that?" I knew why, but I didn't want to confess.

He then said, "If you need encouragement, just let me know, and I will give it to you." Ouch. His words stung. I wanted him to think better of me. My small, "innocent" comment screamed, "Look at me! I'm important! I'm significant!" Have you ever name-dropped to boost yourself up?

Others can hear pride bombs go off a mile away, and they produce the most awful, selfish odor. They reek of self-glorification. As men of God, we are called to a higher standard. He wants us to be humble and to speak with words of grace and thankfulness. I think it's safe to say God wants us to drop encouragement bombs instead of pride bombs. The two bombs are similar, with one exception: the replacement of the word *I* with the word *you*.

Pride bombs say, "I am great."

Encouragement bombs say, "You are great."

If we are truly walking in accordance with the will of God, we will drop encouragement bombs everywhere we go. We will fight the temptation to drop pride bombs.

Will you speak life or death? Encouragement or pride? The choice is yours.

Father, forgive me for dropping pride bombs. Help me find my significance in You and lead me to drop encouragement bombs instead. Amen.

ESCAPE VELOCITY

I can do all this through him who gives me strength.

PHILIPPIANS 4:13

Escape velocity refers to the minimum speed an object needs to break free from the gravitational pull of a planet and venture into space. A rocket leaving earth needs to travel at approximately twenty-five thousand miles per hour to enter orbit. Just as objects need to overcome the force of gravity to soar into space, we need to overcome obstacles that attempt to hold us back from reaching our God-given potential.

Life is filled with challenges that can weigh us down and hinder our progress. These obstacles can take various forms: personal failures, fears, pressures, and expectations. They create a gravitational pull, attempting to confine us within their limits and stop us before we even start. We are called to rise above these limitations and break through.

In Philippians 4:13, Paul affirmed his unwavering belief in the limitless strength he derived from his relationship with Christ. This verse reminds us that we are not alone in our pursuit of overcoming obstacles. God's strength is available to us, empowering us to remove barriers that stand in our way. Just as escape velocity propels objects beyond the gravitational pull, the strength we receive from God propels us beyond the limitations imposed by the world. It enables us to rise above our circumstances, conquer our fears, and embrace the calling God has placed upon our lives.

Remember that you have access to the limitless strength of God. As you lean on Him, you will experience the power of escape velocity, breaking through everything that attempts to hold you back.

Father, thank You for Your strength that gives me escape velocity, helping me overcome obstacles that seem insurmountable. Amen.

IN A SINGLE MOMENT

Put on your new nature, created to be like God—
truly righteous and holy.

EPHESIANS 4:24 NLT

In 1956, as a sophomore lacrosse player at the Naval Academy, my dad made a play that changed everything. His team was down against Syracuse University. Jim Brown, who played for Syracuse, was not only a standout lacrosse player but one of the greatest players to ever play the game. The Orangemen were whipping up on the Midshipmen, and my dad's coach put him into the game to stop Jim Brown.

A few plays later, my dad saw his opportunity. With Jim Brown running toward him, Jim's head turned the other way to catch the ball, my dad knew this was his moment. Running full speed, he knocked Jim into the scorer's table. Bodies flew everywhere; the table flipped over. As a result of the hit, Dad's team was inspired, and they came back and won the game. My dad started every game after that play.

In a single moment, everything can change. One play. One day. One conversation. One event. One person. One moment. And God can use these single moments to change a life forever. My friend Steve Fitzhugh says, "Create a moment for life change, and God can change any life in a moment." As men of God, we must be intentional to create moments for God to work and then remember that He does the changing—not us! Let's expect God to show up and stay on the lookout for when and how He wants to use us.

Father, I desire to create moments for You to show up, and I trust You will change lives through me. Amen.

BRING IT ON

"Your servant has killed both the lion and the bear;
this uncircumcised Philistine will be like one of them,
because he has defied the armies of the living God."

1 SAMUEL 17:36

Life can bring daunting challenges, towering obstacles, and seemingly insurmountable giants. In those moments, we must develop a mindset that says *bring it on*.

The familiar story of David and Goliath shows how to cultivate a bold and unwavering faith in God's power. David, a young shepherd boy, faced a mighty Philistine warrior named Goliath. While everyone else cowered in fear, David's response was different. He didn't shrink back or give in to doubt; instead, he stepped forward with unwavering boldness. David understood that his strength and victory came from the Lord, so he advanced with certainty and confidence.

Like David's confrontation with Goliath, the battles we face are not ours alone. When we have a bring-it-on mindset, we approach challenges with confidence, knowing God is with us. We trust He is greater than any giant that stands in our way. Do you believe and embrace the truth that God equips and empowers you for your battles? This takes surrendering your fears to Him, allowing His strength to flow through you. With this mindset, you can confront challenges head-on, knowing God fights on your behalf.

A bring-it-on mindset also requires a deep reliance on God's promises and His faithfulness. Just as David recalled God's past victories, we, too, can reflect on God's faithfulness and provision. These memories bolster our faith and remind us God is capable of delivering us from any adversity.

Father, help me develop a bring-it-on mindset rooted in unwavering faith and trust that You are bigger than any challenge I face. Amen.

WOULD YOU RATHER?

"If anyone wants to be first,
he must be last and servant of all."

MARK 9:35 CSB

When my kids were young, our family played a great game at the dinner table called "Would You Rather?" We asked questions such as, "Would you rather win a World Series or a Super Bowl?" Once, I decided to ask my three kids, "Would you rather be a great leader or a great servant?"

My ten-year-old, Abigail, said, "Dad, they're the same thing. If you serve someone, you are showing and teaching someone what Jesus would do." Wow! After picking myself up off the ground, I realized she nailed it.

Abigail understood that a great servant is always a great leader, but a great leader is not necessarily a great servant. Maybe the world does not define a great servant as being a great leader, but God always sees them as such.

We need to be men who understand what it means to be a great servant. Being a great servant does not mean serving to become a great leader, but rather, it means sacrificing and dying to self. This is hard! Almost impossible. It means putting the interests of others first. My attitude should be like Christ's by placing others' needs before mine. It is a daily battle, but we need to be men who realize the battle rages every day—the battle to lead or to serve. So I ask you the same question: Would you rather be a great leader or a great servant?

Father, teach me to put the needs of others before my own. Make me a great servant as I seek to follow You. Amen.

AIR SUPERIORITY

Our struggle is not against flesh and blood, but against the rulers,
against the authorities, against the powers of this dark world
and against the spiritual forces of evil in the heavenly realms.

EPHESIANS 6:12

In warfare, gaining air superiority is a critical objective as it provides a significant advantage in achieving victory. In fact, it has been suggested that without air superiority in WWII, the Allies may not have prevailed. Similarly, in our spiritual battles, establishing "spiritual air superiority" through the powerful weapon of prayer is a key to victory. Prayer is our direct line of communication with our heavenly Father. It enables us to bring our concerns, needs, and battles before Him. Through prayer, we access the limitless power and resources of God, who is our ultimate source of strength and victory.

Prayer grants us spiritual authority and dominion over the forces of darkness. It aligns our hearts with God's purposes, activates angelic assistance, and releases divine intervention in our lives and circumstances. Prayer strengthens our faith, fortifies our spiritual armor, gives us wisdom and guidance, and helps us experience God's transformative power.

Ephesians 6:12 reminds us that our fight is won or lost in the spiritual realm. Therefore, we must engage spiritual weapons of all kinds using prayers and requests. Whether it's reading God's Word, praying for ourselves, interceding for others, or engaging in spiritual warfare, we are called to go to war and actively participate in the spiritual battle. As we establish spiritual air superiority through persistent and fervent prayer, we gain the advantage over the Enemy's schemes and tactics. Invite God's presence, authority, and victory into every aspect of your life.

Father, teach me to wage war through prayer, recognizing its importance in establishing spiritual air superiority. Amen.

GUARD YOUR HEART

May these words of my mouth and this meditation of my heart
be pleasing in your sight, Lord, my Rock and my Redeemer.

Psalm 19:14

Just as fruit starts in the root, the condition of our hearts determines the fruitfulness of our lives. To bear much fruit and live a life that honors God, we must diligently cultivate the soil of our hearts.

The heart of man is under attack from virtually every angle. "Everything in the world—the lust of the flesh, the lust of the eyes, and the pride of life—comes not from the Father but from the world" (1 John 2:16). We are tempted to find our value in and satisfy our cravings for physical pleasure, possessions, and power. But none of these pursuits will produce fruit for the kingdom of God. They may build our own little kingdoms, but they will be unsatisfying and a waste of time.

A fruitful life starts with a healthy and pure heart. Our hearts serve as the core of our being, influencing every aspect of our lives—our thoughts, emotions, words, and actions. It's crucial to guard your heart diligently, ensuring it's not exposed to toxic material. Reject harmful temptations. Just as weeds can choke the growth of a fruitful plant, negative influences can hinder spiritual growth. Surround yourself with godly relationships, pursue wholesome entertainment, and be mindful of the impact of the media and culture around you. As we cultivate the soil of our hearts, the fruit of the Spirit—love, joy, peace, patience, kindness, goodness, faithfulness, gentleness, and self-control—begins to flourish.

Father, help me cultivate the soil of my heart so that I may bear much fruit that honors You. Amen.

SOURCE OR SYMPTOMS?

"The beginning of wisdom is this: Get wisdom.
Though it cost all you have, get understanding."

PROVERBS 4:7

Many times when we encounter a running faucet and an overflowing sink that is flooding the room, our instinct is to grab a bucket and mop to soak up the mess. But the most important thing to do first is to turn off the faucet.

Life is full of problems and challenges that require our attention. Instead of addressing the symptoms, true wisdom calls us not just to clean up the mess but to dig deeper and identify the cause. Otherwise, we will never truly solve the problems, and we may face them again. Finding our problems' true source involves examining our thoughts, attitudes, behaviors, and motives. Often, the root causes lie beneath the surface. By seeking God's wisdom, we can gain insight into our own shortcomings, past wounds, or unhealthy patterns that contribute to our challenges.

In relationships, addressing the root causes of issues means seeking understanding and empathy. Rather than reacting to surface-level conflicts, we can approach others with genuine curiosity and a desire to comprehend their perspectives and needs. When someone is trying to express a problem or conflict, responding with simple statements like, "Tell me more" or "Help me understand," can get to the source of the problem rather than just treating the symptoms.

Lasting change depends on getting to the source. It requires courage and humility to confront our own shortcomings or to engage in difficult conversations. However, by facing the cause head-on, we open the door to growth, healing, and transformation in our lives and relationships.

Father, grant me the wisdom to search for, uncover, and solve problems at the source. Amen.

LIFE DETOX

Since we have these promises, dear friends, let us purify ourselves from everything that contaminates body and spirit, perfecting holiness out of reverence for God.

2 CORINTHIANS 7:1

In our pursuit of a healthy life, the concept of following a detox diet to remove harmful substances has gained popularity. This approach can, in certain circumstances, restore health and vitality. But we often face an even greater need for a spiritual detox. Physical detox promotes well-being, but a life detox allows us to live in holiness and honor God. Here's how to do a life detox.

Step one: identify. Discern the harmful influences and behaviors that have infiltrated your life. This includes physical actions and thoughts, words, and attitudes. By recognizing and capturing these toxic elements, you begin the process of renewal.

Step two: remove. Eliminate the toxic behaviors and influences that hinder your walk with God. Just as a surgeon removes cancer, we must remove anything that hinders us from living a life that pleases God. Anger, slander, foul language, lust, greed, jealousy—these are toxic to hearts and minds.

Step three: replace. Removing the bad without filling the void with good puts you at risk of falling back into old patterns. Just as we replace eating sweets with snacking on fresh fruit, we must also replace negative thoughts with positive alternatives. Replace wrong thinking with right thinking, critical words with words of life.

A life detox is a holistic process that purifies us—mind, body, and spirit. As we put off the old and put on the new, we align ourselves with God and experience the fullness and freedom of life in Christ.

Father, purify me from everything that contaminates—mind, body, and spirit—and replace it with thoughts, words, and actions that honor You. Amen.

THE LOVE WIN

Love is patient, love is kind. It does not envy, it does not boast, it is not proud. It does not dishonor others, it is not self-seeking, it is not easily angered, it keeps no record of wrongs. Love does not delight in evil but rejoices with the truth.

1 CORINTHIANS 13:4–6

In 2009, *Sporting News Magazine* published a list of the fifty greatest coaches of all time, and Coach John Wooden was selected as number one. Why Coach Wooden? Maybe it was because he'd won ten NCAA National Championships at UCLA. Maybe because his purpose in coaching was not only to make better players but to make better people. His coaching was marked with love and best reflected by his words: "We can give without loving, but we can't love without giving. In fact, love is nothing unless we give it to someone."[7]

Coach Wooden was committed to teaching, inspiring, motivating, and empowering his players to be the best men they could be. His greatness came from loving his players well.

The love win is when we love others so deeply that everything else becomes secondary. Even if we don't find the word *love* in our job descriptions, we love our coworkers. Even if a relationship gives us strife, we love the other person the way God loves us. Even if we don't win the game, we treat our teammates and opponents with respect. A love win creates a culture of integrity, perseverance, teamwork, belief, and forgiveness. It replaces distrust, bitterness, envy, anger, and jealousy. When we love others, we become more like Jesus.

Father, give me a heart of love so I can love unconditionally. I desire a love win. Amen.

---

7   Fellowship of Christian Athletes, *The Greatest Coach Ever: Timeless Wisdom and Insights of John Wooden* (Ventura, CA: Regal, 2010), 126.

LOVOLUTION

We love because he first loved us.

1 JOHN 4:19

Influence, purpose, strategy, focus, and vision are words commonly associated with leadership. Unfortunately, love is missing from that list. Leaders usually don't talk of creating a culture of love. However, Jesus was the ultimate example of being a love leader. At every opportunity, He drove home the power of love with His disciples. He wanted them to first experience His love and then express His love to others. He created a culture of love everywhere He went.

In Ephesians 5:1–2, Paul revealed how God loves us and said we should imitate Him: "Follow God's example, therefore, as dearly loved children and walk in the way of love, just as Christ loved us and gave himself up for us as a fragrant offering and sacrifice to God." We first must experience God's love. We must be close with Him and not let sin create distance. We must feel His presence daily and walk in love. Then, we can express God's love to others. We will serve without expecting anything in return. We will be the hands and feet of Jesus. Walking in love is a daily exercise as followers of Christ.

Imagine if all leaders would experience and express God's love in this way. Imagine what your household, your workplace, your church would experience. We would create a *lovolution*—that's a love revolution! Let's be men who change the world by our love.

Father, thank You for expressing Your love to me. Help me be Your hands and feet as I show Your love to others. Amen.

IT'S ALL ABOUT HEART

Jesus replied: "'Love the Lord your God with all your heart
and with all your soul and with all your mind.'"

MATTHEW 22:37

When my daughter played her basketball games, I pounded my hand on my heart when she looked over, my sign that encouraged her to play with heart. She always smiled, knowing I meant, "Give it everything you have."

Heart is all about drive, passion, and desire. The Bible talks about the heart over 540 times. Most of us know what it means to give our all on the athletic field, but do we know what it means to give our all when it comes to loving God?

Here are five things I have learned when it comes to loving God with all my heart, soul, and mind:

1. H—Hungry Heart: Do I have a passion for the Word of God, prayer, worship, and fellowship? Do I have a spiritual appetite to feast on things of God?
2. E—Expecting Heart: Do I expect great and mighty things from a great and mighty God? Do I ask for more of God? Do I yearn for God to show up and move in supernatural ways?
3. A—Abundant Heart: Is my heart full of God's love, and is it overflowing with thankfulness? Am I generous and willing to bless others with what I have?
4. R—Real Heart: Is my heart honest, open, and transparent? Is my life whole and complete?
5. T—Teachable Heart: Is my heart tender and teachable? Is my attitude know-it-all or teach-it-to-me?

Jesus longs for us to love Him with our whole heart. Does He have yours?

Father, develop in me a hungry, expectant, abundant, real, and teachable heart. Amen.

FAILURE IS NOTHING

Peter replied, "Even if all fall away on account of you, I never will."
MATTHEW 26:33

Failure is an inevitable part of life. We all stumble, fall short, and face moments of disappointment. Yet our response to failure can make all the difference. The only true failure is giving up.

Peter was one of Jesus' closest friends; he was part of the inner circle. But many people point to Peter for his failures; they use him as an example of speaking before thinking, having little faith, being impulsive, and shrinking back and denying that he ever knew Jesus. That's not what Jesus saw. Jesus could see the future through Peter's failures. He knew what kind of spiritual warrior Peter would become.

When Peter heard the rooster crow, he was crushed by a failure that he had previously claimed would never happen: he denied knowing Jesus. Oh, how the mighty fall. The Enemy was trying to take down one of the most devout followers of Jesus. His plan was to discourage, defeat, and define Peter's very identity by his failure. Satan knew if his plan was successful, Peter would be unlikely to attempt great things. Fortunately, Peter overcame this and helped build the early church and spread the gospel of Christ.

Failure is not the end of your story. Use your failures as fuel for growth and change. Remember that the righteous may fall, but they rise again. Admit your failures, forget the past, and get back in the game. God has great plans for you, and failures cannot hinder what He wants to accomplish through your life.

Father, may my failures serve as stepping stones to growth and success. Amen.

ARE YOU KIDDING ME?

I say, then, walk by the Spirit
and you will certainly not carry out the desire of the flesh.

GALATIANS 5:16 CSB

While watching sports highlights, I saw a scene that made me scream at the TV. *Are you kidding me?* However, it wasn't a great play that caused my reaction. Instead, it was what a player did after his play. With all eyes on him, he reached above his head and pointed to his name on the back of his jersey. I forgot his name, but I didn't forget his gesture. His pride was oozing. It was sickening.

Pride divides. Humility unites. Pride pushes God and others away. Humility unifies relationships. As men of God, we must remember Colossians 3:12 and put on humility every day just like we put on our clothes: "Since God chose you to be the holy people he loves, you must clothe yourselves with tenderhearted mercy, kindness, humility, gentleness, and patience" (NLT). Humility puts our hearts in the right place.

The blessing of humility is intimacy. When we clothe ourselves with humility, there is greater intimacy with Jesus and with others. Don't let pride drive a wedge between you and others. Put others before yourself. Put on humility and watch how God blesses your relationships. Point to His name, not your own. Humility beats pride every single time.

Father, help me give You all the glory all the time. Today, I die to myself so You will live in and through me. Amen.

FENCES AND FREEDOM

Above all else, guard your heart,
for everything you do flows from it.
PROVERBS 4:23

When we moved into our house, the backyard was missing two things: a fence and landscaping. Because of that, we were unable to let our dogs out into the backyard; we would have risked them running into the street and getting hurt or lost, and it would have been an incredible mess. We quickly had a new fence and grass put in.

Once the fence and lawn were completed, we let the dogs out, and they had a blast—running from end to end and exploring every square inch of the backyard. They were finally free! They could run and play without fear and without the possibility of tracking mud into the house. It was a joy to watch.

In Proverbs 4, we are given simple boundaries that lead to life. We are told to guard our heart, be careful with our words, keep on the straight path, and be mindful of where we go. These boundaries are like fences: they bring life, and they help us live a life that is pleasing to God.

God gives us boundaries for our benefit and blessing. Boundaries protect us from dangerous things and give us incredible freedom to enjoy everything within the boundaries. Everything God designs is for our good and His glory. Boundaries provide us a space to be fully alive and creative, a place to fulfill our potential and become our best for God. What boundaries has God given you to experience His freedom?

Father, help me embrace Your boundaries as a blessing meant for my ultimate good. Amen.

INTEGRITY IS HARD

May integrity and honesty protect me,
for I put my hope in you.

PSALM 25:21 NLT

Warren Wiersbe shared in his book *The Integrity Crisis*, "The *Oxford English Dictionary* says that the word [*integrity*] comes from the Latin *integritas*, which means 'wholeness,' 'entireness,' 'completeness.' The root word is *integer*, which means 'untouched,' 'intact,' 'entire.' Integrity is to personal or corporate character what health is to the body or 20/20 vision is to the eyes. A person with integrity is not divided (that's *duplicity*) or merely pretending (that's *hypocrisy*). He or she is 'whole'; life is 'put together,' and things are working together harmoniously."[8]

Living a life of integrity is hard for two reasons:

1. It takes guts to be transparent and not fake it. When you get real, your authenticity will draw others. It always happens. When you become an open book, it doesn't push people away, but instead, it brings them closer. Their respect for, trust in, and love for you will increase. People connect with you when you are vulnerable, transparent, and authentic.

2. Integrity requires courage to do what is right even when it is hard. Many times you'll be the only one pursuing a life of integrity and authenticity. We must be men who are willing to swim against the current. We need to take a stand for what is right and true. Unfortunately, it is getting harder to live a life of integrity. Courage, boldness, and tenacity are key ingredients. As a man of God, it might mean standing alone on your convictions, but God will honor it.

Father, I want my life to be whole and complete. Help me live a life of integrity even when it is hard. Amen.

---

8   Warren W. Wiersbe, *The Integrity Crisis*, expanded ed. (Nashville, TN: Thomas Nelson, 1991), 21.

THE NAME

God exalted him to the highest place and gave him the name that is above
every name, that at the name of Jesus every knee should bow,
in heaven and on earth and under the earth.

PHILIPPIANS 2:9–10

Herb Brooks, coach of the 1980 US Olympic Hockey team that beat the
Soviets and went on to win the gold medal, was known for telling his players
to focus on the name on the front of the jersey, not the name on the back. He
knew the team was more important than the individual. He wanted everyone
to know for whom he was coaching and for whom the players were playing.

I believe it's easier to remember whom we're playing for when we believe
the team name is bigger than our own names. When we put on a jersey, we
represent that name. But there is a name even bigger than a team name. That
name is Jesus, and we represent Him above all else.

In John 14:6, Jesus said, "I am the way, the truth, and the life" (NLT). He
made it clear He is the only path to eternal life. No one comes to the Father
except through Jesus. Many paths may lead to a good life, but only one leads
to eternal life.

Jesus gives us food and drink that satisfy our soul. He gives us wisdom for
every challenge or crossroad we face. He lights our paths. He speaks to us, and
when we listen, we hear His voice. When we put on our jersey, the name on
the front should be Jesus.

*Father, help me live for the name of Jesus. Help me remember I represent You
with my words, my attitudes, and my actions. Amen.*

EYE-POPPING GRACE

God will generously provide all you need. Then you will always have
everything you need and plenty left over to share with others.

2 Corinthians 9:8 nlt

Floyd Harris gave me the same reply every time I asked him, "How are you
doing?": "Better than I deserve." It was his trademark saying. The first time he
answered, I was confused, so I asked him what he meant. He had a one-word
answer: "Grace." Floyd was my godly, eighty-year-old mentor who knew the
secret to life was to live by grace.

Growing up in the church, I have been around the word *grace* a lot. As a
kid, I memorized verses, sang hymns, heard sermons, and read books about
grace—but I rarely took time to understand it. Yes, I knew grace is God's
lavish favor on undeserving sinners, but as I've matured in my faith, I've
learned grace also redeems me, reforms me, and rewards me—even though I
don't deserve it. I have often heard GRACE stands for "God's riches at Christ's
expense," which is a great way to remember God's grace came at a huge
price—Jesus' life!

God has shown me not only that grace is amazing when we receive it but
that it's also eye-popping. We must first experience God's grace before we
express it, and we can only experience grace if we receive it.

Are you experiencing God's grace every day? Remember: grace is simply
getting the good we don't deserve. Ask God for His eye-popping grace today.
If we truly received His amazing, eye-popping grace, then families, schools,
communities, cities, and even countries would be transformed.

Father, help me receive the fullness of grace. Thank You for Your lavish favor.
Your grace redeems me, reforms me, and rewards me. Amen.

GPS

Joseph said to his brothers, "Come close to me...do not be distressed and do not be angry with yourselves for selling me here, because it was to save lives that God sent me ahead of you."

GENESIS 45:4–5

I have a long history of having trouble with directions. It once took me two-and-a-half hours to drive a one-hour trip from Rochester to Syracuse because I made it almost all the way to Buffalo before I realized I was going the wrong way. Today, I don't know what I'd do without GPS navigation. When I enter my destination, it simply calculates the best and fastest route. Whenever I think I know the best way and I ignore the GPS's voice, I hear the familiar "recalculating" prompt that's working to get me back on track.

In Genesis, Joseph probably wished he had a GPS. He encountered a string of wrong turns and detours—his brothers left him for dead, then sold him into slavery, and he was sent to prison for a crime he didn't commit. All along the way, Joseph turned to God as his navigator, and God was with him and showed him favor, especially in the darkest days.

Sometimes we take wrong turns or face detours. Some we have created ourselves and others are the result of other people's decisions. But God always knows where we are, and He has a plan for us. God is always faithful to navigate us to our final destination for His purposes and our ultimate benefit. Don't let a detour derail you from reaching your destination—trust that God's faithfulness will get you there.

Father, may I trust Your voice as You help me navigate the path before me. Amen.

ARE YOU A VRP?

The generous will prosper;
those who refresh others will themselves be refreshed.

PROVERBS 11:25 NLT

In the last several years, there has been a worldwide outbreak of what could be the deadliest disease known to man. Experts say it has the potential to wreak havoc on 100 percent of the world's population. Everyone is vulnerable to it because we're all exposed to those who carry it. This disease is called VDP disease.

VDP stands for "Very Draining Person," and people around the world carry it and transmit it. We have all experienced and felt the devastating effects of being around a VDP. You can identify a VDP by how someone exhibits repetitive negative, pessimistic, complaining, and life-sucking behaviors. It's hard to see VDP disease in the mirror, but others can spot it from a mile away.

Here's the good news: there is one known cure for VDP disease. It's called being a VRP, or "Very Refreshing Person." Large numbers of faith-filled, positive, right-living, energized VRPs are needed to combat the devastating effects of VDPs. VRPs bring healing and relief. They speak words of life into the ordinary and transform it. They breathe encouragement, blessing, and hope into your soul.

Are you a VRP or a VDP? When you walk into a room, do people run, or do they pump their fists into the air, happy to see you? Do you bring life? Your words can unlock God's greatness in others. Be committed to infusing life through your intentional words of nourishment. Let others feast off your encouragement. Be a VRP, not a VDP.

Father, help me be a Very Refreshing Person who blesses others with my words and actions. Amen.

THE POSITIVE TWO

Of the twelve who had explored the land,
only Joshua and Caleb remained alive.

NUMBERS 14:38 NLT

Belief is a powerful force. It's so powerful that God reminds us time and time again to trust in His promises and His power, even when the situations we're facing seem impossible.

In Numbers 13–14, Moses and the Israelites were preparing to enter the promised land. God delivered them from four hundred years of slavery and oppression, and Moses sent out twelve spies to scout out the land. Ten came back with a negative report based in fear. Two came back with a positive report rooted in faith. The positive two, Joshua and Caleb, remembered God's promises and His mighty power to save and deliver His people. In the end, the ten negative complainers were struck down with a plague and died immediately. The rest of that generation wandered around the wilderness until they died just short of experiencing God's promised land. The positive two men, along with a new generation, eventually entered it.

Keeping a positive attitude takes work; it's a mental battle. A positive mindset focuses on the power and promises of God. It confronts challenges head-on. This mindset speaks words of life and encouragement, and it is fueled by a can-do spirit.

When you hear negative reports, make sure your positive voice stands out loud and clear. Be like Joshua and Caleb: rest on God's promises that are found in His Word and rely on His great power over your circumstances.

Father, give me a positive attitude that believes in Your power and promises. Amen.

THE FATHER'S FAVOR

A voice from the heavens said,
"This is My beloved Son, with whom I am well pleased."
MATTHEW 3:17 NASB

The relationship between a father and son is one of the most anointed relationships ever designed by God. In fact, it existed before the creation of the world, as seen in the very nature of God—Father, Son, and Holy Spirit. When Jesus left heaven and became a man, the Father was overjoyed. We see evidence of this when Jesus emerges from the water of baptism and hears His Father's voice.

God's favor rests on His Son, Jesus. In the same way, God's favor and delight rest upon us. When we discover that we are God's beloved, we need to embrace it. Men, have you embraced God's words about how valuable you are to Him? Do you feel His pleasure and affection?

The Father's statement, "My beloved Son," is more than just an approval or validation. It is a manifestation of pure and true love. It's a statement of identity. You are God's beloved; that simply means that you are precious, adored, cherished, treasured, prized, highly regarded, admired, esteemed, and favored. Unfortunately, most men don't experience this and feel they are no good, forgotten, worthless, rejected, and unlovable. No matter what they do, they do not measure up to the Father's expectations. But this is not God's design.

Can you imagine if every man knew he was the Father's beloved? Men would live with security, confidence, and courage. Every man needs and deserves to hear the Father say, "I am pleased with you." Hearing and accepting this will change your life.

Father, I want to know I am Your beloved. Help me fully receive, embrace, and accept this blessing. Amen.

BEHIND THE SCENES

"Your Father who sees in secret will reward you."
MATTHEW 6:18 CSB

The goal of much of what we do in society is to be noticed. Social media is full of our highlight reels, and many of us fall into the trap of caring about views and likes. Even the good deeds we do, if we promote them, can be for attention and rooted in pride. It turns out that self-promotion and recognition aren't very soul-satisfying. Sure, they feel good for a minute, but the feeling never lasts.

It's easy to turn a good thing into a bad thing because of a wrong motive. When we have a desire to do good things in front of everybody so we look good and get the praise, those good things become bad things. And Jesus tells us when we seek the praise and attention of others, we get our reward in full right here and right now.

Jesus tells us to do good things—like pray and give, fast and serve—but to do those things in secret. This is the kind of behind-the-scenes life Jesus modeled. Even when He performed miracles, He often told those He healed not to say anything.

Let's help the behind-the-scenes blessings make a comeback. Don't let everybody know how good you are. Check the motive of your heart. Give anonymously. Pray privately. Make somebody's day. God rewards the good things we do when we don't seek the credit.

Father, help me seek Your pleasure over the praise of others. I want to bless others behind the scenes. Amen.

RUBBER BAND FAITH

Hearing this, Jesus was amazed and said to those following him,
"Truly I tell you, I have not found anyone in Israel with so great a faith."
MATTHEW 8:10 CSB

I think rubber bands are one of the greatest inventions ever. They're simple, practical, and useful. However, rubber bands are useless if they are not stretched. When they extend beyond their standard form, they can hold things together and accomplish their purpose. I always keep a rubber band around my wrist as a constant reminder that God wants to stretch me daily. Faith—like a rubber band—is useless unless it gets stretched.

When we step outside our comfort zones, we are forced to rely on God more than ourselves. This becomes a true test of faith. But God shows up—every time. True faith begins at the edge of our comfort zones. When we are willing to go to the edge and be stretched, God does what we can't do. We need to engage in situations where we whisper, *God, if You don't show up, I am bound to fail. I can't do this in my own strength.*

When we have rubber band faith, we have an opportunity to see God do supernatural things we can't explain. And we'll immediately respond, "Only God could do this!" instead of, "I did it!"

We are made to be stretched.

Men, ask the Lord for rubber band faith—the kind of faith that requires God's Spirit to move. Be bold and courageous. Step out. Let God stretch you so He can accomplish His purposes through you.

Father, I want to live every day with great faith. Today, I ask You to stretch me outside my comfort zone. Amen.

LIMITLESS FORGIVENESS

Peter came to him and asked, "Lord, how often should I forgive someone who sins against me? Seven times?" "No, not seven times," Jesus replied, "but seventy times seven!"

MATTHEW 18:21–22 NLT

Forgiveness is a decision, and we are all called to extend it readily and ask for it humbly. Sometimes it's easy, and other times it's really hard—depending on how serious the issue or offense is.

Some have a hard time finding the humility to ask God to forgive. Others have a hard time forgiving God for things that happened to them. When your pain is fresh, forgiveness can be very difficult. Sometimes you may feel like as long as you hold on to unforgiveness, you can somehow punish the other person. But the truth is that when we withhold forgiveness, everybody loses. We experience the destructive emotions of bitterness, anger, and resentment. The relationship remains divided. If this condition lasts for too long, the relationship could be destroyed.

Matthew 18 gives us a good picture of the kind of forgiveness God expects of us. Peter thought forgiving someone seven times was a huge improvement compared to what the rabbis taught; they only required people to forgive three times. So Jesus' instruction to forgive seventy times seven rocked Peter, especially since the term Jesus used actually meant "countless." Love and forgiveness have no limits.

Forgiveness is easier once we truly realize the size of our sin debt that was canceled at the cross and how much Christ has forgiven us. That gift should motivate us to pass on the same measure of forgiveness to others. God's forgiveness is limitless—shouldn't ours be as well?

Father, Your forgiveness is limitless. Help me willingly extend and ask for forgiveness with humility and grace. Amen.

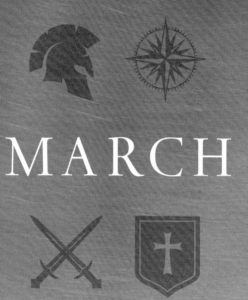

MARCH

GIVE GRACE

Grow in the grace and knowledge of our Lord and Savior Jesus Christ.
To him be glory both now and forever! Amen.

2 PETER 3:18

When my children were young, we taught them how to say grace before eating. This was hard because they had huge appetites and wanted to devour the food before everyone arrived at the table. Even when they said grace, it was often the fastest, shortest prayer ever.

We talk about saying grace, but rarely do we talk, teach, and train on giving grace. Yes, we need to experience grace before we express grace. Ephesians 2:8–9 makes it clear that it is by grace we are saved through faith. Once we have received grace, we need to give it.

Giving God's grace transforms in two ways:

1. Grace shatters a judgmental spirit. I put people into two boxes. The just-like-me box holds the people I like and gravitate toward. I will give them lots of grace. The not-like-me box holds people whom I don't understand and, thus, stay away from. I don't offer them grace, which is judgmental.
2. Grace unleashes a generous spirit. Max Lucado wrote, "Grace walked in the front door, and selfishness scampered out the back…Let grace unscrooge your heart."[9] When we extend amazing grace, it unleashes amazing generosity. We get to lavish favor on the undeserving by being the hands and feet of Jesus.

We are reminded in 2 Peter 3:18 to grow in grace, which is a daily process. Men, let's commit to grow every day in grace—not just to receive it but also to give it.

Father, let Your grace shatter my judgmental spirit and unleash a generous spirit. Show me how to give grace to others. Amen.

---

9   Max Lucado, *Grace: More Than We Deserve, Greater Than We Imagine* (Nashville, TN: Thomas Nelson, 2012), 111–12.

SKIN DEEP

"Woe to you, teachers of the law and Pharisees, you hypocrites!
You clean the outside of the cup and dish,
but inside they are full of greed and self-indulgence."

MATTHEW 23:25

"Beauty is only skin deep." Most of us probably heard that from our parents when we were growing up—especially during our awkward teenage years or when they wanted us to date someone with character and integrity. Even though we all know outward appearance is not always a reflection of what's happening on the inside, we still work really hard to put on a happy face and present ourselves as put together—sometimes hiding who we really are.

Jesus hates it when we spend all our energy on our appearance—the outside versus the inside. He even blasts the Pharisees for looking good in public but being full of greed and self-indulgence. Their outsides were clean, but their insides were corrupt. They appeared to be righteous, but they were actually hypocrites.

Lasting change always comes from the inside out. As Jesus said in Matthew 23, when we clean the inside, the outside gets clean too (v. 26). When our hearts are right, our behavior follows. So often, we try to change our behavior without dealing with the cause of the behavior. Even though it's easier just to cover up the problem, it's much better to deal with the cause. We need to be more concerned with our reality than our reputations. Let's get beneath the surface and become the men of character God made us to be.

Father, help me do the hard work of changing from the inside out. Amen.

THE THREE Rs OF ENCOURAGEMENT

May the Lord grant mercy to the household of Onesiphorus, because he often refreshed me and was not ashamed of my chains. On the contrary, when he was in Rome, he diligently searched for me and found me.

2 TIMOTHY 1:16–17 HCSB

When my wife and I were naming our children, we combed the Bible for some solid, biblical names. When I found my new favorite biblical name, Onesiphorus, for our next child, she quickly said we were not having any more kids!

Onesiphorus is only mentioned twice in the Bible. Obviously, he's not a popular Bible character, but he was well-known to the apostle Paul because of the encouragement he delivered.

From Onesiphorus' example, we learn three key characteristics of encouragement:

1. Encouragement is repeated. Paul wrote, "He often refreshed me." This was not a one-and-done refreshing; Onesiphorus poured out encouragement time and time again. The word *refreshed* means "to cool again"[10] or, as it's also translated, "reviving…like fresh air" (v. 16 AMP). Refreshing needs to be regular and repeated.
2. Encouragement is risky. Paul said Onesiphorus "was not ashamed of my chains." He risked his life by going into prison to refresh his brother in Christ. We need to step out of our comfort zones to encourage others.
3. Encouragement is relentless. The biblical text says Onesiphorus searched hard for Paul. He was relentless in finding his friend, and he did not stop until he found him. Onesiphorus did whatever it took. Encouragers are persistent and tenacious.

Men, we need to be like Onesiphorus and speak words of life—words drenched in hope and healing.

Father, teach me to be an encourager like Onesiphorus—one who brings value and profit with words. Amen.

---

10   Warren W. Wiersbe, *The Wiersbe Bible Commentary: New Testament*, 2nd ed. (Colorado Springs, CO: David C. Cook, 2007), 775.

TEN-TIMES SERVING

She quickly emptied her jar into the trough,
ran back to the well to draw more water,
and drew enough for all his camels.

GENESIS 24:20

Great service is quickly becoming a lost art. But when you get above-and-beyond service, it's like a refreshing glass of ice water on a scorching hot day.

In the story of Rebekah in Genesis 24, Abraham had sent one of his devoted servants to find a wife for his son Isaac. When the servant arrived at his destination, he rested near the well. When Rebekah came to the well, he asked her for water, and she gladly served him.

But what she offered next was remarkable—she offered to get water for his ten camels. At first glance, we may be tempted to say, "That's no big deal." But remember that she had to get the water by hand, and each camel could drink between five and twenty-five gallons of water. Rebekah had no way of knowing how much they were going to drink.

This story is a great illustration of a servant's heart. Rebekah was kind and humble; she responded to the needs of the man, anticipated the needs of the camels, moved quickly, sacrificed, exceeded expectations, and had a pure motive. That's ten-times serving.

A servant always goes above and beyond, especially when he has nothing to gain. That's the kind of life Jesus lived: one of service and sacrifice. As we become ten-times servers, everyone will want to know why we do it. Serving like this will give us opportunities to show the love of Jesus.

Father, help me be a ten-times server and find extraordinary ways to serve others today. Amen.

STEP OUT

We walk by faith, not by sight.

2 CORINTHIANS 5:7 HCSB

In 2002, I was presented with an opportunity to have a larger impact with the Fellowship of Christian Athletes, but it required that our family move from Virginia to Kansas. At first, it felt more like a curse than a blessing because our entire community of friends and relatives lived in Virginia. We were being asked to leave home. Would we respond with great faith or weak faith?

Jesus was astonished only twice in Scripture: once by great faith and once by a lack of faith. In Matthew 8:5–10, we see great faith when the Roman commander had so much faith in Jesus that he asked Him to forgo the journey and just say the words to heal his servant. This was full faith. Big faith. Bet-the-farm faith. In Mark 6:4–6, we see the exact opposite as Jesus was unable to perform many miracles in the synagogue because of the area's lack of faith.

God stretched us in the move. He wanted us to leave the familiar, the safe, and the comfortable. Saying yes was the hardest decision we have ever made as a family, but it has been the most rewarding. God blessed us when we stepped out and walked in faith.

Men, sometimes it's hard to step out because we rely too much on our own strength and play it safe. But ask the Lord to stretch you in all areas of your life and be willing to obey as He leads. It's worth it.

Father, I ask for faith that depends on You showing up. Help me be a man who lives with great faith. Amen.

SITUATIONAL SUFFERING

Join with me in suffering,
like a good soldier of Christ Jesus.

2 TIMOTHY 2:3

Words like *suffering*, *pain*, and *hardships* describe things we generally do not look forward to experiencing. When was the last time you prayed for anything on that list or thanked God for pain, hardship, and suffering? The truth is that most of us will do everything we can to avoid pain and suffering; we would much rather experience God's blessings, favor, and success.

Paul not only experienced these things on a regular basis, but the Holy Spirit also led him into them. I'm not sure I would be eager to do something if God told me that prison was waiting for me. But that's exactly what happened to Paul.

So when Paul instructed Timothy to join him in suffering, Timothy must have known exactly what that meant. He knew there would be suffering if he was bold in his testimony to others about the love of Jesus and that it might even include physical suffering. The comparison to being a soldier must have hit home.

The next time you are suffering through a hardship, remember Paul. God led him into situational suffering to produce everlasting fruit for the kingdom of God. And Jesus taught all the disciples to have the same expectation of suffering. In the end, they knew that their suffering would not be in vain, that a harvest of righteousness would be the result if they did not give up. Are you up for the challenge? Are you willing to go where God leads to testify of His grace, even if it means hard times?

Father, help me see suffering as a means to an end; help me suffer well and be transformed into the likeness of Christ. Amen.

TAMING THE TONGUE

This is scary: You can tame a tiger, but you can't tame a tongue—
it's never been done. The tongue runs wild, a wanton killer.

JAMES 3:7–10 MSG

The average person will have thirty conversations in a day and produce about sixteen thousand words. In one year, these words would fill 132 books with four hundred pages each. Did you know we spend roughly 20 percent of our lives yakking away?

There is a Scottish proverb that says, "When the heart is full, the tongue will speak." Often, people utter something and then quickly say, "I didn't mean that." Actually, they probably meant it; they just didn't mean to say it.

If there is hatred in a person's heart, the tongue will spew criticism. Fear in the heart brings negative words. An impure heart will produce foul speech. An undisciplined heart will result in sloppy language. Hurtful words come from a wounded heart. But, conversely, if there is joy in a heart, encouragement flows. A peaceful heart brings words of hope. Words of blessing come from a secure heart. An honest heart reveals truth.

It's hard to control our words, but God can help us. We need to allow Him to take hold of our tongues and cleanse them. Men, your words can bring daily blessings or curses. The choice is yours—life or death. Every day, others need to hear words of blessing, encouragement, and positivity from you. Don't let a day go by that others don't hear your life-giving words.

Father, thank You for the power of words. Make my heart right so love spills out of my mouth. Amen.

DREAM. PRAY. THINK.

"Absolutely everything, ranging from small to large,
as you make it a part of your believing prayer,
gets included as you lay hold of God."
MATTHEW 21:21–22 MSG

Mark Batterson's book *The Circle Maker* reveals three principles for a purposeful and fulfilling prayer life: dream big, pray hard, and think long.[11]

The first, dream big, helped me ask for the impossible and not limit God. Many things seem like they're too big to ask for, but nothing is too big for God. Here are questions to ask:

- What seems impossible for you that's not impossible for God?
- What giants do you have in your life that are beyond your resources or ability to defeat?

The second, pray hard, helped me not to give up asking, even when nothing seemed to be happening. Daniel prayed for days before the angels were finally dispatched to help win the spiritual battle (Daniel 10:7–14). Here's a question to prime the pump:

- What things have you prayed about casually or inconsistently that you feel conviction to persist in prayer for?

The third, think long, helped me to realize I may not see all my prayers answered now but that I should pray with an eternal perspective. I believe some of my grandma's prayers were answered after she passed away. Here are some questions to consider:

- What prayers are you praying that you may never see the answer to?
- What future prayers are like planting seeds today to bear fruit tomorrow?

When you make your prayer list, ask God for things you think are impossible, stick to it, and trust God for the results.

Father, help me persevere in prayer, expect the best, and never give up. Amen.

---

11 Mark Batterson, *The Circle Maker: Praying Circles around Your Biggest Dreams and Greatest Fears* (Grand Rapids, MI: Zondervan, 2011).

HUMILITY WINS

Don't be selfish; don't try to impress others.
Be humble, thinking of others as better than yourselves.
PHILIPPIANS 2:3 NLT

It is rare but refreshing to see humility demonstrated in the world of sports. I loved watching Matt Stover, former NFL kicker, who pointed to the sky after every kick, regardless of if he made it or missed. It was his way of glorifying God and remaining humble. Matt recognized that God gave him the ability to play, and he pointed to the sky as a regular reminder.

Humility beats pride.

As men of God, we must live out Philippians 2:3 daily. We need to put down our rights and pick up our responsibilities. If Jesus could give up His place in heaven to come to earth, we can give up our pride.

We need to understand that pursuing humility is a lifetime endeavor. Here's a simple list that shows the value of humility over pride:

HUMILITY	PRIDE
Virtue	Vice
Reveals	Blinds
Secure	Insecure
Attractive	Obnoxious
Confident	Arrogant
Responsive	Resistant
Selfless	Selfish
Fruit of the Spirit	Sin

Men, die to self. Never point to yourself. We need to make a total sacrifice of the flesh, pointing toward God. Our lives should bring attention to the only famous one: Jesus Christ. Humility always wins.

Jesus, I want to make Your name great. Remove my pride and selfishness. Amen.

INVISIBLE FENCES

*No temptation has overtaken you except what is common to mankind.
And God is faithful; he will not let you be tempted beyond what you can
bear. But when you are tempted, he will also provide a way out so that you
can endure it.*

1 CORINTHIANS 10:13

Every time I ride my bike, I come across barking dogs. Sometimes they startle me because I get in the zone as I ride; the barking often rudely intrudes on my mental solitude. Every time I see dogs tearing after me, I hope and pray they are either on a leash or contained by invisible fencing. I don't think I would fare too well with my bike shoes, helmet, and spandex bike shorts if there were no fence or leash.

This situation is a lot like temptation. We can often see the temptation coming, and even though we aren't trying to find trouble, sometimes life or even the Enemy brings trouble our way.

But the great news is this: even though temptation will come, we have the power to overcome it. We always have a way of escape. Here are keys to resisting temptation:

- Recognize it early. Now when I ride familiar routes, I know where the dogs live and can anticipate and avoid them.
- Realize that temptation has limits and that you have a choice. Thanks to invisible fences and leashes, those dogs (like temptation) have limited reach.
- Run from it. Sometimes it's best to just get away.

Just like dogs behind invisible fencing have limits, so does temptation. God has given us a way of escape. It's up to us to take it.

Father, thank You for not letting me be tempted beyond what I can overcome or escape. Amen.

FIVE PURITY PRINCIPLES

"Blessed are the pure in heart,
for they will see God."
MATTHEW 5:8

Every year, I develop a one-word vision or theme that narrows my focus for greater impact throughout the year. In 2011, my one word was *pure*. The funny thing was that whenever I shared my word with others, I received silence, blank stares, and awkward conversations. I think they were glad it was my word and not theirs.

Everyone thinks purity deals with one thing: sexual purity. However, sexual purity is only the tip of the iceberg. Purity pertains to every area of life: mind, body, and spirit. It is revealed in our thoughts, words, attitudes, motives, and actions. God revealed five truths during my yearlong experience with purity:

1. Purity ignites intimacy. Fellowship with God demands purity. Sin creates separation and distance. But purity of heart paves the way to transparent, authentic relationships.
2. Purity precedes power. We become God's clear channel of strength and courage when purity paves the way. When we lack purity, we lack spiritual confidence.
3. Purity leads to simplicity. A life of purity is marked with integrity, which brings simplicity. There is nothing more complicated than carrying around sin and secrets.
4. Purity cultivates peace. Sin results in unrest, but purity results in joy. Purity creates a what-you-see-is-what-you-get sense of peace.
5. Purity brings freedom. We discover freedom from guilt and sin when purity is at our core. Too many people are enslaved and entangled in their sin.

Men, pursue purity at all costs. Purity always paves the way to intimacy.

Father, I want intimacy in all my relationships, starting with my relationship with You. Help me pursue purity in body, mind, and spirit. Amen.

GET TO THE ROOT

The heart is deceitful above all things and beyond cure. Who can understand it? "I the LORD search the heart and examine the mind, to reward each person according to their conduct, according to what their deeds deserve."

JEREMIAH 17:9–10

Have you ever picked a weed only to see it reappear a few days later? We all have. I even have weeds that have grown so big they look like trees. If you don't pull the roots, weeds will return. The effort to prune is for nothing.

So often, we try to change our behavior without dealing with our root issues. We're surprised when the same issues surface again and again. We try so hard to stick to a diet, but we fail because we haven't dealt with the fact that we use food as comfort. We put on tons of muscle so we look big or perform on the athletic field, but we don't deal with our fear of failure or rejection and insecurity. We are driven to succeed and spend too many hours at work, but we don't deal with our wounds of never being good enough or failing to meet expectations.

If we don't reach the root, we've wasted our time trying to change our behavior. Even though our lawns may look better if we snip away the weeds, they will return if we don't dig up their roots.

Lasting change requires that we get to the roots of our problems. And in order to do that, we need to let God examine us from the inside out. Only He can reveal what's really going on and help us deal with our roots once and for all.

Father, reveal anything inside me that's preventing me from being everything You have made me to be. Amen.

THREE WAYS OF GUARDING

A judge who says to the wicked, "You are innocent," will be cursed by many people and denounced by the nations. But it will go well for those who convict the guilty; rich blessings will be showered on them.
An honest answer is like a kiss of friendship.

PROVERBS 24:24–26 NLT

When I played professional lacrosse, my coach moved me from offensive to defensive. I quickly learned the fundamentals and how to guard and protect our goal. In sports, we understand the value and impact of great guarding, but do we understand the importance of guarding our hearts?

In the Bible, the Hebrew word for "guard" is interchangeable with the word for "keep," which means "to set a watchman over it." How we guard our hearts is key. Guarding our hearts is done in three tangible ways, all found in Proverbs 4:23–27:

1. Guard your eyes. Access to pictures, videos, internet, TV, and images on social media will affect your heart. If those inputs (like sexual images and immoral behaviors) are bringing impurity, your heart will be polluted. We need to safeguard and protect what we allow our eyes to see. Keep your eyes on Jesus and His path of purity for you.

2. Guard your ears. Messages found in music, media, and other outlets will either build you up or bring you down. Repetitive, negative, or toxic messages will make you sick. Listening to positive or godly messages and lyrics will lift your heart.

3. Guard your steps. The places you go and the things you experience also affect your heart. Using God's Word as a lamp and light will keep you on His path in His footsteps. Be careful about the places you go.

Men, above all else, guard and keep watch over your heart.

Father, guard my heart today because that's where life starts. Amen.

TRUE IDENTITY

The chief official gave them new names: to Daniel, the name Belteshazzar; to Hananiah, Shadrach; to Mishael, Meshach; and to Azariah, Abednego.

DANIEL 1:7

In ancient times, names carried weight. They represented someone's very identity, and they often illuminated a characteristic of God. When the four Israelites were chosen for the Babylonian king's service, their names and their entire identities had to be changed. After all, Daniel means "God will judge"; Hananiah means "the Lord is gracious"; Mishael means "who is what the Lord is"; and Azariah means "the Lord helps."[12]

As Christians, our original identity was restored when we put our faith in Christ. Sin had stolen our true identities; it separated us from God. But you and I have been given a new identity. It's not in name only—God changes the very essence of who we are.

Tragically, millions of people are confused. They have attached their identities to a political party, their favorite sports team, something they possess like a car or house, or a characteristic like skin color or gender. These are all parts of us, but they do not define us. They are not our true identity.

When we place our faith in Jesus, we become a new creation. The old version of us passes away, and a new identity comes. We get set free from our sin and can become everything God designed us to be. We receive the right to be called God's children—part of His family. He adopts us, and we take on His name. As we take on His name, we receive His character.

Father, give me the power and strength I need to stand against the culture and reveal my true identity. Amen.

---

12   C. F. Keil and F. Delitzsch, *Biblical Commentary on the Book of Daniel*, Commentary on the Old Testament 4, trans. M. G. Easton (Grand Rapids, MI: William B. Eerdmans, 1988), 79.

RELENTLESS

We are not those who draw back and are destroyed,
but those who have faith and obtain life.

HEBREWS 10:39 HCSB

When I was growing up, my dad always said, "Work hard. Play hard." We sure worked hard, but I don't remember playing hard. When we did work around the house, he loved to have goals, and we pursued them with everything we had. Nothing got in our way. My dad's middle name should have been Relentless.

It seems as if relentlessness is everywhere these days. There is a Relentless energy drink, Relentless Nike running shoes, *Relentless* movies, and *Relentless* the country music album. But let's define *relentless*. There are several good one-word definitions: "unyielding," "unbending," "determined," "never-ceasing," "persistent."

God wants us to be relentless and move forward, be strong, and not give up. As men, we need to have relentless love, pursue relentless devotion, and be on a relentless mission. We need to have grit and guts. There is no room for fading, melting, rusting, or burning out. We need tenacity and fortitude. We need to reject passivity and rely on God's power in us. No more standing on the sidelines and expecting other people to step up. Relentless men don't go dark and disappear. We take ground for the kingdom of God. Relentless men can absorb the inevitable criticism, obstacles, challenges, and setbacks—and keep advancing. Swimming upstream against the flow gets tiring. However, the relentless don't quit.

Father, teach me how to be relentless. I desire to take ground for You. Amen.

A FEW GOOD MEN

GOD is always on the alert, constantly on the lookout
for people who are totally committed to him.

2 CHRONICLES 16:7–9 MSG

I love the US Marines. They defend freedom around the world. They train and sacrifice and endure the most brutal conditions imaginable, just so they're fully prepared for the enemy. Through training, they become the best of the best. And they don't even pretend to be for everybody—they are for the "few."

Trying to compare Gideon's army with the Marines would be like comparing an orange to a horse. There is almost no similarity. Gideon's army was far from a well-trained fighting machine. Gideon himself questioned God's choice to use him because he was the least in his family, and his clan was the weakest.

When Gideon told his brave group of fighters they could leave if they were afraid, twenty-two thousand left. Then God eventually whittled the remaining ten thousand soldiers down to an intimidating fighting force of only three hundred men. Talk about "a few good men"! With such a small army, Gideon seemed crazy to face the Midianites, who numbered over one hundred thousand. What Gideon did seem to have was a heart fully committed to God. And because God did not want them to boast in their own strength, He created a situation where victory was only possible through faith in Him alone. Faith overcame fear. Gideon's army prevailed.

Whenever God calls us to a task we think is beyond us, we must focus on His unlimited power rather than our limited resources and talent. We don't have to be the smartest, the strongest, or the most talented to be used by God. But we do need to be one of the few.

Father, make me one of the few. Amen.

FOLLOWERSHIP

[Jesus] said to the crowd, "If any of you wants to be my follower, you must give up your own way, take up your cross daily, and follow me. If you try to hang on to your life, you will lose it. But if you give up your life for my sake, you will save it."

LUKE 9:23–24 NLT

"Are you a leader or a follower?" I was often asked that question as a kid. But I don't think the adults wanted an answer. Instead, they were communicating a subtle principle: be a leader, not a follower. But if everyone is leading, then who is following? In our recognition-hungry culture, there are few resources about following. But following is a form of leadership; I call it followership.

- Followership is the beginning of leadership. Following takes intentionally watching, learning from, and imitating others who are walking with the Lord, who live with courage, and who exhibit integrity and compassion.
- Followership starts with humility. Followers are humble. They have a thirst to grow and get better. They don't need glory or recognition; instead, they pass on the praise to those around them.
- Followership grows with serving. Followers have a willingness to serve others in sacrificial ways.
- Followership is perfected with Jesus at the foot of the cross. Jesus followed the voice and will of His Father. He served and sacrificed. He walked with humility and compassion. He served to give, not to get. Jesus never called us to be leaders, just followers. Jesus became the ultimate leader because He was the ultimate follower.

Men, learn how to lead by following. When you follow well, you lead well. That's followership!

Father, I confess I'd rather lead than follow. Teach me what it means to be a follower first. Amen.

WARRIOR VERSUS WHINER

Do not grumble, as some of them did—
and were killed by the destroying angel.

1 CORINTHIANS 10:10

The biggest battle you will ever face is in your mind. It's a war of competing voices. Two voices vie for attention and allegiance: the warrior and the whiner.

The whiner is the complainer. When the going gets tough, the whiner gets loud. This voice reminds you of all the reasons things won't work out; it says you're not good enough and reminds you why you can't. It complains about circumstances, makes excuses, and seeks the easy road. It's always negative, rooted in fear, and it reminds you of all the ways you've fallen short. It's a liar and an accuser. Its favorite words are *can't*, *won't*, and *tomorrow*.

The warrior is the winner. When the heat is on, the warrior says, "Bring it on." This voice turns all the negative into positive. It turns *impossible* into *possible*, *can't* into *can*, and *won't* into *will*. It overcomes obstacles, sees opportunities, and turns adversity into an advantage. It's a truth teller. It believes in the power of God and remembers all the things you've overcome. Its favorite words are *can*, *will*, and *now*.

If you want to have a victorious life, it all starts in your mind. Thoughts change your emotions, emotions affect your actions, and actions determine the results. You must actively silence the whiner and magnify the warrior. Intentionally think on what is good, right, noble, honorable, and true and watch your life transform.

Father, help me get control of my mind. Help me silence the whiner and amplify the warrior. Amen.

IT'S ALL GONNA MELT

*Think about the things of heaven,
not the things of earth.*
COLOSSIANS 3:2 NLT

Being a teenager in the '80s, I was blessed with the arrival of Christian punk bands—a blessing for me but a burden for my parents. One of my favorite bands was One Bad Pig, who had songs like "Smash the Guitar" and "Cut Your Hair." But my favorite was "Ice Cream Sundae" because they sang (okay, screamed) that the world was like an ice cream sundae and would melt one day.

As followers of Christ, we know that what we see will not last. All the stuff of the world will melt one day, but we live as if it is eternal. What we can see is temporary, but what we can't see is eternal. Billy Graham reminded us, "My home is in Heaven. I'm just traveling through this world."[13]

We spend so much time, energy, and attention on the here and now. Yet compared to eternity, it's like a couple of seconds. If your focus is on the seen, you will hold on to things tightly and live a hard life. If your focus is on the unseen, you will hold on to things lightly and live free. The tighter we hold to the earth, the more we quench life. It's all gonna melt. Be resolved to focus on the unseen, not the seen. Ask the Lord to help remove the things that blur your vision. When we focus on the world, we hold tightly. But if we focus on heaven, we hold lightly.

Father, empty me of the desires of the world and instead help me crave the things that are unseen—the eternal things. Amen.

13   Billy Graham (@BillyGraham), "My home is in Heaven," X (Twitter), April 4, 2015, https://twitter.com.

ONE WAY

Jesus answered, "I am the way and the truth and the life.
No one comes to the Father except through me."

JOHN 14:6

There's a scene in the movie *Planes, Trains and Automobiles* where John Candy tries to take off his winter coat while driving and ends up spinning the car around before stopping. When he gets back on the highway, he is going the wrong way. Another driver desperately tries to tell him, but he laughs until he sees two 18-wheelers heading right for his car. It turns out he was indeed going the wrong way![14]

We all want to know which way to go in life. The funny thing is that we all think we're going the right way. Proverbs 14:12 tells us that many times we think we know the right way, but in the end, it leads to death. In this age of tolerance and relative truth, you may hear the common phrases "All roads lead to heaven" or "Whatever works for you." But that's not what Jesus teaches. He teaches that only one road leads to eternal life. Jesus is the way, the truth, and the life, and no one comes to the Father except through Him.

John 3:36 says, "Whoever believes in the Son has eternal life, but whoever rejects the Son will not see life." He's the only one. Not Mohammed. Not Buddha. Not even our own efforts and good deeds. If any of these could be the way, Jesus died for nothing.

Father, help me show people Jesus—the way, the truth, and the life. Amen.

---

14   *Planes, Trains and Automobiles*, directed by John Hughes (Hollywood: Paramount Pictures, 1987), 93 min.

BEWARE, STRONG ONE

If you think you are standing firm,
be careful that you don't fall!

1 CORINTHIANS 10:12

From a very young age, I have been told that becoming the best means maximizing strengths and working on weaknesses. How many of us would admit we turn strengths into weaknesses? But beware, strong one. If you're not careful, your strengths can become weaknesses without warning. Oswald Chambers wisely reminded us, "The Bible characters fell on their strong points, never on their weak ones."[15]

When you take a personal strength to the extreme, it's likely to become a weakness. Often you can't see it; after all, you've been told to focus on your strengths and maximize them. However, unguarded strength can cause a blind spot. My greatest strength is passion, but when I have too much, I become overbearing. My passion, fueled by a will-not-be-denied persistence, can wear people out along the way.

An unguarded strength is a double weakness. When our strengths are out of balance or when we use them in excess, they end up having a negative effect. It's troubling to think that the thing you're best at or the very gift God blessed you with can become a weakness.

A strength, gift, or skill not only can lose its impact but can also take you down. Men, identify and develop your strengths and guard them. When we identify our unique strengths and gifts, keep them in balance, and use them for the benefit and blessing of others, we experience a powerful and meaningful life.

So remember: Beware, strong one. An unguarded strength is a double weakness.

Father, use my strengths for Your glory. I ask that each gift, ability, and strength You have given me becomes a blessing to others. Amen.

---

15   Oswald Chambers, "Is It Not in the Least Likely?" My Utmost for His Highest (website), April 19 devotion, https://utmost.org.

STAY CONNECTED

As the deer pants for streams of water,
so my soul pants for you, my God.
My soul thirsts for God, for the living God.
When can I go and meet with God?

PSALM 42:1–2

I am amazed at how dependent we are on running water. When our ten-year-old well pump called it quits, we couldn't use the toilets or showers, and there was no teeth brushing, dish washing, nor laundry. Life came to a grinding halt because we lost our connection to the water source.

Life also comes to a grinding halt when we lose our connection to Jesus. In fact, Jesus says that apart from Him, we can do nothing. Because life often seems to go on as usual, even when we aren't consistently connecting with Jesus, we frankly don't believe this. We can do *nothing…really*? When we look around, it seems like a lot of people who don't connect with Jesus are successful. They have a great job, nice house, solid reputation, good kids—they appear to have it all. While those things may seem good, they are not how Jesus defines success. Those things are not the fruit that grows from a relationship with God.

The accumulation of material stuff—money, cars, adventures—doesn't truly measure success. And those things don't satisfy for long. The fruit that comes from an abiding, daily walk with Jesus is love, joy, peace, patience, kindness, goodness, faithfulness, gentleness, and self-control (Galatians 5:22–23). The good works we do flow out of that connection. It's an inside-out flow from the wellspring of life.

Father, it's my heart's desire to stay connected to You. Amen.

HEAVEN BOUND

There's far more to life for us. We're citizens of high heaven!
We're waiting the arrival of the Savior, the Master, Jesus Christ,
who will transform our earthy bodies into glorious bodies like his own.

PHILIPPIANS 3:20–21 MSG

Holding this world loosely is a concept that hit home for me several days before my father passed away from his battle with leukemia. I noticed a book about heaven next to his bed; a friend had dropped it off to encourage him. I asked him if he'd read it, and he smiled and said, "Why do I need to read about it when I will be experiencing it shortly?"

His perspective had changed when he knew he was nearing the end.

The things that were important in my dad's life, like people and the things of God, became the most important things in his final days. His walk with the Lord became sweeter. My dad was holding this world loosely, and he was free. He experienced peace because death did not have a hold on his life, nor did this world. Life is short; it's only a mist.

To find peace, swallow a healthy dose of heaven each day. God desires for you to set your mind on things above so you can live freely now. Don't get trapped by this world. Most of us are weighed down by the temporary stuff. If we're honest, we're holding way too tightly to the things that don't count and not investing in things that will live on.

Change your perspective today: think about heaven.

Father, it's hard not to focus on the things of this world. I ask for a godly perspective as I serve You. Amen.

FORK IN THE ROAD

"Small is the gate and narrow the road that leads to life,
and only a few find it."
MATTHEW 7:14

Life is full of choices. Some are between right and wrong while others are just between going right and left. But so many will lead to life or death. The road to death is marked with laziness, compromise, and instant gratification. When we walk this path, we make excuses for not doing what we should. We aren't willing to sacrifice or do what's necessary for success because it's hard. The price seems too high, and it's too much work, so we compromise our standards. And since we don't always see the results of our efforts immediately, we give up. The accumulation of poor decisions made repetitively over time leads to breakdown. We sacrifice deep, long-term benefit for shallow, short-term pleasure.

The road to life is marked with discipline, consistency, and delayed gratification. When we walk this path, we begin with the end in mind. We have a clear picture of what we are shooting for, what we want to accomplish, what life will look like because of the decisions we make. When we make right choices day to day, they lead to blessing. There are no shortcuts; consistent effort, sacrifice, and work are required. Even though we know life may bring obstacles, hardships, challenges, and disappointments, this road gives us the strength to endure, to weather the storms, and to enjoy a peace that surpasses our understanding. We are willing to wait for our reward, knowing we are doing the right things.

Every day we have decisions to make that will lead to life and blessing—or death and breakdown. Choose wisely.

Father, help me pick the path that leads to life. Amen.

TEN PERCENT CLUB

Jesus asked, "Didn't I heal ten men? Where are the other nine?
Has no one returned to give glory to God except this foreigner?"
LUKE 17:17–18 NLT

When I was eight years old, my two older brothers said I could join their club if I jumped off the top of the tree fort and landed on an old mattress. After surviving the jump, I realized no one else had to jump to join the club.

In Luke 17:17–18, we read about one leper out of ten who went back and thanked Jesus. He started a Ten Percent Club. The only thing he did was express his gratitude. But it's like he formed his own little club, except this one required only thanking—not jumping! Jesus was clearly disappointed when only one returned to express gratitude. It's almost like the other nine took their miracle for granted. They wanted to be healed, but they didn't have time to thank the Healer. I am sure they were thankful, but they didn't express it.

Unexpressed gratitude is ingratitude.

Cultivating an attitude of gratitude as a lifestyle is a vital part of our family. Busyness, entitlement, and selfishness are the enemies of gratitude. I teach my children never to miss an opportunity to go back and express thanks because this demonstrates what followers of Christ do. It puts us in the Ten Percent Club, and it pleases God's heart.

It's impossible to be stressed and thankful at the same time. Gratitude is like a muscle: the more we exercise it, the stronger it grows.

Father, I want to be in the Ten Percent Club. Help me always express my gratitude. Amen.

THE MONEY MIRROR

"Store up for yourselves treasures in heaven,
where moths and vermin do not destroy,
and where thieves do not break in and steal.
For where your treasure is, there your heart will be also."

MATTHEW 6:20–21

I recently reviewed my credit card statements and came face-to-face with some hard truths. Whatever I spent the most money on was what I typically loved the most; what I spent the least on, I didn't value as much. I discovered I was selfish—spending a disproportionate amount on car payments, eating out, and other recreational activities. I spent less on supporting important kingdom ministries. My money became a mirror.

If you follow the money, you'll find the heart. And if you follow the heart, you'll find the money. That's exactly what Jesus said in Matthew 6. If someone gets to know your heart, they'll easily be able to predict what you spend your money on. The opposite is also true: if they look at what you spend your money on, they will get to know your heart. How we spend money reveals our character, much like adversity and stress.

Sometimes we have to lead our hearts, and sometimes we need to follow them. When I find myself being selfish, I lead my heart by giving more. When opportunities arise to invest in ministries and families in need, I invest. The more we become like Jesus, the more we want what He wants, and the more we'll give our money to these matters. Over time, what matters to God becomes more important to us.

What is your money mirror showing you?

Father, help me put my money where Your heart is, to invest it wisely, and to have eternal impact. Amen.

GIGO

"A good man brings good things out of the good stored up in his heart, and an evil man brings evil things out of the evil stored up in his heart. For the mouth speaks what the heart is full of."

LUKE 6:45

My college computer teacher introduced me to the acronym GIGO, which stands for "garbage in, garbage out." She stressed the importance of not filling a computer's storage with corrupt files. As an athlete, I got the same talk from my lacrosse coaches. "If you fill your body with junk, that's exactly what will come out. Junk!"

But the concept of GIGO is even more powerful and life-changing when you apply it to your heart.

Sow a thought, reap an action.

Sow an action, reap a habit.

Sow a habit, reap a character.

Sow a character, reap a destiny.

If you put garbage into your heart—jealousy, lying, degrading images, anger, unhealthy competitiveness—that's exactly what will come out. And just as garbage in real life can get stinky, so can your attitudes and actions.

I like to think about GIGO not as garbage in, garbage out but rather as God in, God out. If you are putting God into your heart every day, thinking of Him, studying His Word, talking about Him with others, then God will come out. When you're getting the squeeze, what's coming out of your life—God or garbage? The answer to that question will have everything to do with how you interact with God and with others and how you feel about yourself and the events of each day.

Father, I know my heart is the wellspring of life. Guard my heart from garbage that can creep in. Amen.

HUMILITY. UNITY. COMMITMENT.

Commit your way to the LORD;
trust in him and he will do this.

PSALM 37:5

The journey of Giannis Antetokounmpo from a young boy in Nigeria to a basketball superstar in the NBA is a testament to the power of humility, faith, and family. His story serves as an inspiration, reminding us that with God's help, we can rise above our circumstances and achieve greatness.

Giannis's family emigrated from Nigeria to Greece seeking a better life. Unfortunately, they lived in extreme poverty, but young Giannis did whatever he could to contribute to his family's well-being. He shared the same bed with his three brothers and even shared a pair of basketball shoes with his brother. They would switch shoes when checking in and out of the game, a picture of the humility, sacrifice, and unity they shared as a family.

Through dedication and hard work, Giannis's talent caught the attention of scouts, leading to his selection in the 2013 NBA Draft. Since then, he has achieved remarkable success, winning multiple accolades, including two league MVPs.

Giannis's journey reflects the words of Psalm 37:5: "Commit your way to the LORD; trust in him and he will do this." Despite facing adversity, Giannis remained committed to his dreams and placed his trust in God. Through faith and perseverance, Giannis is a living testimony to God's faithfulness and provision.

Hardship, adversity, and challenges are facts of life. We will each experience our fair share of all three. How we respond to them is what matters most. When we commit our ways (thoughts, attitudes, and actions) to the Lord and trust in Him, He acts for our good and His glory.

Father, help us trust You in the face of adversity and commit our dreams and aspirations to You. Amen.

LEAVE A MARK

Pray that I will proclaim this message as clearly as I should.
Live wisely among those who are not believers,
and make the most of every opportunity.

COLOSSIANS 4:4–5 NLT

I was eight years old when I had a once-in-a-lifetime opportunity to ride my older brother's motorcycle, so I took off with reckless abandon. One hundred yards down the dirt road of my ride to glory, my front tire hit a pothole, and suddenly I was airborne. Thankfully, I landed in a ditch, but the revved-up motorcycle landed on my back.

Because I landed in the ditch, the only part of the motorcycle that touched my back was the muffler. But as the muffler burned through my shirt and then my flesh, I experienced a world of hurt. Almost fifty years later, you can still see a burn imprint on my back.

Each of us also leaves behind an imprint in life. In everything we do and say, we leave a mark on others. Will it be a good impression or a bad impression? That's up to you. For me, the ultimate question is not whether I will leave a good or bad imprint on others. Rather, it's "Will I leave an imprint of myself—or Jesus?" That's what matters in the long run, isn't it?

Will others get more of you, or will they get more of Jesus?

When you touch others' lives, make sure there's no mark of you. Instead, leave a mark of Christ. Everything you say and do has the potential to leave a mark on others. No matter what you do, be committed to leave behind a lasting imprint—the imprint of Christ.

Father, I want to leave behind Your mark and not mine. Amen.

PRAY LIKE THIS

"Give us today our daily bread.
And forgive us our debts, as we also have forgiven our debtors.
And lead us not into temptation, but deliver us from the evil one."

MATTHEW 6:11–13

I remember the days when cell phones didn't exist. Seriously! Moms everywhere made their kids carry a quarter in case they needed to use a pay phone to make a call. Communication was challenging then, but today it's instantaneous. So if communicating with one another is so easy and immediate (and important) now, why is it so tough to communicate with God? It's just as important as making a call to Mom—even more so!

The disciples saw Jesus pray all the time. He would regularly get away to a quiet place to talk with His Father. They witnessed power flowing through Him and the miracles He performed. So when He returned from His place of prayer, they asked Him to spell it out. Jesus started with two prerequisites for prayer:

1. Our hearts must be right.
2. We must be sincere.

We shouldn't pray so other people see us and think we're super spiritual. And God wants to hear from us, but He also wants to speak as well.

Jesus taught us how to pray. He said our prayers need adoration, confession, thanksgiving, and supplication (use the acronym ACTS to remember these four aspects). He gave us the Lord's Prayer. Prayer is our lifeline, and it has the power to change us. Treat prayer as a conversation that keeps you connected to the source of life.

Father, thank You for giving me the freedom to express my heart through prayer. Amen.

DETERMINATION

They were just trying to intimidate us,
imagining that they could discourage us and stop the work.
So I continued the work with even greater determination.

NEHEMIAH 6:9 NLT

Nehemiah was engaged in the great work of rebuilding the walls around Jerusalem, and he experienced incredible opposition from his enemies. They were plotting to harm him and sent messages to try to distract and intimidate him so he would stop the project.

As we pursue our God-given missions and dreams, opposition is inevitable. The Enemy often employs tactics of lies, accusations, intimidation, and discouragement to thwart our progress. But we must meet all opposition with even greater determination. Nehemiah's response gives us a blueprint for how to respond.

- We must recognize the Enemy's lies. When his opponents sought to spread false rumors about his work, Nehemiah didn't fall for them. He recognized that their accusations were lies designed to discourage and distract him.
- We must resist discouragement. The Enemy's primary goal is to discourage us and to make us doubt ourselves and God's calling. Nehemiah didn't allow this discouragement to take root. He rejected his enemies' attempts to instill fear and weaken resolve.
- We must respond with prayer. Nehemiah turned to God in prayer. He didn't rely solely on his own strength, but he prayed for God to strengthen his hands.

Nehemiah's response wasn't to shrink back but to press forward with even greater determination. Opposition was likely a sign that he was on the right track. Determination is a powerful force. It enables us to stand firm in our faith and purpose; it's the antidote to discouragement and opposition.

Father, when opposition comes, strengthen me with even more determination to complete the work. Amen.

APRIL

INNER CIRCLE

Walk with the wise and become wise,
for a companion of fools suffers harm.

PROVERBS 13:20

Bear Grylls, star of the television show *Man vs. Wild*, had always dreamed of climbing Mount Everest, one of the highest and most dangerous peaks on earth. At the age of twenty-three, he became, at the time, the youngest Briton ever to reach the summit. The risk of death is present even for the most experienced mountaineers. And Bear would have died if his skillful teammates weren't there when the ice under his feet gave way and he fell into a crevasse. They literally held Bear's life in their hands as Bear dangled unconsciously from a single rope.[16]

How well we navigate life depends in large part on the quality and character of our friends. The friends we choose, our trusted inner circle, can make or break us, and we can make or break them.

Proverbs is stuffed with wisdom, and it talks a lot about the importance of choosing the right friends. It instructs us

- to be a good friend,
- to spend time with friends who make good decisions, and
- to not have too many friends.

The key is forming an inner circle of close friends with whom you have developed trust over time. Even Jesus, within His group of twelve, had an inner circle of just three—Peter, James, and John. He had a deeper level of trust and closeness with these men. We should be wise and do the same.

Father, lead me to find friends who love You and are walking in wisdom. Help me find an inner circle. Amen.

---

16   Yvonne Gordon, "Even Bear Grylls Gets Scared—Here's How He Climbed Everest Anyway,"
Outdoors.com, October 29, 2023, https://outdoors.com.

DIG IN

"The soil produces a crop by itself—first the blade, then the head, and then the ripe grain on the head. But as soon as the crop is ready, he sends for the sickle, because the harvest has come."

MARK 4:28–29 HCSB

Are you the type of person who looks for the next big opportunity, or are you someone who digs in right where you are and accomplishes what needs to be done? The grass always looks greener on the other side of the fence, doesn't it? That's why many of us are so quick to pursue the next big, great opportunity.

A step of faith often means "stay" not "go."

We rush to make a move, to change the current dynamic. But God looks for men who will dig in where they're planted and stay. He wants the faithful, not the flashy. He wants a sold-out man, not a sell-out. He wants someone who is persistent, not prosperous; patient, not popular. Which kind of man are you?

It's amazing how God uses those who are willing to stay put. You'll grow where God plants you if you give it time. Consistency is important to reaping a harvest. Commit for the long haul. Don't bail. Be faithful. Be consistent. Dig in and make a difference. Then get ready for God's surprises.

Jesus, I am in for the long haul. I ask for big faith as I strive to stay consistent. Amen.

SERVING IS SATISFYING

Each of you should use whatever gift you have received to serve others,
as faithful stewards of God's grace in its various forms.

1 PETER 4:10

Have you ever been around someone who is truly passionate about what they do? You know, the type of person who has a very narrow focus, someone who has become an expert in their field? Someone who eats, breathes, and sleeps what they love to do? People like that inspire me. And I'm even more energized when their gifting and expertise are focused on helping others. Somehow this brings a greater sense of purpose to their passion, and it makes a difference for others.

Countless examples of this are in Scripture, but I love the passage in 1 Peter 4. Peter wrote about living our lives for God compared to living for our own selfish pursuits. He encouraged us to look at all the ways God has gifted us and to use those gifts to serve others. Serving is about meeting the needs of others. It's always about what we can give, not what we can get.

God wants to connect the way He has wired us to what we do. He wants us to take the things we are most passionate about and use them for the good of others and the glory of God. When we operate in our natural gifting, it typically brings us life and bears much fruit. We are most alive when we serve others with our gifts and passions because serving is satisfying; it doesn't only bless others, but it also fills our souls.

Father, help me find ways to turn my passion into serving. Amen.

COMPETITIVE GREATNESS

*"Physical training is good, but training for godliness is much better,
promising benefits in this life and in the life to come."*

1 TIMOTHY 4:8 NLT

Legendary basketball coach John Wooden coined the phrase *competitive greatness*. I sometimes get it mixed up with being great. But competitive greatness is not about being the best in general but being the best *you* can be. There can only be one best, but everyone can achieve being their own best.

Coach Wooden defined *competitive greatness* as "a real love for the hard battle," knowing difficulties offer the opportunity to be at your best when your best is required. These three "Be" principles have helped me grasp competitive greatness:

1. Be prepared. It's not about winning; it's about being prepared. Coach Wooden would spend thirty minutes teaching his UCLA basketball players how to properly put on socks. Being prepared helps you face battles as a man so you can embrace challenges—never fear them.
2. Be disciplined. If integrity is doing the right thing when no one is watching, competitive greatness is working hard when no one is watching. Competitive greatness leads to a disciplined life.
3. Be focused. Competitive greatness focuses on a clear vision; it is not sidetracked or distracted. Focus produces a clear picture of the future, and that produces passion.

Be the best you can be by unleashing the gifts and talents God placed in you. Do it right now and watch Him do an amazing work through you.

Father, You are the great one, the best. Help me be the best man I can be so people will know You are great—not me. Amen.

REMEMBER YOUR WHY

We are God's handiwork, created in Christ Jesus to do good works,
which God prepared in advance for us to do.

EPHESIANS 2:10

In 2005, US Army Medic Kortney Clemons was just a couple weeks away from finishing his tour in Iraq. As he was helping train and orient those who would replace him in active duty, a roadside bomb exploded, killing three soldiers and wounding him severely. Kortney lost his right leg from just above the knee.

Later, his mom reminded and encouraged him that he could have lost his life, but instead, God left him behind for a purpose. His mom's encouragement became a catalyst. He turned his great challenge into an opportunity—an opportunity to rediscover meaning and purpose in his life. This journey ultimately resulted in a trip to London for the 2012 Paralympic Games.[17]

When you remember your why, it helps you overcome your current circumstances and obstacles. It helps you find purpose in your pain. He who has a reason to live can bear almost anything. God has created us for good works that are designed uniquely for each one of us.

Ultimately, our purpose as men is to love God and love others, to glorify God in the way we live. We should know Him and make Him known. But each one of us also carries an individual purpose that surfaces each day—opportunities to extend compassion, help a neighbor, and encourage someone who needs a lift. We're all part of something much bigger than ourselves. Instead of focusing on your problems, focus on your purpose.

Father, help me remember my why so I will never grow weary in doing good.
Amen.

---

17   Charlene Prince Birkeland, "Raising an Olympian: Kortney Clemons," Yahoo Sports, May 24, 2012, https://sports.yahoo.com.

OPPORTUNITY KNOCKS

"If you do what is right, won't you be accepted?
But if you do not do what is right, sin is crouching at the door.
Its desire is for you, but you must rule over it."

GENESIS 4:7 HCSB

We all know what it means to be at the right place at the right time. I heard opportunity knock when I was drafted to play professional lacrosse. Looking back on it, I was simply at the right place at the right time. I probably wouldn't have made any other team in the league, so I seized the opportunity.

Over time, I've learned there are good opportunities and bad opportunities. Just like you can be at the right place at the right time, you can also be at the wrong place at the wrong time. Bad opportunities always come when your guard is down. Satan loves to surprise and ambush you. And he's really, really good at it. But that doesn't mean you have to fall for the bad opportunities.

As God said to Cain, "Sin is crouching at the door." *Crouching* simply means "waiting for the perfect opportunity to spring." So what can you do? You can be on guard. You can build in safeguards and use time wisely instead of wasting it. If you're fulfilled and satisfied with your life and the way it's going, you'll be less likely to jump at a bad opportunity. Before you open the door of opportunity, you'd be wise to take a good long look at it through the peephole first.

Father, I need wisdom to discern the difference between good and bad
opportunities. Help me choose the good and steer clear of the bad. Amen.

GET READY

Don't you realize that in a race everyone runs, but only one person gets the
prize? So run to win! All athletes are disciplined in their training. They do
it to win a prize that will fade away, but we do it for an eternal prize.

1 CORINTHIANS 9:24–25 NLT

Having spent nearly twenty years in the fitness industry, I've met folks who
exercise for all kinds of reasons. But I've met very few, if any, who say they're
training "to be ready." The most common answers people give for training
are to lose weight, to look better, to get healthier, to be stronger, and even to
compete in an event. Some need to exercise because their doctors told them
that if they didn't, they'd face a chronic illness. But rarely is readiness the
reason people hit the gym.

"Ready for what?" you might be asking. Well, ready for the challenges of
every day, ready to help somebody who might need it, ready in case of an
emergency, and ready for life. Abraham Lincoln is considered to have once
famously said, "Today I will prepare, and someday my chance will come."

The challenge for each one of us is this: Will we have the "strength for
two"? What will we do to make sure we're strong enough in mind, body, and
spirit to help others when the time comes? Push beyond your normal limits.
To gain muscle, you must lift heavier weights. To grow in faith, you must step
outside your comfort zone. To grow in empathy, you must step into others'
shoes. If it doesn't challenge you, it will never change you.

Men, others are counting on us to be ready for the demands of life.

*Father, help me train my mind, body, and spirit so I am ready to see a need
and meet it. Amen.*

WALKIE-TALKIE

I urge you to imitate me.
1 Corinthians 4:16

When my brothers and I were kids, we invented a game called Walkie-Talkie. We would walk side-by-side through the house with our arms over each other's shoulders and say, "Walkie-Talkie," out loud with each step. The way to win was by suddenly tripping the other person, throwing them to the ground. One time, my brother won when he threw me face-first into my mom's showcase furniture. Almost fifty years later, there's still evidence: my front tooth took out a chunk of wood!

Sometimes it feels like I'm playing spiritual Walkie-Talkie. Over the years, I've walked shoulder-to-shoulder with people (coworkers, teammates, family, friends) who have later tried to "take me out" because a competitive spirit developed between us. I confess I can quickly get sucked in. But instead, what I really need is a good friend to walk with me—someone who sees how I live, gets to know me well, and is trustworthy to hold me accountable.

I always thought Paul's statement in 1 Corinthians 4:16 was rather arrogant. After all, he was telling people that they should imitate him. Then I realized what Paul was really saying: "Hey, if you want to walk with me for a couple hours, you'll get a full understanding of what the life of Christ is all about." I want people to walk with me and find out I'm the real deal. I want to become more like Christ every day so His light and love shine through to others. No tripping each other up, just walking side by side.

Father, help me find people to lean on, people who want to walk side by side with me. Amen.

DO THE WORK

On October 2 the wall was finished—
just fifty-two days after we had begun…
Our enemies…realized this work had been done with the help of our God.

NEHEMIAH 6:15–16 NLT

Vince Lombardi is famous for saying, "The harder you work, the harder it is to surrender."[18] I've found that statement to be true. Partly because we're willing to work hardest for the things that matter most. That makes giving up, giving in, or quitting out of the question—at least not without a fight.

Winners work. Quitters don't work. They whine. Dedication and discipline are two things that generally separate the winners from the quitters. Dedication requires consistency of effort and action. Work is never dependent on how you feel. In fact, we all have plenty of days when we don't feel like showing up and putting in the work. But if we truly want results, we must be dedicated.

Nehemiah is the epitome of what it looks like to work wholeheartedly for a cause that honors and glorifies God. He was called to rebuild a wall, and he didn't quit. Like Nehemiah, God has planted a vision in us and given us the passion to go for it. He wants us to get to work. When we obey, He multiplies our effectiveness and magnifies His name in the process. God does more than we can ever ask or imagine as we surrender to His plan and get to work. God's people completed the rebuilding of the wall around Jerusalem in an astonishing fifty-two days. They were determined and disciplined, and they refused to be distracted or discouraged.

Let's pursue God-sized goals and get to work.

Father, help me work hard, do my best, and take advantage of every opportunity that comes along to truly make a difference. Amen.

---

18   Vince Lombardi and Vince Lombardi Jr., *What It Takes to Be Number One* (Nashville, TN: Thomas Nelson, 2012), 70.

THE THREE DS OF DEVOTION

I long for Your salvation, LORD,
and Your instruction is my delight.

PSALM 119:174 HCSB

My dad loved to engage God daily. But it was not always that way. For most of his life, he was an overcommitted businessman who squeezed in a quick, two-minute devotion in his car before he started his day.

That all changed with the help of his friend Brad Curl. When Brad saw that my dad was skimming when it came to his devotions, Brad literally grabbed my dad by the collar, put him against the wall, and said, "Ed, you need to stop playing with God. You are a Christian leader, and you need to start diving into God's Word daily. No more giving God leftovers!"

That day marked my dad. The quick devotions were done. He started digging in.

My dad always shared the three Ds of devotions: drudgery, discipline, and delight. He would say, "Getting up daily and doing a quiet time starts out as drudgery. You won't like it, but you just do it. Then, gradually, it grows into a discipline. It becomes a part of life. Then, if you stay at it long enough, it will become a delight. It is a joy to be with the Savior. It goes from a have-to to a need-to to a want-to."

Engage God daily—no matter what!

Jesus Christ is waiting to empower you with His presence. He desires to be with you. Why not engage God today? He longs to be with you and me much more than we long to be with Him.

Father, I desire to be with You. Give me discipline and delight to spend time with You. Amen.

THE PURSUIT

Commit to the LORD whatever you do,
and he will establish your plans.

PROVERBS 16:3

In 2013, my oldest son, Jimmy, was contemplating trying out for the Liberty University Lacrosse Team. He was wrestling with doubts but made the decision to go for it. He had both the vision and passion for being part of that team. Following his decision, Jimmy went to work. He pushed his body harder and competed with an intensity and focus like never before. He made the team, and we celebrated! I believe God honored his effort and helped him in unseen ways.

Watching my son overcome doubts and pursue a goal that really mattered to him uncovered three keys to success:

1. Pick your prize. It all starts with setting a wildly important goal—a goal that stretches you beyond your comfort zone. You will only be dedicated to something that is very important to you, so you must know your "why." Achieving goals isn't about trophies; it's about testimonies (1 Corinthians 9:23–25).

2. Count the cost. Everything worth pursuing costs something. In fact, nothing worth achieving will come easy. So examine the cost. What will be required of you to make it happen? Jesus encourages us to consider what it will take before we begin (Luke 14:27–29).

3. Pay the price. Once you have set the goal and counted the cost, the real work begins. Making daily progress toward your goal, regardless of how you feel or what setbacks you encounter, is what will keep you on track. Crush the distractions and excuses and the little compromises. Celebrate small successes and go to work every day.

Get in the pursuit!

Father, help me pursue things wholeheartedly as if I am working for You. Help me pursue Your version of success. Amen.

THE BIGGEST GIVER

I will most gladly spend and be spent for you.
If I love you more, am I to be loved less?
2 Corinthians 12:15 HCSB

Stephen Paletta is a special guy in more ways than one. In April 2008, in the finale episode of the ABC reality show *Oprah's Big Give*, Stephen won the premiere title as "the biggest giver." He'd made it through eight episodes and survived the competition of nine other bighearted contestants. But that's only the tip of the iceberg.

I first met Stephen in 1992 while playing lacrosse in a summer tournament. During that tournament, God got hold of Stephen. Even though Stephen already had a big heart, he realized he needed God's heart. Stephen says that moment was an "aha" in his life.

Since 1992, I've been privileged to watch Stephen's heart for God grow. He's a man who knows what it means to serve with a heart yielded to Christ. When he gives, he gives big because he knows you can't out-give God.

So when the *Oprah's Big Give* opportunity came along, Stephen approached it with that same attitude. He once said to me, "I went into the show with a servant's heart. I said, *God, whatever it is You want me to do with these folks, let it happen.*" The show revealed Stephen's heart. His love for people naturally flowed. That's what big, deep giving is all about.

To serve others and to give of yourself is true worship. Oswald Chambers once said, "Worship is giving God the best that He has given you…Whenever you get a blessing from God, give it back to Him as a love-gift."[19]

Jesus, I ask for a big heart so I can be a blessing. Show me what it means to be rich in good deeds. Amen.

---

19 Oswald Chambers, "Worship," My Utmost for His Highest (website), January 6 devotion, https://utmost.org.

SUCCESSFUL FAILURE

We know that in all things God works for the good of those who love him,
who have been called according to his purpose.

ROMANS 8:28

"Houston, we've had a problem." Jim Lovell, the mission commander for NASA's Apollo 13, said these famous words in April 1970 as the space flight crew was on its way to the moon. On April 13, just nine minutes after signing off for the night and two hundred thousand miles from earth, disaster struck, causing substantial damage that put the crew in grave danger.

From that moment on, the mission to land on the moon was over; the new mission was survival. They needed a miracle. Gene Kranz, Apollo 13's flight director in Houston, would not accept failure.

When the astronauts returned safely to earth, the mission was renamed NASA's "successful failure." They had survived extreme cold, sleep deprivation, dehydration, a lack of oxygen, and food rationing, all while making repairs and modifications to the spacecraft as directed from Houston.

God loves to turn our failure into success, disappointments into determination, and challenges into character. In fact, the Bible is full of stories of successful failures. A successful failure is when you fail while attempting something big for God. Then look for God to turn that failure into future success. You choose to look at failure differently. You refuse to let it define or discourage you.

With God, ultimate failure is not an option. God is ready to turn what we might consider our worst failure into our greatest victory. Don't let failure define or defeat you. Instead, let God turn your circumstances into success.

Father, help me be willing to risk failure, knowing You will do great things as I go for it even if things don't go as planned. Amen.

FOCUS ON ONE THING

No, dear brothers and sisters, I have not achieved it, but I focus on this one thing: Forgetting the past and looking forward to what lies ahead, I press on to reach the end of the race and receive the heavenly prize.

PHILIPPIANS 3:13–14 NLT

The hardest thing for me to do as a leader is to narrow my focus and just do one thing. I pride myself on being able to multitask and not needing to choose between two things. Why do one when you can do two? The power of *and*, not the weak *or*, is a life principle of mine.

However, I have learned over the years that my coaches were right: "Keep your eye on the ball." When I took my eye off the ball, turnovers were inevitable. In a complex and complicated world, the discipline of narrowing our focus to one thing is the secret to transformation. It seems like we get more responsibility added to our lives every day, and the pressure increases. When we develop laser-like focus, we create clarity. Like Oswald Chambers wrote, "Simplicity is the secret of seeing things clearly."[20] Focus creates power and purpose, which always drives life change.

The apostle Paul discovered the power of narrowing his focus to just one thing. In Philippians 3:13–14, Paul confessed he was still on this journey to figure it out, but he was forgetting the past, looking ahead, and focusing on the goal to win for Jesus Christ. I can hear Paul saying, "Keep your eye on the prize!"

What's the one thing? It is simply to have laser focus on one goal, one prize: the upward call of God—becoming more like Jesus every day.

Father, give me laser-like focus to become more like Jesus every day. Amen.

---

20   Oswald Chambers, "Arguments or Obedience," My Utmost for His Highest (website), September 14 devotion, https://utmost.org.

NO PAIN, NO GAIN

I consider that our present sufferings are not worth comparing with the glory that will be revealed in us.

ROMANS 8:18

I've heard it said that pain is just weakness leaving the body. When I was a young competitive athlete, "No pain, no gain" was the standard expectation in the gym. I had to push beyond my limits to get better. I had to break my body down in order to build it up.

We must be stretched beyond our current capabilities to increase our capacity. In order to grow, sacrifice, struggle—and yes, even some pain—are necessary. This is true in training, and it applies in all aspects of life. Here's how you can grow spiritually, relationally, mentally, and emotionally:

- To grow spiritually, our faith must be tested; we must engage in situations where we need God more and depend on our own strength less.
- To grow relationally, we must be willing to consider the needs of others above our own.
- To grow mentally, we need to seek new learning opportunities and engage with others who know more than we do.
- To grow emotionally, we must be willing to experience pain, disappointment, and even loss to be able to comfort others.

The apostle Paul knew pain, and he knew gain. In 2 Corinthians 11:23–28, Paul described what he experienced as a follower of Jesus—physical pain, loneliness, fear, betrayal, danger, hunger, thirst, and even homelessness. But his greatest pain was the burden he felt for reaching unbelievers with the gospel. He was emboldened to build up believers. Paul knew that in the end, no matter what he experienced, it would be worth it. Pain brings gain.

Father, don't let me take the easy road but help me use the pain of struggle, sacrifice, and challenges to more fully depend on You. Amen.

BAGS OF BIBLES

"It is the same with my word. I send it out, and it always produces fruit.
It will accomplish all I want it to, and it will prosper everywhere I send it."

ISAIAH 55:11 NLT

When I was eight years old, my grandfather Pop took me to the Baltimore airport to distribute Bibles. Pop explained the right way and wrong way to hand out Bibles. He said to never ask, "Do you want a Bible?" Rather, he trained me to say, "I have a gift for you. I would like for you to have a Bible." Not a question but instead an invitation.

I was petrified, but saying no to Pop wasn't an option. So we dressed up to look our best and arrived at the airport with bags of Bibles. We prayed and asked God to use every copy of His Word to penetrate the hearts and minds of those who received it. After two hours of gifting God's Word to strangers, I was surprised I wasn't mocked, ridiculed, or humiliated. Instead, I learned firsthand the incredible power of blessing others with God's Word. I don't think a single person said no. Maybe it was Pop's training or that I was an eight-year-old boy, but people accepted the gift.

Not only did my grandfather model a passion for distributing God's Word, but my father also did the same. Now as a third-generation Bible distributor, I have the same passion to share God's Word, and I have taken thousands of Bibles around the world.

How is God calling you to equip those you meet with His Word? It's never too late.

Father, use me to get Your Word out. May it produce fruit in the lives of those who receive it. Amen.

BE TRUE

> "I have been crucified with Christ and I no longer live, but Christ lives in me. The life I now live in the body, I live by faith in the Son of God, who loved me and gave himself for me."

GALATIANS 2:20

Everybody wants to be somebody. Some people really want to be somebody else. In fact, most of us spend an incredible amount of time not only searching for identity but also trying to create it. We are desperate to create a "brand" that projects a certain image or, more accurately, projects who we want to be. But often, we're trying to be something we're not.

The simplest definition of *identity* that I've heard is "who someone really is." It's the true you.

The true you can only be found on the inside. It's easier to create a false identity on the outside than do the hard work of becoming like Christ on the inside. It's easier to change appearances than realities. Change your shirt, your team, your weight, your friends—piece of cake. But change your character? Now that's a different story; that can be painful and time-consuming. The true you is about who you are, and the false you is about what you do.

Changing the outside appearances and circumstances never changes the inside. But what's going on inside always shows up on the outside. As Christians, we've had our original identity restored. The sin that stole your true you, separating you from God, has been cleansed by the blood of Jesus on the cross. Now you have a new identity. So stop worrying about appearances and start focusing on being the real you. Be true.

Father, thank You for restoring my true identity as Your beloved child. Help me be true to that. Amen.

DREAM ON

"Are you really going to reign over us?" his brothers asked him. "Are you really going to rule us?" So they hated him even more because of his dream and what he had said.

GENESIS 37:8 HCSB

When I was eight years old, I did a lot of dreaming. My dad took me to watch college lacrosse games, and I stood down by the field and said over and over again, "One day I wish I could play on that field!"

My dream drove me for ten years until I finally had the opportunity to fulfill it. When I was eighteen years old, I stepped onto that exact field to live my dream as a college lacrosse player. Not only did the ten-year-old dream come true, but God's plan for me was much bigger than my dream. God allowed me to use my gift of lacrosse to reach thousands for Him through the Fellowship of Christian Athletes. All because of a dream He had for me!

Joseph had a dream at age seventeen, but his dream was not fulfilled for more than twenty years. He stayed faithful to the vision God gave him. Here are five principles of dreaming as you dream big for Jesus:

1. Dreams come from God.
2. Dreams ignite energy, passion, and drive.
3. There is always a season of preparation with dreams.
4. Celebrate the fulfillment of the dream when it comes true.
5. Dreams should glorify God, not us.

Let the dream ignite your passion but let your actions be the fuel that converts your dream into a reality. Go ahead—dream big!

Father, I know all dreams come from You. Continue to ignite the passion in my soul to dream the dreams You have for me. Amen.

LIVE LIKE JESUS

We all, who with unveiled faces contemplate the Lord's glory,
are being transformed into his image with ever-increasing glory,
which comes from the Lord, who is the Spirit.

2 CORINTHIANS 3:18

Jesus living in us gives us the power to live for Him. The old identity passes away, and God's transformational work is underway. Your heart, mind, thoughts, and attitudes will be changed. You have been set free from your sin and can become everything God designed you to be.

God made each of us uniquely. He has a purpose and a path He wants us to follow. He doesn't want us to cave in to pressure. Establishing a healthy identity in Christ helps you live like Jesus. Living like Jesus requires you to pay attention to three things:

1. Do I *think* like Jesus? Sometimes our old ways of thinking steal our new identity and leave us discouraged, pessimistic, and negative. Jesus wants us to be transformed by the renewing of our minds. Right thoughts lead to positive words.
2. Do I *talk* like Jesus? Sometimes the old words we spoke brought death instead of life. Jesus wants us to say only what builds people up, including ourselves. Positive words lead to godly actions.
3. Do I *act* like Jesus? Sometimes our old ways of doing things prevent us from making changes. We get stuck in old habits that tear us down. God wants us to honor Him by presenting our bodies as a living sacrifice. Godly habits lead to the true you.

If you want to live like Jesus, seek Him first. Ask Him to transform the way you think, the words you speak, and the things you do.

Father, help me be the person You have made me to be. Amen.

GLORY HOUND

"I am the LORD; that is my name!
I will not give my glory to anyone else."

ISAIAH 42:8 NLT

Gary Brasher did the unthinkable: he completed three Ironman triathlons in three consecutive days for a total of 421.8 miles. Most cars don't even travel 421.8 miles in three days. I was at a conference with Gary for a few days while he was training. One morning, I was heading out for a 6-mile run, and he was working on his daily six hours of training.

After spending my whole life around athletes, I know one thing for sure: there's always a bit of "glory hound" in competitors. We compete to impress others and get recognition. One of the awesome things I discovered about Gary was that he is not a glory hound. He wasn't doing 421.8 miles for himself. He was doing it for the Lord.

Don't steal the glory.

If anyone in the Bible could have been justified in being a glory hound, it would have been Nehemiah. But he was smart and godly enough to give God the credit God deserved. And therein lies the secret of greatness: God did it. Not me.

We may never do a triple-iron triathlon. We may never accomplish a huge task like building the wall of a city in fifty-two days. We must ask ourselves: Am I a glory hound or a glory reflector? It's simple. It's either "God did it" or "I did it." Which route will you choose?

Father, change my perspective from "I did it" to "You did it." Help me be not a glory hound but a glory reflector. Amen.

PUBLIC FAITH

I am not ashamed of the gospel, because it is the power of God that brings salvation to everyone who believes: first to the Jew, then to the Gentile.

ROMANS 1:16

Before his championship lacrosse game, my son quietly knelt down in front of the bench and prayed. No fanfare. It was simply a public display of his private love for God. He was unashamed about devoting his effort, his attitude, and his play to the glory of God in a public setting.

Our faith in God is personal but not private. When we accept the idea that faith is a private thing, we don't have to be accountable to anyone or actively live out our faith. We hide behind our "right to privacy," and we don't get forced out of our comfort zones.

Jesus never intended for our relationship with Him to be private. He doesn't just want secret devotion; He wants faith in action. In fact, faith without action is worthless. We need to exercise our faith so it grows and makes an impact.

Our love for Jesus in the privacy of our hearts should produce a public display of love for Him. Our thoughts, words, and actions are an overflow of our hearts. Showing love for Christ can take courage. But we are called to love like Jesus did—to make our faith public. Faith shows up in humble serving, anonymous giving, and unselfish sacrificing for others. Can others see your faith in the words you say and things you do?

Father, I pray for the courage to make my faith public. I want my love for You to overflow in a natural, authentic way. Amen.

TWENTY-EIGHT-YEAR MIRACLE

Let us not become weary in doing good,
for at the proper time we will reap a harvest if we do not give up.
GALATIANS 6:9

God's delays are not God's denials. In the 1990s as I played professional lacrosse, one of my coaches was Coach Hoffy. He was the type of coach who lived by the motto, "Work hard, play hard."

During the four years I played, I was the weird Christian on the team who didn't "play hard" off the field with the rest of the team. Coach Hoffy's wife and son loved Jesus, and we often prayed for a miracle in Coach's life and in the lives of my teammates.

Twenty-eight years later, we took an FCA lacrosse team to Israel to serve in the World Cup of Lacrosse. Wouldn't you know it—Coach Hoffy and his son Josh came. Amazing ministry took place during the two weeks, and we shared God's love with hundreds of players through outreaches and competitions. Meanwhile, God was working on Coach Hoffy.

The miracle of all miracles happened when our team went to the Sea of Galilee for a tour. We offered the opportunity for our players to get baptized. Once we all got into the water, Coach Hoffy said he wanted to be baptized. His son and I had the blessing of baptizing him that day. I witnessed a twenty-eight-year miracle.

Spiritual seeds planted with obedience and faith will always produce fruit. For Coach Hoffy's miracle, it happened twenty-eight years later. What spiritual seeds have you planted yet given up on? Maybe the miracle is right around the corner. Don't give up hope!

Father, help me have the faith to believe seeds planted many years ago can still produce a harvest. Amen.

MOVE THE CHAINS

Go to the ant, you sluggard; consider its ways and be wise!
It has no commander, no overseer or ruler,
yet it stores its provisions in summer and gathers its food at harvest.

Proverbs 6:6–8

My youngest son played in a flag-football league with a bunch of his friends, and I coached. One of the keys to football is getting a first down by moving the ball across midfield so you can get four more downs to score. When you get a first down, a pole with a chain moves to indicate your position on the field. Getting first downs is critical because they keep drives alive.

Those who practice, prepare, and perform with the most consistency generally outplay their opponents. Consistency leads to continual forward progress. It's defined by being steady, reliable, and persistent. Inconsistency, on the other hand, is the enemy of excellence. It's one step forward, two steps back. Unfortunately, many of us don't realize that what we do today affects who we become tomorrow. Little things do affect our character, health, and future. Sometimes the effect is immediate; other times it may take time to surface.

A moving-the-chains mentality means we do the little things that lead to growth. We do hard things—even when we want to quit, even when we don't feel like it, even when we're tired, even when we can't see results, and even when things aren't going the way they should. God rewards us when we seek Him. A consistent life leads to both internal transformation and external influence. Men, take action and do the little things that lead to excellence. Move those chains.

Father, help me take small steps that lead to small changes, believing each action will all make a difference for You. Amen.

THE ISOLATION TRAP

Bear one another's burdens,
and so fulfill the law of Christ.

GALATIANS 6:2 ESV

In 1989, I graduated from college and moved back to my hometown to start serving with the Fellowship of Christian Athletes. Realizing I needed fellowship, I connected with three friends every Friday morning for Bible study. However, our weekly meeting quickly became a powerful accountability group where we dove into each other's lives as we pursued Christ with reckless abandon.

For more than three years, we opened up our lives to one another and invited accountability—we didn't demand it. We put our "junk" on the table instead of hiding it under the table. We were living out James 5:16: "Confess your sins to one another and pray for one another, so that you may be healed. The prayer of a righteous person is very powerful in its effect" (CSB). There was lots of confessing, crying, and healing. We discovered life is a "we" thing, not a "me" thing. When we see life as a "me" thing, we isolate. Pride says we can live our faith through our own power. As a result, we distance ourselves from those who know us best.

Isolation makes us believe we can commit sins and be free of consequences. King David had that mindset until the prophet Nathan showed up and told him exactly how badly he was messing up. Isolation convinces us we're the only ones wrestling with a problem. We believe no one will understand, so why open up and seek help? Men, don't fall into the trap of isolation. Living the Christian life is not a "me" thing; it's a "we" thing. We are always better together.

Father, bring me at least one accountability partner with whom I can do life. Amen.

WALK THIS WAY

Teach these truths to other trustworthy people who will be able to pass them on to others.

2 TIMOTHY 2:2 NLT

Barry Spofford, a friend and spiritual mentor, passed away on April 25, 2015. On April 30, hundreds of people attended his celebration service in Colorado to honor a life well lived. Throughout his journey with cancer, his focus was always on his sweet Jesus.

For twenty-three years, I had the joy and honor to serve with Barry in FCA. God used Barry as a spiritual coach in my life to show me the importance of spiritual disciplines, especially prayer. Barry taught me how to develop a deep prayer life by showing me prayer is not a last resort but a first response. Spending hours of prayer on my knees with Barry in the early '90s, I saw God move mountains.

We didn't talk about prayer, but we prayed. Barry would slip off his old Timex watch and set an hour on the timer, put it on the table, then get on his knees. No talk; just prayer. He modeled that our lives need to be built on prayer. Barry, who was twenty years older than me, was an example of a man of God who sought the Lord's face daily—always laying a foundation of prayer. Barry shaped and molded me into the man of God I am today.

Now I have others who have picked up that torch and are helping me live a godly life. And now I am passing on to others what others have taught me. Are you walking with the wise? Are you sharing wisdom?

Father, I want to walk with the wise and learn from them so I can pass wisdom to others. Amen.

THE FOUR Os OF LIFE

If you need wisdom, ask our generous God, and he will give it to you.
He will not rebuke you for asking.

JAMES 1:5 NLT

Every day we experience four Os when we face decisions: opportunity, opposition, obedience, and outcome. When we truly understand these four Os, we can live courageously despite the circumstances.

1. Where do opportunities come from? God orchestrates and provides all opportunities. They come from Him alone. He will use us, but opportunities are God's part, not ours.

2. Opposition will always come. Opposition follows every opportunity. We have three main enemies that give us opposition: the world, the flesh, and the devil. Each one has a goal to prevent us from succeeding.

3. Obedience is saying, *Yes, God!* When the going gets tough, the tough start obeying. Sometimes we shy away from an open door of opportunity because we can see the opposition. Courageous living requires obedience to walk with the Spirit through the open doors of opportunity, even in the face of opposition. Remember: obedience is our part.

4. Outcomes are God's part, not ours. The God of the universe is responsible for how things turn out. When we are obedient, we can rest in His results. There is peace when we know the Lord is taking care of the outcome. The harvest is coming.

Father, I ask for opportunities to grow, courage to face opposition, resolve to obey, and trust in Your outcome. Amen.

MR. IRRELEVANT

*"In the same way, let your good deeds shine out for all to see,
so that everyone will praise your heavenly Father."*
MATTHEW 5:16 NLT

Since 1976, the NFL has given the Mr. Irrelevant award to the very last player selected in the NFL Draft. In 2009, the award went to kicker Ryan Succop from the University of South Carolina. He was picked number 256 in the last round by the Kansas City Chiefs. At the draft, he received an official NFL jersey with the number "256" and "Mr. Irrelevant" on the back.

Can you imagine getting tagged with the title Mr. Irrelevant? His response was this: "I don't mind it. I don't plan on being irrelevant…I plan on making an impact right away."[21] He proudly put on his NFL jersey, and today he is considered one of the most successful final draft picks in history. God prepared him for his assignment so he could respond with power and might, not weakness. He didn't let others define him. Do you?

People might give Ryan the title Mr. Irrelevant, but in God's eyes, he is Mr. Impact. In fact, to replace the jersey he received from the NFL, I presented him with an official jersey with a number one and "Mr. Impact" on the back when he arrived in Kansas City.

Instead of thinking of yourself as irrelevant, why not think of the impact God wants to make through you? You are set up for maximum impact. Step out in faith and believe it.

Father, I want to impact those around me. I throw off irrelevant and pick up impact. Amen.

---

21   Associated Press, "Succop Taken 256th Overall by Chiefs," ESPN, April 27, 2009, https://www.espn.com.

TIME-OUT

*"Come with me by yourselves to a quiet place
and get some rest."*

MARK 6:31

Have you ever reached a point in life where you needed to call a time-out? When you were overwhelmed by your to-do list, or when you needed to be in two places at once? Some of us push so hard, we should call back-to-back time-outs! We've all been there.

God knew we needed regular rest in order to be at our best; He designed us that way. But our frantic schedules and busyness tear us down. The noise from technology prevents us from unplugging. This isn't His design. God gave us two primary gifts to ensure we can unplug and escape: sleep and Sabbath. When He created the world, He incorporated a rhythm of rest for both our daily and weekly routines. Each day, God gives us light and dark. We all have an internal clock that regulates our wake-sleep cycles. And He told us to set aside a day for rest each week.

If we follow His plan, we will be regularly refreshed and renewed in mind, body, and soul. The more we know about the effects of proper rest, the more we marvel at God's perfect design. Sabbath is a once-a-week opportunity for God to breathe life back into our weary souls and for us to show we trust Him. He wants us to set our minds and hearts on Him so our priorities get reset and our souls revitalized. Sleep is a reward for a good day's work. These two gifts ensure we operate at our best.

Father, give me the strength to change my priorities for sleep and Sabbath. Amen.

BIGGER. FASTER. STRONGER.

Love the LORD your God with all your heart
and with all your soul and with all your strength.

DEUTERONOMY 6:5

When I got to high school, I realized I had to train differently to be competitive and make the teams. I needed to get bigger, stronger, and faster. So my brother and I got a membership at the Nautilus health club and went to work.

In sports, we spend 95 percent of our time training to compete. But spiritually speaking, most of us spend very little time training. We spend 99 percent of our time living and less than 1 percent of our time training. Why don't we approach our spiritual life as a training program?

We read devotions, but we aren't devoted. We call it quiet time, but we rush through it as we tackle the noise of the day. If we're honest, most of us don't even have a plan. As a result, we're often spiritually unprepared for life's challenges. The bottom line is that if we want the results, we need to do the work. We need to put ourselves in position for God to do what only He can do—transform us from the inside out. But we need to show up, put in some time, and make a training plan. While the plan can have freedom and flexibility, there are some essential exercises: reading the Word, prayer, confession, meditation, praise, and thanksgiving.

If we want to experience real life change, we must train. Make a plan and show up for the workout. Your soul will get bigger, faster, and stronger, and you'll be ready for whatever comes.

Father, give me the discipline to show up and train spiritually. Amen.

RUNNING ON EMPTY

"Come to me, all you who are weary and burdened,
and I will give you rest."
MATTHEW 11:28

Marco Andretti became the youngest driver to win a major open-wheel race at the 2006 Indy Grand Prix at Sonoma. Andretti was running very low on fuel near the end of the race, but a yellow caution flag allowed him to conserve enough to cross the finish line in first place. You could say that he was running on fumes.

Sometimes life feels like this—like that little fuel light is always lit on our dashboard. Running on empty can be exhilarating for a short while, but as a strategy for life, it wears you out. The things we think will fill up our tank rarely do. Success, money, recognition—all these things are nice, but they don't truly satisfy for long. When we try to fill our own tanks with things of this world, it's like putting diesel in a tank that calls for premium unleaded. We desperately want it to make the car go, but it simply won't.

Running on empty is running a race we can't win. We can only run on adrenaline and the applause of men for so long before we hit the wall and run out of gas. And once that warning light comes on, we have fewer options and limited time to refuel. The only way to get the car, and our life, the fuel it needs is to spend time with Jesus. Abiding in Christ means filling up on fuel that brings life. He is the only one who can fill your tank so you can finish the race victoriously.

Father, fill my tank with the fuel I need to complete Your mission today. Amen.

MAY

ALL ACCESS

*Confess your sins to each other and pray for each other
so that you may be healed.*

JAMES 5:16 NLT

It was a one-of-a-kind wristband. My hometown Kansas City Royals were playing against the famous New York Yankees, and my friend had given me an all-access wristband. And I mean all access! On the field for batting practice, in the dugout with the coaches, or in the locker room with the players—I could go wherever I wanted and be around any coach or athlete on the team. All I had to do was lift my arm to show my all-access wristband, and security let me in. Nothing was off limits. I had permission to wander and explore.

We often talk about God having all access to our lives, and yes, the Lord should have all access. When we surrender our lives to Jesus Christ, we are giving Him permission to wander through, explore, and enter any room of our heart. Nothing is off limits. However, it's another thing to give another human being all access. Nancy Leigh DeMoss insightfully wrote, "Humbling yourself by letting others into your life and allowing them to help you and hold you accountable will release the sanctifying, transforming grace of God in your life."[22]

All of us are one step away from making a stupid decision. Friends with an all-access pass to our hearts help create moral margin and keep us at a safer distance from stupid. They expand our safety zone. Men, are you willing to give someone you trust all access into your life so you can be who God has called you to be?

Father, I want to be more like You. Show me whom I can trust with an all-access pass to my heart. Amen.

22   Nancy Leigh DeMoss, *Holiness: The Heart God Purifies* (Chicago: Moody Publishers, 2005), 129.

LIFE IS A GIFT

How can I repay the Lord
for all the good he has done for me?
PSALM 116:12 CSB

My father, Edward T. Britton, passed away at 7:52 a.m. on May 2, 2008. Eight days later, more than eleven hundred people attended his celebration service to honor a life well lived. Throughout his eighteen-month journey with leukemia, he always talked about God's goodness, God's greatness, and God's graciousness. His favorite verse that he often quoted was Psalm 116:12. He was so thankful for his life and God's rich blessings.

Dad was totally focused on finishing well. Every time I called him during his final two months of life and asked how he was doing, he would say, "Contending." It was his way of saying he was fighting the good fight, running the right race. He lived every second as if it were his last—and not just when he became sick but throughout his lifetime. His favorite saying was "Life is God's gift to us. What we do with it is our gift back to Him." His life's ambition was to repay the Lord with a life surrendered to Him.

What a great challenge for us who still have life. What are you doing with your life? Is it a blessing to God? Are you investing your life in things that please God? What does it mean for you to lay down your life at the feet of Jesus? Your life is indeed God's gift to you. But what you do with it is your gift back to Him. What would you like that gift to be?

Father, thank You for the gift of my life. Help me know how to gift it back to You. Amen.

FAITH > FEAR

"Do not be afraid of them;
the LORD your God himself will fight for you."

DEUTERONOMY 3:22

It has been said, "Fear defeats more people than any other one thing in the world." Many of us have a fear of failure. But many of us are equally afraid of being rejected or not fitting in. The Bible is full of stories of faith overcoming fear. And God regularly puts us in situations where we are in over our heads so we have to depend on Him. He wants to grow our faith to overcome our fear.

In 1 Samuel 17, David, a teenager, faced down Goliath while the entire army of God looked on from the sidelines, and David's faith overcame the nation's fear. In Judges 6, God grew Gideon's faith by reducing his army from thirty-two thousand men down to three hundred to fight an enemy that would number over one hundred thousand—and the faith of the nation strengthened. In the book of Esther, Esther risked her life to stand up to the king and saved Mordecai and the Jewish people. In Numbers 13–14, Caleb and Joshua were the only two of twelve spies who told Moses they could possess the promised land.

Being courageous doesn't mean you don't face fear; it means you act by faith in the face of fear. No matter what challenge you are facing today, have a brave heart. Take a risk. Attempt something important for God. And remember that God is with you wherever you go. The Lord Himself will fight for you.

Father, develop in me the faith of David, Gideon, Esther, Caleb, and Joshua. Help me be strong and courageous even when I feel afraid. Amen.

THE RING

"What good is it for someone to gain the whole world,
yet forfeit their soul?"

MARK 8:36

Every sport at every level has a championship. Sure, there's the Lombardi Trophy, the Stanley Cup, and even the Green Jacket. But just about every competitor wants their own ring. Winning championships is the name of the game. Some say rings serve as a status symbol and even personal validation. Players who dominate their sport are still questioned if they haven't won a championship—if they don't have a ring. UCLA Hall of Fame football coach Henry "Red" Sanders once said, "Winning isn't everything. It's the only thing."[23] And many players today agree.

Wanting to win isn't a bad thing. But when the pursuit of "the ring" becomes the ultimate thing, we've got a problem. We have to compete for the right prize. The ring is the wrong prize because it never satisfies. Winning is temporary, and the feeling always fades.

Many of us place our sense of identity in our accomplishments. But God never designed the "rings" in our life to satisfy us. When we put all our energy and passion into chasing rings, success, or records, we will be disappointed and empty. It's never healthy to exchange the things that satisfy the soul for the temporary things of this world.

Jesus is the only prize that satisfies. He's the only thing worth pursuing with our whole heart. When we know Christ and experience His love, we are satisfied. We feel full and complete. And we are empowered to serve and bless others. Stop chasing after the rings of temporary pleasure and success. Stop searching for substitutes that never satisfy. Keep your eyes on the prize.

Father, change my heart to love and pursue things that will last forever.
Reorder my priorities and efforts so I put You first. Amen.

---

23   Jerry Bryan, "Sanders Gives Prescription for His Grid Success," *Birmingham News*, November 9, 1948.

NOTHING BEATS TEAMWORK

I will know that you are standing together with one spirit and one purpose, fighting together for the faith, which is the Good News.

PHILIPPIANS 1:27 NLT

When I was in Cambodia training sport leaders, I noticed a place by our hotel called Teamwork Coffee. The next morning, I needed coffee and couldn't wait to see what Teamwork Coffee was all about. The coffee was outstanding, the service was great, and the staff truly worked together as a team. They were living out their name! It still makes me smile when I think about seeing that classic teamwork principle plastered on the wall: "Teamwork makes the dream work."

Teamwork does make the dream work, but there are four enemies of teamwork that we must recognize:

1. Lone rangers want to do things alone instead of including others.
2. Blockers don't help others advance. They find it hard to share credit and feel threatened by stronger leaders.
3. Me Monsters are self-absorbed. They have difficulty trusting and believing in others.
4. Hoarders have a scarcity mindset over an abundance mindset and believe resources are limited. They think, *If others receive something, there is less for me.*

Ninety-four verses in the New Testament mention *one another*—love one another, accept one another, serve one another, and encourage one another, to name a few. Two-thirds of those verses deal with the church getting along and Christians loving each other. Lock arms with friends, family, coaches, and teammates because God's heart explodes when His children work, play, and serve together. Nothing beats teamwork!

Father, teach me to be a great teammate. Remind me that Your children accomplish more when we work together. Amen.

GO FOR IT

"With man this is impossible,
but with God all things are possible."
MATTHEW 19:26

Not only did doctors and scientists say that breaking the four-minute mile was impossible, but they also said that one would die in the attempt. On May 6, 1954, twenty-five-year-old medical student Roger Bannister broke the insurmountable barrier in a time of 3:59.4. His incredible feat shattered that limiting belief, redefined what's possible, and inspired other competitors to push their own limits.

Ten years later, high school runner Jim Ryun ran a 3:59.0 mile. By 2024, seventeen other kids have done the same, and the world record, set in 1999, is 3:43.13. International runners routinely run a sub-four-minute mile; what was once impossible is now common.

Roger's achievement teaches us an important lesson about the human spirit and our capacity to exceed our own limitations. We are called to go beyond what is comfortable and strive for greatness. We often face challenges and obstacles that seem insurmountable. We may doubt our abilities or fear failure. But we are called to break through the barriers that hold us back.

God's Word encourages us to pursue the impossible and rely on Him for strength. Striving for the impossible requires a new mindset. We must reject the limitations, negativity, and excuses so we can truly believe that, with God, all things are possible. We must push ourselves beyond what we think is achievable. When we strive for the impossible, not only do we experience growth, but we also inspire those around us. Our pursuit of greatness becomes a testimony to God's power and faithfulness.

Father, help me be courageous as I attempt the impossible, rely on Your power, and inspire others to do the same. Amen.

NO OTHER WAY

"If you love me,
obey my commandments."
JOHN 14:15 NLT

Growing up in the church as a young boy, I have fond memories of singing the classic hymns of the faith. One of my favorites was "Trust and Obey," written by John Henry Sammis, a Presbyterian minister, in 1887. "Trust and obey, for there's no other way to be happy in Jesus, but to trust and obey."

A biblical definition of *obedience* is simply "hearing God's Word and acting accordingly." The problem isn't hearing but acting. As men of God, we either lead lives of obedience or lives of disobedience.

There are hundreds of reasons to obey, and if we love Jesus, then we will obey His commandments. Here are ten reasons obedience reveals the supernatural power of God:

1. Obedience invites the favor and blessing of God (Joshua 1:8).
2. Obedience always pleases the heart of God, who loves me (John 14:21).
3. Obedience will always, in time, bring a harvest (Galatians 6:9).
4. Obedience is the ultimate expression of my love for Christ (2 John 6).
5. Obedience is the pathway for intimacy with God (1 John 2:3).
6. Obedience always delivers what it promises: freedom and blessing (James 1:25).
7. Obedience leaves a legacy (Psalm 112:1–2).
8. Obedience to prayer is powerful and effective (James 5:16).
9. Obedience guides the direction of my life (Colossians 1:10).
10. Obedience means God succeeds (Galatians 2:20).

Men, I challenge you to obey. There's no other way. Others are counting on you to hear God and act.

Father, help me obey You. Obeying You brings clarity, and disobeying You brings confusion. Bring clarity to my life. Amen.

A VIRTUOUS WOMAN

A wife of noble character who can find? She is worth far more than rubies.

PROVERBS 31:10

Proverbs 31 outlines a description of a virtuous woman. This passage provides valuable insights for men seeking a woman who has qualities that reflect godly character, wisdom, and strength. Here are some virtuous qualities to look for:

- Trustworthiness: A virtuous woman is trustworthy and dependable. She is faithful in her commitments and keeps her word. She builds a strong foundation of trust in all her relationships.
- Industriousness: A virtuous woman is hardworking and diligent. She strives to provide for her family and contributes actively to her household. She uses her talents for the greater good.
- Wisdom: A virtuous woman exercises wisdom and discernment in her decision-making, seeking God's guidance and making choices based on biblical truth. She navigates life's challenges with maturity and godly wisdom.
- Compassion and Kindness: The virtuous woman is compassionate and kindhearted. She extends love and care to others and displays genuine empathy and generosity.
- Strength and Dignity: A virtuous woman is strong, both in character and resilience. She faces adversity with courage and grace, demonstrating inner strength.
- Humility: A virtuous woman does not seek attention or praise for her deeds but humbly serves those around her. She demonstrates humility, recognizing true greatness comes from serving.
- Fear of the Lord: Above all, the virtuous woman's life is characterized by her reverence for and relationship with God. Her faith in Him influences every aspect of her life.

Look for and celebrate women in your life for their virtuous qualities. This will lead to harmonious, Christ-centered relationships.

Father, thank You for revealing the qualities of a virtuous woman. Amen.

PASS IT ON

For our benefit God made him to be wisdom itself.
Christ made us right with God;
he made us pure and holy, and he freed us from sin.

1 CORINTHIANS 1:30 NLT

The most memorable moments happen in the midst of real life. Wisdom isn't something you wait to acquire when you get "old." Wisdom is passed on in everyday moments, through everyday events, and by everyday people like you and me. Everything you experience is an opportunity to dig deeper, connect the dots of faith and life, and pass on your most important beliefs. It takes intentionality.

That's exactly how Jesus turned the world upside down and started a worldwide movement of people who put their faith in action. His early followers saw their relationships with Jesus as an intricate part of their lives. They didn't join God's team to sit on the bench. They yearned to contribute. Their thoughts and words, the way they did business, how they interacted with their neighbors and handled temptation—you name it—all reflected their faith and the condition of their hearts.

Jesus didn't just let life happen. He was intentional. Whether He was walking on the paths, telling stories, teaching to a crowd, eating a meal in the upper room, or healing the sick, Jesus was walking wisdom. He taught His followers to be intentional too. Through His parables, He passed on the wisdom of God. You can too. In fact, it's crucial that you do. More people than you know are counting on you to share.

Father, I want to pass on the wisdom You've given me. Help me show others what it looks like to walk with Jesus. Amen.

GAME OVER

Humble yourselves before God.
Resist the devil, and he will flee from you.

JAMES 4:7 NLT

Mariano Rivera of the New York Yankees is the greatest closer of all time with over six hundred saves. As a Yankees fan, if I saw Mariano coming out of the bullpen, I knew it was game over for the other team. In life we have three opponents: the lie of the devil, the lure of our flesh, and the love of the world. Second Peter 1:3–4 tells us we have divine power and what we need to live a godly life.

We have power over our flesh. Whether it's a sexual temptation, a desire for alcohol or drugs, excessive food, or even laziness, our flesh is insatiable. But God always gives us a way out—a closer.

We have power over the world. The Enemy loves to appeal to our sense of pride in what we've done and what we own. But material things never satisfy for long.

We have power over the devil. Our enemy is not to be taken lightly. His singular purpose is to destroy us. First Peter 5:8 says the Enemy is prowling around like a lion, looking to devour.

We must walk in the Spirit so we can see the attempts of the Enemy. Our strength is not enough; we need the power of the Holy Spirit living in us to overcome our flesh, the world, and the devil.

Father, with the power of the Holy Spirit, help me overcome the lies of the devil, the lure of my flesh, and the love of the world. Amen.

STAYING POWER

"As for you, be strong and courageous,
for your work will be rewarded."

2 CHRONICLES 15:7 NLT

In 2007, I took my first mission trip to Ukraine, and it opened my eyes. The trip was a game changer as God captured my heart for the nations. During that trip, we walked through a back door into an old gym, and we saw a young man doing basketball ministry with a group of boys. I approached him and said, "Andriy, you are doing FCA in Ukraine!"

He replied, "What is FCA?"

Two years later, Andriy joined FCA staff to start FCA Ukraine. Today, his team is impacting thousands of coaches and athletes throughout the country. Andriy keeps showing up and remaining faithful to the calling God has put in his heart. He is a living example of the power of showing up. Andriy has maintained his commitment despite difficulties, and as a result, his life is marked with resolve, resilience, fortitude, and grit. So many people get distracted and lose their focus. Sometimes it is harder to keep showing up because you must press into the known, deal with the mess, and figure out how to make it work. If we want to make an impact, we need to show up, remain faithful, and stay focused.

What hangs in the balance if we don't stay? Families. Loved ones. Friends. Coworkers. Teams. Church communities. Just imagine what God could do through us as men if we decided to keep showing up and stay focused.

Lord, I commit to show up. Mark my life by unwavering commitment that will not crumble under changing or difficult situations. Amen.

NO EXCUSES

When Jesus saw him and knew he had been ill for a long time, he asked him, "Would you like to get well?" "I can't, sir," the sick man said, "for I have no one to put me into the pool when the water bubbles up. Someone else always gets there ahead of me."

JOHN 5:6–7 NLT

George Washington Carver is famously known for saying, "Ninety-nine percent of failures come from people who have the habit of making excuses." We make excuses for everything. We point the finger at everybody else and fail to take responsibility for the part we played. Every time we make an excuse, it's easier the next time.

In John 5, Jesus found a man who had been crippled for thirty-eight years. The man didn't even answer Jesus' question about getting well. He immediately offered excuses. A simpler answer would have been "Yes, I want to be healed!"

Excuses never make you better. And they don't change your circumstances—they solidify them. When making excuses becomes a habit, we run on a road to failure. These three words are always followed by an excuse: *could've*, *would've*, and *should've*.

One of the ten guiding principles at my kids' school is "Take full responsibility for your actions and their consequences." Or saying "No excuses" would work just fine. When we take responsibility, we assume ownership. When we make changes, we assume responsibility.

Benjamin Franklin is credited with saying, "Those who are good at making excuses are seldom good at anything else." So take this warning: don't get good at making excuses. Instead, take responsibility and make changes. Excuses lead to failure. If it's important enough, you'll find a way. If not, you'll find an excuse.

Father, show me areas where I am making excuses, and help me take personal responsibility instead. Amen.

WALK WITH JESUS

You were called to this, because Christ also suffered for you,
leaving you an example, so that you should follow in His steps.

1 PETER 2:21 HCSB

Can you imagine what the disciples felt as they gradually realized they were walking with the God of the universe, the creator of heaven and earth, the Savior of the world? At first, they had no idea who He really was, but His call compelled them to immediately leave everything they knew and follow Him. There was something special, something different about Jesus. He could see things in people they couldn't see and do miraculous things they couldn't do. No wonder they were irresistibly drawn to Him.

Day after day, they walked with Him along dirt roads, gathered and ate meals, and laughed and listened as they learned an entirely new way of doing life. Along the way, their souls were satisfied because their longing for that "something more" was gone. Jesus had what they wanted. He breathed life, purpose, passion, and power into otherwise boring, unfulfilling lives. The disciples tasted greatness. They touched eternity. And they were never the same.

Your time with Jesus will inspire you to walk in His footsteps, hear His voice, and do what He did. You'll be challenged as a man to love unconditionally, live with integrity, pray powerfully, and do things greater than you've ever imagined. Walking with Jesus will transform the way you think, feel, and live. What are you waiting for? Dive in today and follow the God of the universe, the only one who can fill that deep longing in your heart.

Father, help me walk with You like the disciples did. I want to experience You filling every need, desire, and longing of my heart. Amen.

MAKE IT FUN

"Rejoice in that day and leap for joy!"
LUKE 6:23 HCSB

In Sweden, they converted a set of stairs leading to a subway into an actual working piano keyboard with black and white "keys." With each step you took, it played a note. At first, people were hesitant to step on it, but within two days, it took off. Sixty-seven percent of the commuters started taking the stairs (the hard way) instead of the escalator (the easy way).[24] Almost no one chose the stairs when they were plain old stairs. But when they were transformed into something fun, people literally jumped for joy—all the way up the steps.

God's version of fun is wrapped up in the word *joy*. Joy is the deep feeling of great pleasure, satisfaction, and happiness—regardless of the circumstances. Joy is something we experience on the inside that overflows on the outside. We shouldn't be able to contain it. That's what I want. How about you?

Sometimes it feels like we've sucked the fun out of the Christian life. But I propose that if we're going to make it for the long haul, we'd better make it fun. If you hate it, you may not make it. Devotions shouldn't be drudgery. We should look forward to church. In our life, our joy should overflow. Legendary self-improvement author Dale Carnegie once said, "People rarely succeed at anything unless they have fun doing it."[25] Work can be hard, but it better be fun too. Faith goes the same way—make it fun!

Father, thank You for being a God of joy and fun. Help my contagious joy point all to Jesus. Amen.

---

24   "The Piano Stairs Experiment: Making Life More Fun," Academy 4SC, accessed November 13, 2023, https://academy4sc.org.

25   Dale Carnegie, *How to Win Friends and Influence People*, hardcover ed. (New York: Simon & Schuster, 2009), 71.

WISDOM WALKING

Blessed are those who find wisdom, those who gain understanding,
for she is more profitable than silver and yields better returns than gold.

PROVERBS 3:13–14

Life is a series of forks in the road. Some directions and decisions are clearly right or wrong; others are merely multiple paths you could take. But all decisions take you down one of two paths. That's why it's so important to walk in wisdom every day.

Walking in wisdom is a lifelong journey. Here are three essential ways to walk in wisdom daily:

1. It all starts with desire. Galatians 5:25 says, "Since we live by the Spirit, let us keep in step with the Spirit." Your life should reflect the fruit of the Spirit, not the works of the flesh. "Let us keep in step" means the desire to walk with Jesus every moment and in every area of life.
2. It's fueled by devotion. Walking as Jesus did is an all-or-nothing proposition. It's not about adding God into your life or sprinkling Him into your plans when you have time. When you say, "Whatever you want, God, not what I want," expect Him to take you up on that offer.
3. It's about setting your direction. Just as coaches take athletes to a higher level of competition they couldn't achieve on their own, Jesus Christ has a game plan to take us from point A to point B.

When you're filled with God's wisdom, surrendered to His will, and know your ultimate destination, you live a life worthy of Jesus.

Father, help me find wisdom and gain understanding so I can be the man You desire for me to be. Amen.

IN THE FIRE

In all this you greatly rejoice, though now for a little while you may have had to suffer grief in all kinds of trials. These have come so that the proven genuineness of your faith—of greater worth than gold, which perishes even though refined by fire—may result in praise, glory and honor when Jesus Christ is revealed.

1 PETER 1:6–7

Character is uncovered in crisis and formed in the fire. It will be revealed and refined. When we encounter pressure, we're given a chance to grow and mature. God brings to the surface all things that need to be refined.

In Daniel 3, Shadrach, Meshach, and Abednego faced one of the hottest trials in history. When they refused to bow down and worship a false god, the king ordered his soldiers to literally throw them into a fiery furnace. When the men took their stand and fell into the fire, the heat of the flames instantly killed the soldiers who threw them in. But the big three were unharmed. The trial produced not death but life. The trial set them free from what was holding them back and elevated the name of God.

God uses trials to make us unshakeable and Him unmistakable. Don't try to get out of anything prematurely. Let the fire do its work. Anybody can avoid adversity or tackle trials on their own—but they remain ordinary. God wants to produce the extraordinary out of our adversity. Trials come in many shapes and sizes, but one thing is for sure: trials will come. Sometimes we choose them, and sometimes they seem to choose us. God will make us complete, expand our faith, and bring glory to His name. Let your character be formed in the fire.

Father, I know trials are not optional but inevitable. Form my character through the fire. Make me look more like Jesus. Amen.

SPIRITUAL SHIFT

If you confess with your mouth that Jesus is Lord and believe in your heart that God raised him from the dead, you will be saved. For with the heart one believes and is justified, and with the mouth one confesses and is saved.

ROMANS 10:9–10 ESV

When I was eight years old, my mom was leading a Bible club as an outreach for the neighborhood kids. What she didn't expect was for her son to say the simple prayer with her to accept Jesus. However, it was not until I was fourteen years old while at a church camp that I completely surrendered everything in my life to Jesus. To symbolize my decision, I threw a wood chip, representing my life, into a bonfire. With tears streaming down my face, I now understood the prayer I'd prayed with my mom at age eight. Since then, life has never been the same. I still have the little yellow card I signed that evening at camp that says, "All I am, all I have, and all I ever hope to be, I now and forever dedicate to the Lord Jesus Christ for His use and glory, absolutely, unconditionally, now and forever."

Have you experienced that spiritual shift in your life? Is there a moment in time as a man that you called on the name of Jesus? If you would like to trust in Jesus now, here is a prayer I recommend:

Father, I realize I'm a sinner and that I can't save myself. I need Your forgiveness. I believe You loved me so much that Jesus died on the cross for my sins and rose from the dead. I put my faith in You as Savior and Lord. Today, I surrender my life. Amen.

WINNING MARGIN

Blessed is the one who does not walk in step with the wicked or stand in the way that sinners take or sit in the company of mockers, but whose delight is in the law of the LORD, and who meditates on his law day and night.

PSALM 1:1–2

Flash back to the closest finish in the history of swimming: Michael Phelps, in pursuit of eight Olympic gold medals at the 2008 Beijing Games, finished his flip turn in the hundred-meter butterfly in seventh place and trailed the other swimmers by almost a full body length. Incredibly, Michael closed the gap, literally winning by the tip of his finger. When the giant scoreboard posted the times, everyone was stunned. Even the underwater replays seemed to defy logic.

When a margin of victory is tight, it's an adrenaline rush. For the winners, it's time to celebrate. For the losers, it's agonizing. But in life, walking a tightrope between winning and losing can have devastating effects. The winning margin is the distance between doing the right thing and doing the wrong thing. God wants us to keep our distance from temptation, not see how close we can get. He wants us to flee to get out of compromising situations. One small mistake can bring a tidal wave of guilt, shame, and brokenness.

When Joseph found himself in a compromising situation with Potiphar's wife, he fled. When David looked on Bathsheba's beauty, he moved closer to the line of sin and eliminated his margin of victory. When he crossed the line, he left a wake of destruction behind. Our goal with temptations is to create a significant winning margin.

Father, help me draw the line far from temptation and sin so I have distance between what I know to be right and wrong. Amen.

THE PACER

Enoch walked with God.

GENESIS 5:24 ESV

Approaching the starting line, I saw runners wearing bright green shirts and holding up signs with numbers representing competition times. They were the marathon pacer runners, who help runners achieve their goal times. Never having run with a pacer, I decided this was my only chance to reach my goal. I finally found a pacer with my goal on his sign. Zach would maintain the pace I needed to achieve my goal. Ten runners gathered around Zach, and he kept us on track. No stops, no breaks, no waiting for stragglers. He set the pace, and it was our job to stay with him.

I stayed on Zach's hip, stride for stride. Zach took care of everything. He encouraged us, motivated us, and gave us tips throughout the run. All I needed to do was run with Zach, step by step. When eight runners fell back, Zach didn't slow. He maintained the pace needed to accomplish the goal on his sign. Only two of us crossed the finish line with him.

In the same way, we need to get into stride with Jesus, being in step with Him. When we decide to walk with God, we must know His pace and His ways. When we get into His stride, the only thing that matters is the life of Christ. Get in stride with the pacer; run with Jesus.

Father, help me run the race of faith You've marked before me. I commit to run with You. Amen.

TOXIC FRIENDS

Do not be misled:
"Bad company corrupts good character."

1 Corinthians 15:33

You've probably heard the phrase "Birds of a feather flock together." That saying means that we naturally gravitate toward people like us. People who have similar interests, ideas, characteristics, or behaviors tend to find each other. American entrepreneur Jim Rohn says we are the average of the five people we associate with most. Our friends influence us subtly yet powerfully, and that influence can be negative or positive.

Toxic friends show up in a lot of different ways. Toxic friends are false friends. They have no desire to help you become the man God has made you to be. In fact, misery loves company. God says bad company corrupts good morals. Toxic friends are complainers, criticizers, or tempters.

Complainers never have anything positive to say and see the glass as half empty. They see problems instead of potential and obstacles instead of opportunities. Criticizers find all your faults and drag you down. And the tempters push you to do things you have decided not to do. "A companion of fools suffers harm" (Proverbs 13:20). Like it or not, toxic friends tear you down.

It's time to evaluate your friends and have real conversations about the value of the friendship. Expose the negativity or ways your friendships have become toxic. Address it. Sometimes, once people see it, they deal with it, and things get better. Other times, it may not be so simple, and you'll need to change how much time you spend together. Either way, finding like-minded, encouraging friends is a key strategy as you walk with Jesus on the narrow path.

Father, help me be a great and godly friend and weed out those who are dragging me down. Amen.

GOOD FOR NOTHING

Don't worry about anything, but in everything,
through prayer and petition with thanksgiving,
let your requests be made known to God.

PHILIPPIANS 4:6 HCSB

During my freshman year at college, I was so stressed out that I was ready
to explode. Seventy-five players were competing for thirty-five spots on the
University of Delaware lacrosse team. If that wasn't tough enough, almost the
entire team had returned with only a few spots to fill.

So I phoned my mom. "I don't think I'm going to make the team," I told
her. I worried that my dream of playing college lacrosse was dying, so I did
what I do really well: I began to question everything. *Why did I come to
Delaware? What will people think if I get cut? Should I transfer if I don't make
the team?* Worry consumed me.

Worry has no redeeming value. It's good for nothing. Worry will not help
us or protect us from danger. Worry is plain wrong. It rots and destroys the
mind. It drains us and ties us down. It becomes cancer. According to the
Cambridge Dictionary, the word *worry* is derived from the German word
wurgen, which means "to strangle" or "to choke." Worry strangles our hearts
and minds with the world's viewpoint and chokes out God's viewpoint.

The good news is that we cannot control the future. If we knew with
certainty what the future holds, we wouldn't need to trust God. Worry is
believing God will screw up. Where there is worry and anxiety, there is fear
and a lack of trust. When you have faith and trust, you have peace and joy.
Men, refuse to worry. Instead, trust God and pray about every part of your life.

Father, drain the worry out of my heart. You are in control, and I am not. Amen.

PROTECT THIS HOUSE

The weapons we fight with are not the weapons of the world.
On the contrary, they have divine power to demolish strongholds.

2 CORINTHIANS 10:4

Under Armour commercials blasted the question, "Will you protect this house?" Every competitor responded, "I will. I will. I will." We love the battle. We love the competition. And we love the fight. In sports, we prepare our bodies and our minds for the battle. We know what to expect, and we get ready. We stand our ground. We take our shots. We "man up." There's no backing down or giving in. If you let your guard down, you can get beat. Life is no different.

Unfortunately, many of us don't view life as a battle. We think we're on a vacation cruise ship instead of a battleship. We don't approach the battles we face with a competitor's mindset or from a spiritual perspective. We are often unaware of the spiritual battles that rage in and around us. As a result, we are unprepared to "protect this house."

We have an enemy within us—the lust of the flesh. Our flesh wants what it wants when it wants it—now! You can think of it as cravings. Paul described our internal struggle in Romans 7:21–23, saying, "The moment I decide to do good, sin is there to trip me up" (MSG). The Spirit always wars against self. And our old nature always has a craving for sin. God never tempts us; instead, we are tempted by our old nature. When we're prepared to protect this house, we fight with spiritual weapons of prayer, praise, and the sword of the Spirit.

Father, get me ready to protect this house, using the spiritual weapons that break strongholds. Amen.

BETTER OR DEADER

You too consider yourselves dead to sin
but alive to God in Christ Jesus.

ROMANS 6:11 HCSB

Coach Sleepy Thompson coached football at my high school for thirty-two years. His teams boasted twenty-nine winning seasons, twelve conference titles, and three undefeated seasons. I loved playing for Coach Thompson. I always had an internal drive to become a better football player. He coached in such a way that he took the entire team to a higher level of competition.

I'm fascinated with what makes a great coach. According to the *Merriam-Webster Dictionary*, the word *coach* actually comes from the word *wagon* or *stagecoach*, implying that they take passengers from point A to point B.

In life, our master coach, Jesus Christ, also has a clear game plan for us. We think God wants us to get better—to improve, to become better people, or to be nicer Christians. But His call goes much deeper than that. He says to get deader not better!

If you want to live, Jesus said you must die. The apostle Paul wrote in Galatians 2:20, "I have been crucified with Christ and I no longer live, but Christ lives in me." That's what it means to get deader. When Paul wrote this, he was talking about dying to desires. Getting deader is dying to self daily. Dietrich Bonhoeffer, who died for his faith, wrote, "When Christ calls a man, he bids him come and die."[26]

Nowhere in Scripture does Jesus encourage us to surrender our life to Him and just get better. All of us need to wake up each day and say, "I choose to die today!" The world is longing to see men that are dead to self. But it's all-or-nothing. You can't do it halfway.

Father, give me the courage to die to the things of this world. Amen.

---

26   Dietrich Bonhoeffer, *The Cost of Discipleship* (New York: Touchstone, 1995), 89.

FINISH STRONG

He will also keep you firm to the end,
so that you will be blameless on the day of our Lord Jesus Christ.

1 CORINTHIANS 1:8

In 1982, ABC's *Wide World of Sports* introduced the world to the Ironman Triathlon. ABC spotlighted the leader, Julie Moss, as she agonizingly crawled toward the finish line. Moss held the lead just yards away from the finish line, but unfortunately, she was passed by eventual winner Kathleen McCartney. After Kathleen passed her, Julie literally willed her body to cross the line. Her mind would not let her fail. She reached her goal even when her bodily systems were shutting down. Millions watched her incredible finish and were inspired to start the sport. Julie, then a twenty-three-year-old college student, is now an Ironman Hall of Famer.[27]

When we look at the Bible, the greats always finish strong. They may not have started well, or they may have stumbled along the way, but they all have one thing in common: they finished strong. Take Paul, for example. When Scripture first introduces us to Paul, his name was Saul, and he was persecuting followers of Christ. It took a personal encounter with Jesus to change his heart; physical blindness gave him eyes to see his new passion and purpose. He started bad, but he finished well. King David started strong, stumbled, then finished strong. Peter started fast and followed Jesus immediately, stumbled in his three-time denial, then finished strong by boldly sharing Christ.

If you have the desire to actually finish what you've started, you can do it. Start and finish strong each day. Days lead to months, and months to years. Finishing strong happens one step at a time.

Father, give me what I need to finish the race and keep the faith. Amen.

---

27   Pam Kragen, "Ironman Vet Julie Moss Recounts Her 1982 'Crawl of Fame' in New Memoir," *San Diego Union Tribune*, October 2, 2018, https://www.sandiegouniontribune.com.

MIRROR, MIRROR

Anyone who listens to the word but does not do what it says is like
someone who looks at his face in a mirror and, after looking at himself,
goes away and immediately forgets what he looks like.

JAMES 1:23–24

Have you ever seen those guys in the gym who just can't seem to take their
eyes off themselves? You know, the ones who are always flexing in front of the
mirror or the ones who look past you at their own reflection as they talk to
you? I always get a kick out of the guys who suck in their guts and push out
their chests as they walk through the weight room.

What makes us so fascinated by our own reflections? We're literally
obsessed with our appearance. Think about how much time we spend making
sure we look just right—we wear fashionable clothes and comb our hair
perfectly. We need to sport trendy sunglasses and to drive the right car. And
we put on a happy face so people think we have it all together. But how many
times do we go back to the mirror, forgetting what we look like? A lot. Are we
that mesmerized with our appearance, or is it rooted in a deeper insecurity?

God tells us in His Word that He cares much less about external
appearances and much more about the internal conditions of our hearts.
The condition of your heart can't be seen in the mirror. The most important
changes happen in your mind and heart, not your body. God values your
character over your appearance. Align your heart and do the same.

*Father, help me focus on developing a heart that cares about the things that
matter most to You. Amen.*

THE LARRY PRINCIPLE

"The last will be first,
and the first last."
MATTHEW 20:16 CSB

Larry, at only thirteen years old, made a significant impact on my life. It happened at a Fellowship of Christian Athletes camp. The last night featured an open mic session when campers could come forward and share how camp influenced their lives. It was time to hear how God had worked in the campers' hearts throughout the week. I'll never forget when Larry got up to share. Larry was a five-foot-tall seventh grader from inner-city Kansas City, and he was a hit with the other campers. He was funny, lovable, charming, and outspoken. His contagious laugh and raspy voice made him stand out from the others, and he became the camp favorite.

The open mic session had already gone thirty minutes too long when Larry stood to be the last in line to share. Larry was never short of words, but when he leaned into the microphone, he shared a single transformational leadership statement: "If you ain't serving, you ain't leading!" Then he turned around, walked off the stage, and sat down. Larry, the Great Theologian, had spoken. I was in awe. In seven words, he'd communicated one of the most profound concepts I've ever heard on leadership. That was a watershed moment for me. It's all about serving, not leading. Everybody wants to be a leader, but no one wants to be a servant.

Men, let the Larry Principle burn in your hearts: "If you ain't serving, you ain't leading!"

Father, I ask for a heart to serve. When I serve, I am leading. Amen.

ACT LIKE MEN

Be watchful, stand firm in the faith,
act like men, be strong.
1 CORINTHIANS 16:13 ESV

It's no secret that men have been in the line of fire for a long time. Modern society has deconstructed and demonized traditional ideas of what a man really is. When a man shows strength, honor, and courage, people label him as having toxic masculinity. None of this should matter to a man of God because he should only care what God says and pay little attention to the nonsense of the world and current culture. God has designed men and women to be different. We are different in obvious ways in a physiological sense, but we're also different in the responsibilities and roles we are assigned.

Make no mistake: we are all equal in the sight of God. God has created us all to be image-bearers, clay on the Potter's wheel. We are His masterpieces. We all have equal value. At the same time, our roles and responsibilities are different, and we desperately need both masculine men and feminine women. Men are designed to protect, provide, and pastor. Scripture refers to us as watchmen, warriors, and shepherds. First Corinthians 16:13 implores men to be men—to be watchful, stand firm in the faith, act like men, and be strong. These are very specific admonitions. And it's time for us to step up into these roles and refuse to let culture emasculate us.

We need men who understand the times and know what to do. We need men who are strong in body and spirit, who aren't afraid to hold to a standard and call others to that standard too.

Father, help me unapologetically rise into my role as a strong man of God. Amen.

WHO'S YOUR ONE?

Two are better than one because they have a good reward for their efforts.
For if either falls, his companion can lift him up; but pity the one who falls
without another to lift him up.

ECCLESIASTES 4:9–10 CSB

Do you have at least one trusted friend who knows you inside and out? We all need at least one person to share our hearts with—someone who has the green light to the door of our life, someone with whom no subject is out-of-bounds or off-limits. This is someone who lifts us up when we stumble and holds us down when we stray. They are absolutely, totally committed to our spiritual, physical, mental, and emotional success.

You can't demand accountability from someone. It never works! There can be no judgment or condemnation, only tough love and compassion; the Holy Spirit does the real work—and we are not Him. You need friends who will hold you accountable in the areas of purity, faith, and integrity—people who will fight for these things in their own lives. Accountability is more than asking tough questions. It's staying engaged and involved in the messy areas of struggle until victory is won. True accountability requires humility and a willingness to admit your mistakes and learn from them.

For more than three decades, I have had at least one man of God in my life who is my accountability partner. Accountability has allowed me to align my beliefs with my behaviors and my convictions with my conduct. Find at least one because two are better than one. Who's your one?

Father, I need at least one friend who will hold me accountable. Show me who that person needs to be. Amen.

POTTER AND CLAY

You, Lord, are our Father. We are the clay, you are the potter;
we are all the work of your hand.

ISAIAH 64:8

I can still remember when each of the kids gave us gifts from art class—a carefully crafted coffee mug or something else they'd molded and knew we'd love. Never "perfect" like you'd buy at the store but infinitely more valuable. We immediately recognized the love and thoughtfulness that went into their creations, and that's what made them so valuable.

We are the clay, and God—our Father—is the potter. This analogy reminds us of the divine craftsmanship involved in shaping our lives. God is creating masterpieces out of us, and we can trust His creative process. Just as a skilled potter molds clay with intention and purpose, God does the same with our lives. He shapes us into vessels that can carry His love, grace, and purpose in the world. In the process of molding clay, the potter applies pressure and removes parts that hinder the desired shape. God allows challenges, difficulties, and even trials to shape us into vessels of greater strength and purpose; these experiences teach us to grow in faith and resilience.

Many times we aren't happy with the way we look on the wheel. The finished product may not be "perfect" according to our human idea of perfection. But in God's eyes, we are of infinite value. Every creation is made in the image of God with divine purpose. In the end, we can be confident that He who began this good work in us will bring it to completion.

Father, shape me, mold me, and transform me into a vessel that brings glory to Your name. Amen.

THE PRESENCE

The LORD replied, "My Presence will go with you,
and I will give you rest."
EXODUS 33:14

Everybody knows a car can't run without gas—or electricity for some. Cars need power. Even if the fluids are topped off, the tires have air, and the battery is new, without gas or electricity, it simply won't go. In the same way, our Christian lives need the Holy Spirit.

Moses knew he needed God's presence. In fact, he was afraid to do anything without it. He witnessed firsthand how God went ahead of him and the Israelites through a pillar of cloud by day and a pillar of fire by night. He had witnessed God part the Red Sea by His power. Moses knew that apart from God, they were powerless.

Following Jesus' death and resurrection, the Spirit of God now lives in us (John 14:15–26); this is the same Spirit who hovered over the waters during the creation of the universe, who set the Israelites free from Egyptian slavery, and who raised Jesus from the dead. The Holy Spirit will fill, control, and empower us as we seek Jesus, humble ourselves, confess sin, and fully surrender to His leadership. He leads, guides, corrects, and directs.

The life of a person who is controlled and completed by the Holy Spirit enjoys the fruit of that filling: love, joy, peace, patience, kindness, goodness, faithfulness, gentleness, and self-control (Galatians 5:22–25). The Holy Spirit gives us wisdom, courage, and power (Acts 4–7). Now that's the kind of life I want, a life marked by God's presence.

Father, fill me with Your Spirit so I can have the wisdom, courage, and power to live for You. Amen.

FIRE IN THE BELLY

The words are fire in my belly, a burning in my bones.
I'm worn out trying to hold it in. I can't do it any longer!
JEREMIAH 20:7–10 MSG

"Do you have fire in your belly?" I've heard this question hundreds of times from my coaches. It never required an actual answer. It was a challenge to play with passion. My coaches wanted to know if I had determination and commitment.

It's one thing to talk about fire in the belly when it comes to sports, but it's another thing when we apply it to spiritual life. Jeremiah had a fire burning so strong for God that he couldn't contain it. This is encouragement for us: spiritual grit and spiritual tenacity need to burn so strong in us that we can't hold it back.

The fire is the presence of the Holy Spirit, and we must remember that the fire within comes from Him. We must lay ourselves on the altar and ask God to consume us with His fire. I am so inspired by the story about the great preacher John Wesley, who preached to large crowds during the Great Awakening. It was said he would be so on fire for the Lord that people would come watch him burn.

How do you stoke a fire and passion for Jesus? Just like you stoke a fire by adding wood, put your faith into action in your everyday walk, and it will keep burning. Spending personal time with the Lord adds wood and stokes the fire too.

Men, are you on fire for Jesus? Do others want to come and see you burn for Him?

Father, I desire for Your fire to burn within me. I want a spiritual fire in the belly that can't be contained. Consume me. Amen.

JUNE

SPEAK LIFE

The tongue can bring death or life;
those who love to talk will reap the consequences.

PROVERBS 18:21 NLT

In the back seat of our minivan, I heard my daughter cut down her brother. Immediately, I said, "Abby, were you speaking life or death?"

She responded, "Death, Daddy!"

She knew what was coming next when I said, "Now speak life to your brother." When our kids were young, I made sure they understood that their words brought life or death. If they spoke death, they would have to replace it with words of life. This became one of our key family principles.

God wants us, as men of God, to speak life, not death. Our conversations should bless, encourage, motivate, and inspire others. We should look for opportunities to bring life to every conversation. Instead of letting our words drip with negativity, we should drench them in the edification and blessing of others. I can name several people in my life whom I actively seek out because of the encouragement they offer. They are gifted to build others up with authentic, genuine, encouraging words. The effect is love, joy, compassion, blessing, and motivation.

If we are truly walking in accordance with the will of God, we will speak life everywhere we go, and He will use our words to bring healing and restoration to our work, our teams, our family, our churches, and even our communities. May we all be committed to bringing life change with words of life. I firmly believe everyone is underencouraged, so there is a lot of work to be done. Today, will you speak life or death? The choice is yours.

Father, please forgive me for speaking death. I know You want me to speak life and bring blessing, encouragement, and love. Amen.

OUTSIDE DEFICIT DISORDER

The heavens declare the glory of God;
the skies proclaim the work of his hands.

PSALM 19:1

Joe De Sena, the founder of Spartan races, is famous for promoting outside workouts and competitive races. I have a theory that we don't have deficits in attention; we have ODD—outside deficit disorder. This theory has proven true in the practical and experiential laboratory of obstacle course racing. I've become an avid Spartan racer and have reaped the benefits and blessings of completing courses up to thirteen miles and conquering over thirty obstacles along the way. There's something inspirational about army crawling under barbed wire in muddy, rocky terrain, clawing your way out of mud pits, and climbing the mountains in majestic venues across the country. It's good for the body, mind, and soul.

Most men have been shamed into believing their masculinity is toxic. That's utter nonsense. But if you spend enough time indoors staring at a phone or computer screen while sitting at a desk, it's easy to lose your heart and spiritual connection to God's creation. Men and boys need to be outside to feed their souls. God gives us room to breathe and relieves our stress, and our encounters with nature fill us with an awe and reverence for Him. Plus, I've found I hear clearly from God when I'm outside.

Pick the activity—it really doesn't matter—but get outside and into the wild. I've come to love outdoor workouts; the worse the weather, the more satisfying the workout. Snow, sleet, rain, wind, and even the sunny days are a blessing. Seeing the expanse of stars while sitting at the fire pit cures ODD. Pick up your head and see what God has made. It's majestic.

Father, breathe new life into my soul as I intentionally experience Your creation outside. Amen.

FEARLESS, NOT FLAWLESS

Though the righteous fall seven times,
they rise again.
PROVERBS 24:16

In Major League Baseball, a hitter with a career batting average over .300 is considered a Hall of Famer. In fact, hitting the ball successfully only three out of every ten times is enough to attain greatness. Babe Ruth was one of the greatest baseball players of all time, but he struck out almost twice as many times as he hit a home run. So what made him a success?

What made Babe Ruth arguably the greatest player ever was his willingness to keep swinging. He never let a strikeout prevent him from swinging for the fences his next time up. His last time at bat was gone and forgotten; he couldn't let that "failure" prevent him from going for it next time.

Sometimes we let our failures prevent us from taking risks when the next opportunity comes. But God doesn't expect us to be flawless; he wants us to be fearless. The fear of failure and striving for flawlessness crushes our spirit. Perfectionism hinders performance by instilling fear of failure and paralyzing us. It breeds self-criticism, anxiety, and discontent. As that fear grows, we start to dread tomorrow and rob ourselves of the gift of each day and each opportunity.

By striving to be fearless rather than flawless, we can grow and thrive. We are liberated to take risks, learn from failures, and develop resilience. As we seek progress, we see everything as an opportunity to win or grow. This is the ultimate growth mindset that sets us free from fear and anxiety.

Father, thank You for reminding me to be fearless, not flawless, because fearlessness leads to a life of freedom. Amen.

POSTING UP

God, You are my God; I eagerly seek You. I thirst for You;
my body faints for You in a land that is dry, desolate, and without water.
PSALM 63:1 HCSB

Even though lacrosse was my primary sport, I loved to play basketball as a kid. I invested hours in front of the driveway hoop over our garage. At six foot one, I didn't have much height for a forward, so I quickly learned the art and importance of posting up against the defense. Even though I don't post up on the court like I used to, I do a different type of posting up every day. It's a battle, and it's for positioning, but it's not about basketball. This kind of posting up involves the Lord and me. Every morning, I post up to get the Word of God in me. Since I joined His team, I need to be ready, prepared.

In 1 Timothy 4:7–8, Paul said physical training has some value, but spiritual training has double value—for this life and the life to come. When we work out with God, spiritual sweat is created, and a transformation takes place when we engage God. Our spirit grows and becomes strong. We spiritually prepare ourselves to be in shape for the game of life. God loves spiritual sweat.

Make space for Him to speak to you. Practice the discipline of posting up. Understand the power it brings. Remember that the Lord loves to see His players establishing position, calling for the ball, and making a play.

Father, teach me the discipline of posting up. Help me box out the competition. Nothing is more important than connecting with You. Amen.

TOXIC STUFF

A righteous person who yields to the wicked
is like a muddied spring or a polluted well.
PROVERBS 25:26 HCSB

For thirty days—three meals a day—Morgan Spurlock ate nothing but McDonald's food. And then he produced a documentary called *Super Size Me* that tracked the results of his experiment. About halfway through, he began to feel sick, and by the end of the month, his health had deteriorated significantly. He gained twenty-four pounds, his body fat percentage doubled, his cholesterol went up sixty-five points, and he experienced huge mood swings, cravings, and headaches. His energy levels plunged, and he even became depressed. He was a train wreck in just thirty days. Worst of all—it took him fourteen months to undo the damage.[28]

When we expose ourselves to toxic stuff, we will eventually get sick. Proverbs 25:26 tells us, "If the godly give in to the wicked, it's like polluting a fountain or muddying a spring" (NLT). We are made to be vessels of living water that refreshes, but when toxic material enters, we become morally muddy and personally polluted. Not only do we get sick, but we can make others sick as well.

Toxic stuff looks good, but it goes bad. We can expose ourselves to toxic stuff on TV, on the internet, in movies, and on our phones. When we go shopping, we may feel that we need to buy something now, but that's just temptation. We search for a substitute to satisfy our cravings. Stuff always overpromises and underdelivers. It never satisfies. It's time to cut off the toxic sources in our lives and get rid of them. Let God reveal the toxic material in your life and get clean.

Father, reveal specific material in my life that needs to go. I want to be clean and refreshed by the work of Your Holy Spirit. Amen.

---

28   *Super Size Me*, directed by Morgan Spurlock (Los Angeles: Samuel Goldwyn Films, 2004), 98 min.

LEADER OR FOLLOWER?

"The Son of Man did not come to be served,
but to serve, and to give His life—a ransom for many."
MATTHEW 20:28 HCSB

While attending a youth conference in New Mexico, I joined hundreds of the best youth leaders in the world to learn from the leadership giants who were going to invest in us for several days. On the second day, I heard one of the keynote speakers, Dan Webster, challenge all the leaders on the concept of leadership of the heart. From that weekend in New Mexico, God graciously allowed Dan and me to become great friends. Now as one of my spiritual mentors for over twenty years, Dan has taught me that the most powerful thing about leadership is being a great follower. And he has been a true example of what it means to follow well.

What society is missing is that following is the beginning of leadership. The best leaders have mastered the art of following. Following does not mean doing what everyone else is doing. Following means that you intentionally watch and learn from others. You observe those who are walking in a manner worthy of the Lord, who live with humility and courage, who exhibit integrity and compassion, who make wise decisions—and then you choose to follow in their footsteps.

As men, it is hard to follow because we are made to lead. We think following is weak, second place, and for others—not us! However, following is God's design, plan, and purpose for us.

Father, whenever I want to lead, not serve or follow, please transform my heart. Teach me how to follow. Amen.

JARS OF CLAY

We have this treasure in jars of clay to show that this all-surpassing power is from God and not from us.

2 CORINTHIANS 4:7

Paul painted a vivid picture of our human condition by comparing us to jars of clay. Though we are seemingly fragile and vulnerable, within us lies an extraordinary treasure: the Holy Spirit, who resides in the hearts of all believers. Life can often make us feel like fragile clay jars, susceptible to the pressures and challenges that come our way. We encounter hardships, disappointments, and moments of weakness. Yet in the midst of our weakness, we possess a treasure that sets us apart from the world: the presence and power of God dwelling within us. He enables us to endure trials, overcome temptations, and rise above circumstances that might otherwise crush us.

As jars of clay, we don't boast in our strength because our weaknesses make us dependent on God. In our weakness, we can be strong. The treasure within us demonstrating the power to navigate life's challenges and fulfill God's purposes does not emanate from our own efforts but from God's limitless power. Our weaknesses become opportunities for His strength to be magnified. When we face difficult situations and remain steadfast in faith, the world witnesses a testimony that points not to our own merits but to the divine power at work within us.

God's power is most evident when we surrender completely to His purpose, allowing Him to work through our lives. As you face challenges, remember that His strength is made perfect in your weakness.

Father, thank You for choosing to dwell in me. Fill me with Your Holy Spirit and empower me to be Your vessel. Amen.

SHOWTIME

*If anyone thinks they are something when they are not,
they deceive themselves. Each one should test their own actions.*
GALATIANS 6:3–4

Jon Foreman, lead singer for Switchfoot, shares in his song "Free" that we need to ask God to set us free from the prison inside. For most men, the shell they live in has a cell inside. We often feel the pressure to perform and be someone we aren't. Since the show must go on, we fake it until we make it…and life becomes a show.

The front stage (what we present to others but not the real us) is the enemy of the soul. We want others to see us better than who we really are. The front stage (our outside or false self) contradicts the backstage (our inside or true self). This battle rages within us, which creates an enormous amount of unhealthy inner tension. And we feel trapped. Our life becomes a daily show on the main stage, with the goal to impress others. The act is rehearsed and choreographed to bring pleasure to the viewing audience. A foundational principle of the front stage is to impress at a distance but never up close.

Pastor Rick Warren's words ring true: "Our culture today is overrun with fake products—they look like the real thing, but they're cheap imitations. Fake may work fine in some areas of your life, but when it comes to your faith, fake simply doesn't work."[29]

Men, we must replace the backstage and front stage with Christ's stage. The front stage is the enemy of our souls, but Christ is the lover of our souls. And He loves us too much to let us stay the way we are.

Father, I confess I have a backstage that doesn't honor You. I ask You to do Your work in my life to bring wholeness. Amen.

---

29   Rick Warren, "'Real Faith versus Fake Faith' with Pastor Rick Warren," Pastor Rick, posted May 30, 2020, YouTube video description, 37:28, https://www.youtube.com.

LIMITLESS REACH

Here is a trustworthy saying that deserves full acceptance:
Christ Jesus came into the world to save sinners—of whom I am the worst.

1 TIMOTHY 1:15

Paul had a profound sense of just how big the love of Christ actually is. He knew the condition of his heart and the reality of his actions before Jesus saved him. He never wanted to limit Jesus' ability to do for others what Jesus did for him.

It's easy to feel like you must clean up your life before you come to Jesus, but the exact opposite is true. Come to Jesus, and He will heal your soul. It's easy to say, "But you don't know what I've done," but there's nothing that can separate you from the love of Christ. No one is so far gone that God can't reach them. People can seem so distant from God—lost in their struggles, burdened by their mistakes, and feeling unworthy of His love. But no soul is too far for God's reach. He is the relentless pursuer of hearts.

God can find anyone. Many feel lost, but Jesus is the Good Shepherd who leaves the ninety-nine to find the one lost sheep. No matter how far someone has strayed, God's love and grace can lead them back. No one has done something so bad that God can't forgive them. Guilt and shame often weigh heavily, and the Enemy lies and says God could never forgive *that* sin. However, Christ's sacrificial love on the cross covers all sins—past, present, and future.

Let us be ambassadors of God's limitless reach, love, grace, and forgiveness. We can bring hope to the hopeless, healing to the broken, and reconciliation to the lost.

Father, thank You for Your grace, which is sufficient for all of us. Amen.

SECONDHAND GLORY

Not to us, Lord, not to us, but to your name give glory
because of your faithful love, because of your truth.

PSALM 115:1 CSB

Growing up with two older brothers meant I never got anything new. Nothing!
I was given secondhand items all the time, including clothes, sporting
equipment, and toys. It was hand-me-down living at its best. Since there is
no such thing as a hand-me-up, I never had the chance to return the favor.
However, I do remember getting a few new pairs of socks, so I had that going
for me.

The concept of secondhand means something had a previous owner (i.e.,
my brothers). Secondhand can never be new. We clearly understand this
principle when it comes to possessions and even when it comes to secondhand
information. But what does *secondhand* mean when it comes to God? He
doesn't want secondhand, passed-down glory. You know what I'm talking
about: taking the credit when God should be getting it. This can be subtle
and quick—giving credit to God after we take it first. Of course, we're always
"spiritual" enough not to keep the glory for good…just long enough to enjoy it.

The key, though, is to reflect His glory, not absorb it. We need to be
mirrors, not sponges. We should reflect God's glory—and He should see
Himself in us. If we are sponges, we absorb His glory and rob Him of the glory
due His name. So, men, reflect God's glory; don't steal it. Our Father delights
to see Himself in you. It doesn't get any better than that.

*Father, forgive me for giving You secondhand glory, keeping some for myself
before giving credit to You. I don't want to steal from You. Amen.*

THE PROTECTOR

Those who fear the LORD are secure;
he will be a refuge for their children.

PROVERBS 14:26 NLT

As men, we are called to protect mind, body, and spirit. Our role extends far beyond physical strength; it is a sacred duty to safeguard our loved ones on every level. The Scriptures provide us with powerful guidance and encouragement in fulfilling this noble calling.

Protecting our mind and the minds of our families is vital. The world is full of negative influences and distractions. Most of the attacks of the Enemy go after our mind, our way of thinking, our beliefs about who God is, and our identity. By cutting off the source of these lies and focusing on what is true, noble, and pure, we create an environment that fosters mental well-being and spiritual growth.

Protecting our physical well-being and that of our families is our duty. We must lead by example, promoting a healthy lifestyle and respecting the bodies God has given us. But more than that, we must be prepared to defend them in the event of a real physical threat.

Protecting our spirit and the spirits of our families is of utmost importance. We are called to be spiritual leaders, guiding our loved ones toward deep and meaningful relationships with God. By putting on the full armor of God and leading our families in prayer, worship, and the study of His Word, we equip them to withstand the spiritual battles they may face.

God Himself is our ultimate protector. He creates a secure refuge in times of uncertainty or danger, giving us confidence in His presence and power.

Father, help me rise up with courage and strength as a protector. Help me create a safe and secure environment for my loved ones. Amen.

SCOREBOARD

"You didn't choose me. I chose you. I appointed you to go and produce lasting fruit, so that the Father will give you whatever you ask for, using my name."

JOHN 15:16 NLT

Known as "The Flying Scotsman," Eric Liddell ran to victory in the 1924 Paris Olympics. He won a gold medal for Great Britain in the 400 meters, set a new world record with his time of 47.6 seconds, and won a bronze in the 200-meter race. He was an amazing athlete who was not only a runner but also a rugby player and a missionary to China.

Eric ran, spoke, and lived with incredible faithfulness. He never wavered from his commitment to Jesus Christ. His life was defined by his desire to please God in his competition. After competing, he went to China as a missionary, where he taught children in school, worked with extremely poor people, and rescued victims of war. Whatever he did, his goal was to become like Jesus.

For Eric, winning wasn't the scoreboard, medals, records, or awards. He had a different definition of *winning*. His spirit was captured in the movie *Chariots of Fire* when the actor playing Liddell said that God "made me fast. And when I run, I feel His pleasure…To win is to honor Him."[30]

When we sense and feel God's pleasure in us while we live, lead, and compete, the scoreboard changes. We become the hands and feet of Jesus. As a man, it's hard not to buy into the world's definition of *winning*. Jesus has "appointed you so that you might go and bear fruit—fruit that will last" (John 15:16). Winning is simply becoming more like Jesus.

Father, I desire to win by becoming more like Jesus. Help me be Your hands and feet to bear fruit that will last. Amen.

---

30 *Chariots of Fire*, directed by Hugh Hudson (Los Angeles: 20th Century Fox, 1981), 124 min.

THE NINTY-NINE

"What do you think? If a man owns a hundred sheep, and one of them wanders away, will he not leave the ninety-nine on the hills and go to look for the one that wandered off?"

MATTHEW 18:12

My mailbox is number ninety-nine, and every time I get the mail, I am reminded of the parable about the shepherd who leaves his ninety-nine sheep to search for the one that wandered off. This story reveals the depth of God's love for each of us and the relentless pursuit of His lost children. We are not lost in the crowd. God knows us intimately and loves us uniquely. Our struggles move his heart, and He pursues us with an unwavering determination to bring us back.

Leaving the ninety-nine sheep behind may seem risky, but the shepherd's compassion drives him to sacrifice his time and effort for the sake of the lost one. This exemplifies the sacrificial love of God, who gave His Son, Jesus, to seek and save the lost. We are called to show compassion and willingness to sacrifice for others. The shepherd does not give up on the lost sheep. He diligently searches until he finds it and joyfully brings it back to the fold. Similarly, God never gives up on us, pursuing us with His grace and mercy even when we have strayed. This shows us the immense value of each individual soul to God.

As we walk in God's love and grace, let us actively engage in seeking the lost, demonstrating His redemptive power in a world that desperately needs His love.

Father, help me seek after the one who may have walked away from You. Amen.

MARK OF EXCELLENCE

Do your best to present yourself to God as one approved, a worker who does not need to be ashamed and who correctly handles the word of truth.

2 TIMOTHY 2:15

After a hard workout session at an FCA sports camp, one of the coaches challenged the campers to compete with excellence. "Practice makes permanence," he said. "Perfect practice makes perfect." I always heard it as, "Practice makes perfect." But if you're practicing something wrong, it doesn't matter how many times you do it; it just makes it permanent, not perfect. The key is doing it right by doing it with excellence. God deserves our best, not our leftovers.

If we want excellence, we need to be men of excellence who are committed to pursuing excellence over the long haul. To achieve this, we must answer three questions:

1. Whom do you serve? If your answer is Jesus Christ, then also ask yourself, *Is the Lord well pleased?* We should present ourselves approved to God alone.
2. How's your work? Doing the Lord's work with excellence and a faithful heart is the goal. We should be compelled to pursue excellence in all we do. Is your work well done?
3. What's your foundation? If your answer is the Word of God, then are you using the Word well? We need to have a passion for the truth and to handle the truth with accuracy.

When we're committed to excellence, we naturally desire to leave the kind of mark on others that will have an eternal impact.

Father, I know being excellent requires the total release of all my talents, gifts, and abilities. Help me become more like Christ. Amen.

IMAGO DEI

God created human beings in his own image.
In the image of God he created them;
male and female he created them.

GENESIS 1:27 NLT

From the very beginning of creation, God intentionally formed humanity in His own image. This divine imprint means we have inherent worth and purpose; it's called *imago Dei*. Knowing we are fearfully and wonderfully made empowers us to approach life with confidence, understanding that our lives have a unique and valuable purpose in God's grand design. Scripture calls us to put on a new self in Christ, continually renewing our knowledge of God and growing in His image. By pursuing godliness, compassion, and love, we mirror the attributes of our Creator. We are vessels through which God's character can shine forth into the world, impacting those around us for His glory.

The truth of *imago Dei* challenges us to value and respect every life. It calls us to treat others with dignity, love, and kindness, recognizing that every individual bears the divine imprint of the Creator. This truth can transform our interactions and bring unity and harmony.

God's ultimate plan for us, as men created in His image, involves being conformed to the likeness of Christ. Through redemption in Jesus, we are called to grow in holiness and reflect Christ's character more and more. Let us embrace the truth of *imago Dei*, rejoicing in the knowledge that we are fearfully and wonderfully made. May this revelation fuel our pursuit of godliness, compassion, and love—shining the light of Christ in every aspect of our lives. As we walk in the reflection of God's image, may we inspire others to encounter His love and experience the transformative power of His grace.

Father, may my thoughts, attitudes, words, and actions reflect Your image in my life. Amen.

HAY IN THE BARN

My son, if you accept my words and store up my commands within you…
then you will understand the fear of the LORD
and discover the knowledge of God.

PROVERBS 2:1, 5 HCSB

The day before the Kansas City marathon, I met with a friend who was also a runner. I was fired up for the race but a bit anxious about trying to run a personal record (PR). As I reflected on my training leading up to the race, I mentioned I wished I'd done more long runs, more conditioning, more everything.

He smiled big and leaned across the table. "Dan, at this point, the hay is in the barn. The race is tomorrow. Nothing you can do now." The formal training was over, and there was no looking back—nothing more to do but execute on race day.

Hay in the barn is a powerful principle in every area of life—especially our spiritual lives. Spiritually, the hay is the Word of God, and the barn is our heart. Sometimes, however, we fall into the trap of wanting a spiritual PR without putting in the spiritual investment. I admit it—sometimes I want God to show up and do something miraculous without my having to invest the time to know Him better.

We must dive into the Word and store up His commands. Too many men skim—going through the motions. It becomes a matter of getting through today, not thinking about tomorrow. Running on spiritual fumes becomes the norm. Carve out the time. Make an investment. Go deeper. Start putting spiritual hay in the barn. Your tomorrow depends on your today.

Father, I want spiritual hay in my heart so I can finish strong. Help me go deeper in my walk with You. Amen.

BE WELL

You were bought at a price.
Therefore honor God with your bodies.

1 Corinthians 6:20

I've heard *wellness* defined as "the absence of disease" or "adding years to your life and life to your years." But I think Jesus said it best: life to the full (John 10:10).

Ultimately, as our verse today shows, God calls us to honor Him with our body. And while this verse specifically refers to us maintaining sexual purity, it has a much broader application: stewardship of our health. Since our body is the temple of the Holy Spirit, how we take care of our health can be an expression of worship.

Living a healthy lifestyle affects virtually every area of our life. Exercise and proper nutrition affect our mood, mental focus, weight, immune system, and even decision-making. God created food for our bodies to give us energy, sustain life, prevent disease, and facilitate healing. As we incorporate key health practices into everyday life, we are more prepared for life's challenges. When built on a foundation of living for Christ, we maintain the right motives. This is a spiritual act of worship.

Being a good steward of our physical health helps us accomplish our mission and fulfill our unique calling in this life. When we are physically unhealthy, we often lack the energy and endurance to perform at our best. But when we're healthy, we're more positive, optimistic, and hopeful. We become more productive and can maximize each day.

Take some steps today to pursue optimal health and honor God with your body. You will be setting an example for others and living a fuller life.

Father, help me be a good steward of the body You've given me so I have energy to complete what You've asked of me. Amen.

TRIPLE THREAT

Be joyful always; pray continually;
give thanks in all circumstances,
for this is God's will for you in Christ Jesus.
1 THESSALONIANS 5:16–18 NIV1984

When I was a twelve-year-old aspiring basketball player, I heard NBA Hall of Famer Adrian Dantley teach about basketball's "triple threat." I learned that when you have the ball, you have three options: dribble, shoot, or pass. As men of God, we can be a spiritual threat every day. Our opponent, Satan, wants to defeat us and take us out. He is working overtime to make sure you and I are discouraged and overwhelmed. But in 1 Thessalonians 5:16–18, Paul gave us a great spiritual triple threat: be, pray, give.

Threat one: be joyful. It would have been easier to live this out if Paul wrote, "Be joyful," not, "Be joyful always." Many times, my joy depends on my circumstances. Remember that joy is more than happiness. Joy is internal, and happiness is external. Do not let anyone or anything rob you of the joy God has placed in you.

Threat two: pray continually. There should always be a prayer in your heart and on your lips. Prayer is not telling God what He already knows but God revealing to us what we do not know. Are your prayers shaking the gates of hell? When you pray, is Satan knocked back on his heels?

Threat three: give thanks. We need to use our words to build up others, bringing praise. When we speak, we either speak life or death. Giving thanks means speaking life in every situation.

Put Satan on his heels today. There are family members, coworkers, friends, and neighbors who depend on you to be joyful, pray continually, and give thanks.

Father, help me be a spiritual threat. Amen.

FIRE FROM HEAVEN

The fire of the LORD fell and burned up the sacrifice, the wood,
the stones and the soil, and also licked up the water in the trench.

1 KINGS 18:38

In 1 Kings 18, Israel was plagued by a severe drought, and King Ahab blamed Elijah for the crisis. However, Elijah remained steadfast in his faith, knowing he served a God of immeasurable power and provision.

Elijah challenged the prophets of Baal to a showdown on Mount Carmel. The 450 prophets built an altar and called upon their false god to send fire to consume the offering, but there was no response. Elijah, with unwavering confidence, mocked their futile efforts, knowing the God of Israel would soon reveal His power.

Elijah then took his turn, rebuilding the altar of the Lord and drenching it with water. Then, with a simple prayer, he called upon God, and the fire of the Lord fell from heaven, consuming the sacrifice and even licking up the water. God displayed his power in a remarkable way, leaving no doubt that He is the one true God. Elijah's boldness reflects his intimate relationship with God. Elijah's confrontation with the prophets of Baal reminds us to be vigilant against false teachings and beliefs in our society.

We are called to be bold witnesses for the truth. Like Elijah, we must stand firm in the promises of God, trusting He is in control—even when circumstances seem dire. God's faithfulness is unwavering, and He will fulfill His word in His perfect timing.

Father, help me stand firm in my beliefs, be bold in prayer, challenge falsehood, and trust in the mighty power of Your name. Amen.

LUST PATROL

Whoever sows to please their flesh, from the flesh will reap destruction; whoever sows to please the Spirit, from the Spirit will reap eternal life.

GALATIANS 6:8

A common sermon illustration attributed to the late Paul Harvey tells the graphic story of how an Eskimo kills a wolf:

> First, the Eskimo coats his knife blade with animal blood and allows it to freeze. Then he adds another layer of blood, and another, until the blade is completely concealed by frozen blood. Next, the hunter fixes his knife in the ground with the blade up. When a wolf follows his sensitive nose to the source of the scent and discovers the bait, he licks it, tasting the fresh frozen blood. He begins to lick faster, more and more vigorously, lapping the blade until the keen edge is bare… So great becomes his craving for blood that the wolf does not notice the razor-sharp sting of the naked blade on his own tongue, nor does he recognize the instant at which his insatiable thirst is being satisfied by his OWN warm blood. His carnivorous appetite just craves more— until the dawn finds him dead in the snow![31]

What a picture of what lust can do. It can feverishly consume us. Lust is often associated with sex. But the concept of lust can be applied to almost every area of life. As men, we understand the law of the harvest. It's about "later" and "greater." It always delivers.

But the law of lust is about the "now" and the "foul." It never delivers what it promises. Lust says you can have anything instantly and that it will satisfy. Lust takes what God has made for good pleasure and distorts it.

Sin never delivers what it promises, but obedience does. Let's be men known for our obedience—known for pursuing purity and holiness—not lust.

Father, give me self-control and trust that great things will spring forth at a later time because of my obedience today. Amen.

---

31   Chris T. Zwingelberg, "Consumed by Their Own Lust," Bible.org, February 2, 2009, https://bible. org.

IF SHE CAN DO IT

"Who knows, perhaps you have come to your royal position
for such a time as this."

ESTHER 4:14 CSB

Esther fearlessly stood up to the most powerful ruler of her time. Her bravery and unwavering faith in God offer valuable lessons as we navigate our own journeys of courage and integrity. A young Jewish woman, Esther found herself in a precarious position as the queen of Persia during the reign of King Xerxes. When an evil plot to annihilate her people, the Jews, came to light, she faced a life-altering decision. She could remain silent to protect herself or risk everything by standing up for justice and the welfare of her people.

Esther didn't allow fear or self-preservation to overshadow her commitment to righteousness. Recognizing that she was uniquely positioned "for such a time as this," Esther resolved to approach the king uninvited, a decision that could have resulted in her death. Esther understood that her position as queen was not by accident. She believed God had placed her there for a purpose, and she trusted His timing. We, too, have been placed purposefully right where we are, and there will be moments when we must step forward with courage and faith.

Esther was willing to sacrifice for the greater good. Are you? As men, we are called to love and protect those around us, even when it requires personal sacrifice. Today, there will be a cost to stand up for Jesus and righteousness. We must be willing to pay the price and stand firm in our faith and convictions. Esther's bold stand changed the course of history. If she can do it, you can too.

Father, give me the courage to stand tall for You. Amen.

PRAY REAL QUICK

Pray hard and long. Pray for your brothers and sisters. Keep your eyes open. Keep each other's spirits up so that no one falls behind or drops out.

EPHESIANS 6:13–18 MSG

"Let's pray real quick." We hear it all the time. It's part of our lingo, and we don't even realize we're saying it. We are all guilty of uttering these words. The underlying message is "Before we get to the important stuff, let's rush through the God stuff." It becomes a rote habit that bypasses our hearts. We look spiritual but lack power. Prayer isn't something to rush through so we can get to work. Prayer is the work! I believe these words grieve God's heart because He desires a continuous conversation—not lip service.

Martin Luther was once asked what his plans for the following day were, and he is said to have answered, "Work, work, from early until late. In fact, I have so much to do that I shall spend the first three hours in prayer." The busier he got, the more he prayed. Prayer needs to be the driving force in our lives. It's our greatest weapon. We need to move from mini prayers to mighty prayers, short prayers to long prayers, and shallow prayers to deep prayers.

Prayer makes us.

Prayer molds us.

Prayer matures us.

Paul encouraged us to pray long and hard. He told us to keep the lines of communication with the Father open at all times, in every circumstance. Our lives should be one continuous prayer. It's our foundation and our covering. It's our first response, not our last resort. Be quick to pray, not to pray quickly.

Father, help me be quick to pray and not to rush through prayer. Teach me to pray. Amen.

NO PRESSURE, NO DIAMONDS

Consider it a great joy, my brothers and sisters, whenever you experience various trials, because you know that the testing of your faith produces endurance. And let endurance have its full effect, so that you may be mature and complete, lacking nothing.

JAMES 1:2–4 CSB

If there's one thing we all have in common, it's pressure. Some people hate pressure and try to avoid it at all costs. Others seem to enjoy it and even thrive under it. But one thing's for sure: we will all face pressure in life.

I've come to believe it's impossible to develop character, to create greatness, or even to mature without adversity and pressure. People who have the most wisdom, make the best decisions, have the greatest performance, and make the biggest difference for others have almost always experienced great pressure and adversity. Character is uncovered in crisis and formed in fire. It's here that character is revealed and refined. When we are squeezed, what comes out shows what's inside. And it gives us a chance to let God change us, especially when we don't like what we see.

No pressure, no diamonds. God forms our character in the same way He forms diamonds. The word *diamond* comes from the Greek word *adamas*, which means "invincible" or "unconquerable."[32] Diamonds are formed from a single element: carbon. Not only do diamonds take time, but they need extreme heat and pressure to transform. When carbon is forced deeper beneath the surface of the earth (100 miles down), it encounters extreme temperatures (2,200 degrees Fahrenheit) and pressure (725,000 pounds per square inch). Those extreme conditions make diamonds. And when it rises again to the surface, it displays the brilliance of the light.

Father, use pressure in my life to forge godly character. Amen.

---

32   David Bressan, "The Origin of Geological Terms: Diamonds," *Forbes*, April 30, 2016, https://www.forbes.com.

THE YES FACE

God's chosen ones, holy and loved, put on heartfelt compassion, kindness, humility, gentleness, and patience.

COLOSSIANS 3:12 HCSB

Chuck Swindoll once shared a story that went something like this: When President Thomas Jefferson and several companions were traveling across the country on horseback in the early 1800s, they approached a large river that they intended to cross. A stranger appeared who also needed to cross the river. He looked at the president and asked if he could get a ride across the river. Thomas Jefferson said, "Sure, hop on!"

As the stranger slid off the horse on the other side, one of the companions questioned why he asked the president for a ride. The stranger replied, "I didn't know he was the president. All I know is that his face said yes, and all your faces said no!"[33]

For some of us, our faces say no many times. Our face has already spoken before we even open our mouths. Too many Christians were baptized in lemon juice—they have a scowl on their faces and pursed lips. Everything about them says no—their attitudes, countenances, demeanors, postures, and facial expressions.

A yes face is a blessed face because blessed people bless people. Others watch our nonverbal communication. They know what we are saying without us speaking a word. They watch from a distance and want to know if they can trust us to get on the horse and get a ride across the river. Our countenance should exude our confidence in Christ. A yes face has a Spirit-filled heart. What does your face say about you? Men, let's see those yes faces!

Father, I want a yes face, but I realize it starts with the heart. Please change my heart so my face can show it. Amen.

---

33   Charles R. Swindoll, *The Grace Awakening* (Nashville, TN: Thomas Nelson, 2003), 4.

TELL THE TRUTH

Whoever walks in integrity walks securely,
but whoever takes crooked paths will be found out.

PROVERBS 10:9

"You can't get where you want to go until you stop lying about where you're at." My coach knew the right words, and they served as a catalyst for change. He saw gaps between my desire and my discipline. He saw gaps between my words and my actions. He then began to expose the excuses I made that I had disguised as reasons for why I fell short. Good intentions don't produce integrity.

The single greatest limiting factor that prevents a person from fulfilling their potential is their unwillingness to tell the truth about their current reality. We are afraid to face the facts not only about where we are but also about what we'll need to do to get where we want to go. The Bible is full of passages that speak to the idea of living with integrity. But Proverbs 10:9 always stuck out to me. When we walk in integrity, we walk securely. In other words, we never have to worry that someone will catch us living in a way that is inconsistent with what we say we believe.

Living with integrity is hard. Doing the right thing when no one else is looking—regardless of the consequences—is the standard. It's not easy to do what we say we will do or live in such a way that our actions line up with our words, values, and beliefs. But that is what we are called to do. People with integrity live in such a way that God is glorified. I know that's the type of man we all want to be.

Father, help me always tell the truth and live with integrity. Amen.

GREATEST COACH EVER

A good name is more desirable than great riches;
to be esteemed is better than silver or gold.

PROVERBS 22:1

On June 26, 2010, thousands gathered to remember the life of legendary coach John Wooden and his ninety-nine years. He lived well, died well, and understood his eternal fate. He once said, "There is only one kind of life that truly wins, and that is the one that places faith in the hands of the Savior."[34]

Just two weeks before he passed away, we had read him the manuscript of the FCA book *The Greatest Coach Ever*. The book features forty tributes from athletes, coaches, and other influential leaders who shared how Coach Wooden's example challenged and changed them. After hearing their words, Coach said, "I am happy being remembered as a man of integrity. I like that!" Coach knew a good name is better than national championships, undefeated seasons, and Hall of Fame honors. To be called a man of integrity was better than being considered the greatest coach ever.

What a gut check! I was so convicted by his reaction, so challenged by the simplicity and clarity of his life. Even today, his legacy inspires me to be the best I can be, to invest in others, to give my life away. His purpose in coaching was always to instill greatness in others. He understood that the fruit of a leader grows on other people's trees.

Coach Wooden left a legacy of faith, integrity, and love. We remember who he was, not what he did. What about you? How would you finish the sentence "I want to be remembered as a man of…"? May your answer shape your future and your legacy in a way that honors the Lord.

Father, I desire a good name more than any titles or accomplishments. I want to be remembered as a man after Your heart. Amen.

---

34   John Wooden and Jack Tobin, *They Call Me Coach* (Chicago: McGraw Hill, 2004), 95.

THE DOMINO EFFECT

"A little yeast works through the whole batch of dough."
GALATIANS 5:9

As a kid, I enjoyed setting up rows of dominos on the floor and weaving them around chairs and under tables. But the real fun was watching them fall one by one with just a small nudge of that very first domino. It certainly took a lot more time to set them up than it did to knock them down!

Life is all about small decisions. One small decision can often lead to consequences that we never would have expected—for better and for worse. But we often think that one small choice is independent, a stand-alone decision; in other words, we think one small choice won't lead to other similar compromises. In fact, we often make small compromises and don't seem to experience any negative consequences. But over time, we are emboldened to make other compromises, and eventually the consequence shows up.

One thing always leads to another. Sin always leads to more sin. As yeast works its way through the dough, sin works its way through your life. When we give in to temptation or to our cravings, it never fully satisfies us; we always want more. And it's easier to compromise the next time or to cross the line again once we have crossed it. As believers, we cannot afford to push the dominos.

When we make wise little choices, they lead to more wise choices. And they give us momentum to do the right thing. Compromises always lead to the next compromise. Stand your ground.

Father, help me make a good decision today. Stop the negative domino effect in my life. Amen.

ARE YOU LIMITED?

I protested, "Oh no, Lord God! Look, I don't know how to speak since I am only a youth." Then the Lord said to me: Do not say, "I am only a youth," for you will go to everyone I send you to and speak whatever I tell you.

JEREMIAH 1:6–7 CSB

In an age obsessed with leadership, it is hard to find someone willing to talk about leadership in an authentic, transparent way—especially men. Any sign of weakness means you are not a leader who is large and in charge. We are taught never to admit we don't know something because if we do, then we just might be called a limited leader.

But if you are tagged with that moniker, you might have discovered one of the greatest leadership secrets of all time. What the world sees as a liability, God sees as an asset. I believe all great leaders have the awareness of their personal limitations and inadequacy. The limited leader realizes he is not all-powerful and doesn't have all the answers. A limited leader realizes he has gaps, blind spots, and problems. He doesn't try to pretend to have it all together. Instead, he sees his limits as an asset because they produce dependence on God. God does not need our strength. He simply needs our availability, humility, faith, and trust.

We are limited; God is limitless. Life is a trust walk that forces us to completely rely on Him. Corrie ten Boom is believed to have said, "When I try, I fail. When I trust, He succeeds." The world is waiting for God-trusting, limited leaders.

Father, teach me to embrace my limits so I can trust in You. Amen.

WATCHMAN

Unless the LORD builds the house,
those who build it labor in vain.

PSALM 127:1 ESV

In biblical times, watchmen played a crucial role in warning people about physical threats and impending danger, including the approach of enemies or invaders. The term *watchman* referred to individuals assigned to keep watch over cities, towns, and fortified structures—such as city walls and watchtowers. The primary duty of a watchman for physical security included conducting surveillance, sounding the alarm, and defending the city. Watchmen were stationed on high vantage points to have a clear view of the surrounding landscape. Their task was to scan the horizon and observe any potential dangers or suspicious activities.

If the watchman spotted approaching enemies or any imminent threat, his responsibility was to sound a warning signal, often using a trumpet. Their early warning allowed the city's inhabitants to prepare for an attack, secure the gates, and organize a defense against invading forces. It often was the difference between victory and defeat. The prophet Isaiah described watchmen as being vigilant in observing and sounding the alarm when they saw enemy forces approaching.

The watchman was vital for the safety and security of the community. Watchful eyes and timely warnings provided crucial time for the people to respond and take appropriate measures. As a result, the watchman's responsibility was highly regarded and valued in biblical times.

This is a role we must play in modern times. We need to understand the times and know what to do. We must be like spiritual watchmen over our families, churches, and communities.

Father, help me be like the watchmen of old, helping protect those You've entrusted to me. Amen.

SERVANT OF SERVANTS

"Among you it will be different. Those who are the greatest among you should take the lowest rank, and the leader should be like a servant."

LUKE 22:26 NLT

We love leading, but do we love serving? We attend leadership conferences and workshops, and we read books and blogs on becoming a better leader. But when was the last time you attended a serving conference?

Over the thirty years of doing ministry and meeting leaders from over one hundred countries, I have met amazing leaders who have modeled what it means to be a servant. They view themselves as plain old servants. They are not obsessed with titles, positions, accolades, and accomplishments. They are humble, God-glorifying servants.

God is calling us to be bondservants who have no rights—*a servant of servants*. We must develop a willingness to serve others in sacrificial, humbling ways. A servant of servants not only is willing to be a servant but is willing to be treated like a servant without complaining or murmuring. This person has no need for praise, thanks, or encouragement.

Barnabas was a servant of servants. He served Paul and the church, and he expected nothing in return. Luke described him in Acts as a man full of the Holy Spirit and faith. No task was beneath him. He had nothing to prove. He served to give back to others, not to get. A true servant of servants, he sought to develop a Christlike character, not a man-made reputation.

God calls us as leaders to serve. Many men are servants of servants, and they are changing the world. Are you one of them?

Father, teach me to be a servant of servants. I want to serve and help transform those around me. Amen.

JULY

PERFORM OR PERISH

May God himself, the God of peace, sanctify you through and through.
May your whole spirit, soul and body be kept blameless at the coming of
our Lord Jesus Christ.

1 THESSALONIANS 5:23

"I hate tennis!" Why would one of the world's best tennis players say that? Because Andre Agassi was trapped. In his book, *Open: An Autobiography*, Agassi said, "I play tennis for a living, even though I hate tennis, hate it with a dark and secret passion, and always have."[35] As early as age seven, he wanted to quit the game he eventually dedicated his life to. The unrelenting pressure from his overbearing dad created a hatred for the game he played so well. Finally, at age thirty-six, he revealed his truth: he was playing tennis for others.

There is always pressure to perform when leading—no matter what we are doing. We prepare hard to perform well, and we quickly learn there are two outcomes: perform or perish. We begin to think the goal is to impress coworkers, friends, family, and neighbors. But that's called transactional leading, and that type of leading traps us in a destructive cycle. It destroyed Agassi.

Remember: we live for an audience of one. No more performing. No more pretending. Sacrifice your image and restore your heart. Stop faking it and get real. God does not need our performances to advance His kingdom. But He does need our hearts. Ready. Set. Stop. Stop performing. Performance-based living will kill you from the inside out. It will rob and steal your joy for living. It's time to get real and be honest. Let Christ reign in your life.

Father, I am finished with performing. Sanctify me through and through.
I want to live wholeheartedly. Amen.

---

35   Andre Agassi, *Open: An Autobiography* (New York: Knopf Doubleday, 2009), 3.

THE PROVIDER

Lazy hands make for poverty,
but diligent hands bring wealth.

PROVERBS 10:4

Our role as providers should not be a source of anxiety or excessive worry. God knows our needs intimately, and He promises to take care of us as we seek His kingdom and righteousness first. Trusting in God's faithfulness and provision allows us to approach our role as providers with confidence and a reliance on His guidance. But we also have a responsibility to work hard and be diligent.

Providers are called to be generous and compassionate, sharing our blessings with those around us. By embracing a spirit of generosity, we participate in God's abundant provision and experience the joy of being a conduit of His blessings. Provision goes beyond our material needs; it extends to equipping us for every good work. As providers, we are called not only to meet the physical needs of our families but also to support and encourage them in their spiritual growth. Relying on God's abundant blessings empowers us to be effective and fruitful in all aspects of our role as providers.

God's faithfulness endures throughout generations, and He has a track record of providing for His people. We can take comfort in the assurance that God will never forsake the righteous. As we seek to fulfill our role as providers, we can trust God's hand is guiding and sustaining us, ensuring all our needs are met. As we embrace our role, hard work and diligence produce a return for our efforts. It's up to us to take responsibility, roll up our sleeves, and do the work.

Father, help me be diligent and work hard to provide for my family's needs, knowing You are the ultimate provider. Amen.

BUILD YOUR DREAM TEAM

Let us not neglect our meeting together, as some people do, but encourage one another, especially now that the day of his return is drawing near.

HEBREWS 10:25 NLT

"Dream Team" was the nickname given to the 1992 United States men's Olympic basketball team. It was the first American Olympic team to feature active NBA players, and the results were awesome. As they dominated their way to the gold medal, they beat their opponents by an average of forty-four points. The most amazing thing about this team was their chemistry. They played unselfishly. Since the original Dream Team, the United States has sent numerous teams with the best and most talented players to the Olympics, but USA basketball has never been able to repeat the success of the original Dream Team.

Jesus did the same thing when assembling His dream team—the twelve disciples. He wasn't looking for perfect people, not by a long shot. But He chose men whose hearts would be His. Peter, James, and John became Jesus' inner circle.

Every man needs a dream team. We need a small inner circle of friends to do life with. If we want to be our best, we need the help of others. Getting godly men on your team who understand the role they play is essential. Life gets complicated quickly, and without key people, it gets overwhelming.

Now is the time to recruit teammates. Find friends who won't let you isolate. Find friends who are pursuing God, walking in wisdom, and making decisions that honor God. Assemble your dream team now.

Father, help me identify people You want as part of my dream team. Teach me how to be a great teammate. Amen.

LIFE, LIBERTY, AND THE PURSUIT OF HAPPINESS

It is for freedom that Christ has set us free. Stand firm, then, and do not let yourselves be burdened again by a yoke of slavery.

GALATIANS 5:1

Many of us are blessed to live in a country that treasures and upholds certain inalienable rights. Life, liberty, and the pursuit of happiness are not merely ideals but gifts from God rooted in His design for humanity. The sanctity of life is woven into the very fabric of our existence. God carefully created each of us in our mother's womb. We are fearfully and wonderfully made, and our lives are meant to be cherished and protected. Let us stand for the value of every life, from conception to natural death, acknowledging that every individual is a precious creation.

In Christ, we find true freedom and liberty from sin and its chains. Through His sacrifice, we are set free to live abundant lives, liberated from the burden of guilt and condemnation. Let us walk in the freedom of Christ, avoiding any form of slavery to sin or worldly pressures.

In Psalm 37:4, we learn God desires our joy and fulfillment in Him: "Take delight in the LORD, and he will give you the desires of your heart." When we delight in the Lord, our hearts align with His will, and He grants us the desires that are in harmony with His plan for our lives.

In gratitude for God's gifts of life, liberty, and the pursuit of happiness, remember to value and protect the lives of others, stand firm in the freedom Christ has given us, and seek happiness in Him.

Father, thank You for the gifts of life, liberty, and the pursuit of happiness. Amen.

MIRACLE IN THE MOUNTAINS

Then I heard the voice of the Lord saying, "Whom shall I send?
And who will go for us?" And I said, "Here am I. Send me!"
ISAIAH 6:8

In 1991, God moved several lacrosse coaches in the back room of a small pizza place to answer the same question Isaiah did: "Whom will I send?" Little did we know that the following summer, God would use our willingness to step out of our comfort zones and impact the sport of lacrosse. It's something we now call Miracle in the Mountains.

What happened during the Miracle in the Mountains is still the most powerful ministry experience of my life. God miraculously showed up in July 1992 in Vail, Colorado, not only to teach a lacrosse team of twenty players that He can do the impossible but also to plant seeds of ministry that led to a harvest FCA is still reaping today. All we had to do was utter these life-altering words: "Here I am. Send me."

There are so many spiritual lessons I learned from Miracle in the Mountains. Here are my top five takeaways:

1. God loves to take us out of our comfort zones and put us into faith zones.
2. God longs for us to say, "Here I am. Send me."
3. God makes a way if we are willing to take the next step.
4. God desires to create champions, not to win championships.
5. God does far beyond all we can ask or imagine.

It all started with the Lord asking, "Whom will I send?" It's an invitation that continues today. Let's all respond like Isaiah: "Here I am. Send me!" We just need to take the next step.

Father, here I am. Send me. Amen.

TRUST OTHERS

"The LORD, the God of Israel, commands you [Barak]:
'Go, take with you ten thousand men of Naphtali and Zebulun
and lead them up to Mount Tabor.'"

JUDGES 4:6

In Judges 4, the nation of Israel was distressed and oppressed by the king of Canaan, Jabin. As a prophetess, Deborah received a divine message from God instructing her to call Barak, a valiant warrior, to lead the nation's armies against their oppressors. Deborah's wisdom and strength came not from her own might but from her unwavering faith in the Almighty. Her summons to Barak was not a mere suggestion. It was a command from the Lord.

Barak hesitated to take up the mantle of leadership, but Deborah reassured him that God had gone before them and would ensure victory. Barak trusted that God spoke through her, so he led the army into battle. Together, they routed Jabin's forces and experienced the fulfillment of God's promise.

Like Barak, we may find ourselves facing daunting challenges and uncertainties. We may doubt our abilities and feel inadequate for the tasks ahead. Trusting that God speaks through others is a sign of maturity. As men, we are called to be leaders in various aspects of life—at home, in the workplace, and in our communities. But we need the wise counsel of others to operate with confidence.

Deborah's obedience to God's call and her certainty gave Barak the confidence and courage to step up. She empowered Barak by affirming God's presence and promises. As leaders, let's encourage and uplift others, reminding them of God's faithfulness. Let's also surround ourselves with people who can do the same for us.

Father, help me discern Your instruction from others and trust in Your power as I step into my calling. Amen.

TOUGH OR FLUFF?

Give it everything you have, heart and soul. Make sure you carry out The
Revelation that Moses commanded you, every bit of it. Don't get off track,
either left or right, so as to make sure you get to where you're going.

JOSHUA 1:1–9 MSG

When I first met Peter, I realized there was something special about him. He
had a fire in his heart, conviction in his voice, and urgency that stirred passion
in others' hearts. Peter was imprisoned seven times in his Southeast Asian
country because of his faith. He endured beatings and interrogation as a result
of doing ministry, yet his fire burned bright. He taught me what it means to be
all in to fulfill the calling God put on your heart. He is a modern-day apostle
Paul who radiates Jesus Christ. He motivates me to be a stronger and more
courageous leader.

Peter is a walking, talking, living example of being tough for Jesus. He is all
tough and no fluff. I have learned three principles from Peter:

1. The tough train. The tough press in and do whatever it takes to
   advance the kingdom of God. When the going gets tough, the tough
   don't quit. The tough train; the fluff quit.
2. The tough trust. The tough have big faith in a big God. When our
   trust increases, our experience of God increases. The tough trust; the
   fluff doubt.
3. The tough testify. The tough love to share about God's goodness.
   When we pass the test, we get a testimony. The tough testify; the fluff
   complain.

Tough times don't last, but tough people do. What about you? Are you
tough, or are you fluff?

*Father, help me train and not quit, trust and not doubt, testify and not
complain. Amen.*

ABUNDANCE MINDSET

"The thief comes only to steal and kill and destroy;
I have come that they may have life, and have it to the full."

JOHN 10:10

Jesus invites us into a relationship with Him so we can enjoy a "rich and satisfying life." He promises us abundance in the areas of life that matter most. The abundant life is a life of joy and peace, a life of fulfilling work and close relationships, and an attitude of gratitude. It's a life filled with influencing others to find and follow Jesus. God is a generous Father; sometimes He gives us what we want, but He always gives us what we need.

The abundance mindset is a belief in the generosity and goodness of God. It's a certainty that God has more than enough for everyone to enjoy, that when someone else has success, you can have success too. It gets rid of the idea that the "size of the pie" or opportunity is fixed. God's pie is unlimited.

The scarcity mindset, on the other hand, sees God as unfair. It's a belief that all resources are limited. When the outcomes aren't the same, we often get jealous or even angry. When someone else has success, we believe there is less opportunity for us. That is a lie from the thief. He is trying to make us think small and steal our joy.

The abundance mindset is critical for a fulfilling life. Don't let the thief steal your rich and satisfying life. Don't be jealous when God is generous to others because He is also generous to you.

Father, give me the abundance mindset and help me make the most of every opportunity. Amen.

CABIN PRAYER MEETING

Devote yourselves to prayer,
being watchful and thankful.
COLOSSIANS 4:2

In 1806, five students from Williams College gathered in a field to pray and discuss how to impact Asia with the gospel. When a thunderstorm arose, they took shelter under a haystack as they continued to seek God for direction. What seemed like a small, spontaneous prayer meeting gave birth to the first-ever American missions agency and sparked the mobilization of one hundred thousand college students through the Student Volunteer Movement, which was one of the greatest missionary movements in history.

God loves using small, spontaneous things for His purposes because divine appointments birth divine assignments. Even though I have never had a prayer meeting under a haystack, I experienced a powerful prayer meeting in a stone cabin. In 2007, I was traveling with a group of FCA staff, and we toured a facility in northern Italy in an area with rich spiritual roots. We visited the stone cabins the Waldensians used as a Bible college during the twelfth century to train hundreds of missionaries to be sent throughout Europe. Then it happened: a small, spontaneous prayer meeting broke out. As we knelt on the stone floor of one of the cabins, we began to seek God's divine direction. This divine appointment birthed a divine assignment—a college summer sports internship.

Since our "cabin prayer meeting," FCA has equipped and empowered hundreds of college interns to influence thousands across numerous countries. God has launched young leaders into ministry, coaching, education, and business as a result of this spontaneous prayer meeting.

What might seem like an interruption may actually be God's invitation. What might seem spontaneous, God positions as strategic. What might seem small, God sees as significant.

Father, teach me to be devoted in prayer while being watchful and thankful. Amen.

DROP THE WEIGHT

Let us throw off everything that hinders and the sin that so easily
entangles. And let us run with perseverance the race marked out for us.

HEBREWS 12:1

Back in the 1980s, I was being trained by a guy who was preparing for a tryout
with the Dallas Cowboys. He often made me strap on a forty-pound weighted
vest and run the stairs; adding weight was one way to accelerate my growth.
Once I was free from the added weight in my workouts, I could compete at my
absolute best. In a similar way, once we shed the added weight of life burdens,
we can live a life of freedom—mentally, emotionally, and spiritually.

Negative words from others, or even yourself, reinforce fear and doubt,
and these can tempt you to quit. Negative emotions caused by stress, anxiety,
and the pressure to perform make you feel like a failure, like you'll never be
good enough, or that the challenges you face are too big to overcome. Negative
experiences from the past—if you hold on to them—can weigh you down and
affect your future. When things don't go our way, additional weight leads to
excuses and blame. We find ourselves looking for reasons why we failed. But
getting rid of mental noise, emotional pain, and past burdens helps us run our
race with perseverance.

Jesus said, "Come to me, all you who are weary and burdened, and I will
give you rest…For my yoke is easy and my burden is light" (Matthew 11:28,
30). Jesus came to set us free from the weight of anxiety and worry, our pain
and our past, and even sin and death.

*Father, help me drop the weight of past regrets, present problems, and future
worries. Amen.*

WHAT'S YOUR SQUIRREL?

My ambition has always been to preach the Good News where the name of Christ has never been heard, rather than where a church has already been started by someone else.

ROMANS 15:20 NLT

Every morning, I have a discipline of running, which I developed after graduating college. Since I run very early, I usually run alone. This changed when my oldest daughter rescued a dog from the animal shelter. Huxley became my running partner.

Our run includes a long trail through the woods. Huxley stays alert, looking for moving creatures to pursue. At times, I think the leash will break because he's pulling so hard. Lots of things get his interest—rabbits, foxes, other dogs—but his passion is squirrels. When he sees one scampering across the trail, he goes from me pulling him to him pulling me. Energy and drive arise when his passion lies ahead.

Huxley's ambition for squirrels has made me realize how focused, committed, and determined we can get when we wholeheartedly desire something. One morning I was laughing at how he was practically dragging me after he saw a squirrel when I heard a small whisper from the Holy Spirit: *What's your squirrel?* The laughing turned into conviction as I thought about my sole ambition. What am I sold out for?

In Romans 15:20, Paul said his ambition was to bring the gospel to places where no one had heard it—to the unreached people of the world. Every morning, Huxley's ambition is squirrels. What's your ambition?

Father, show me what to run after with relentless passion and desire so I bring You glory and praise. Amen.

NEVER SAY NO

"I tell you, keep on asking, and you will receive what you ask for.
Keep on seeking, and you will find.
Keep on knocking, and the door will be opened to you."

LUKE 11:9 NLT

We have a family principle we all live by: never say no for someone else, meaning we don't assume how someone's answer without asking them. When my kids were young, they would miss out on opportunities because instead of asking, they assumed and answered for someone else. When I asked them how they knew my answer, their responses ranged from, "But Dad, you would never let me have that!" to "I never thought you let me go to the party with them." They said no for friends, family, and even strangers—all the time, everywhere, for every situation.

When we say no for others, we become negative, limit our options, and isolate ourselves. This principle is applicable not only when dealing with people but also when dealing with God. How many times do we say no for God? We never pray for God to say no, but we think it: *The Lord would never allow that to happen. God wouldn't do that for me.*

We answer for God without ever asking Him; however, God is longing for us to simply utter the request. I'm not sure if God gets frustrated with us like I did with my kids when they said no for me and others, but I do know He rejoices when we simply ask. God can do mighty things when we ask, even if it's a weak, feeble ask. Never say no for someone else, and never say no for God.

Father, I ask for the faith to keep asking. Forgive me when I say no for You and others. Amen.

BREAK THE HUDDLE

"Go and make disciples of all nations, baptizing them in the name of the
Father and of the Son and of the Holy Spirit."

MATTHEW 28:19

The modern-day circular huddle we see in sports was created in 1894 by
Gallaudet University football player Paul D. Hubbard. It was his strategy for
protecting his team's play calling from the opponents. However, people have
been huddling up since the beginning of time for many different reasons.

Huddling up is important, but so is breaking the huddle. You can't stay in a
huddle forever. Nobody wants all talk and no action. The power of the huddle
is what happens *after* you break it. Time reveals the impact of the huddle.

In the church, there has been a huge emphasis on small groups for
over thirty years. We have seen small groups get people out of rows and
into circles. Sharing and sharpening one another in small groups has been
transformational. However, we often stop at circling up. Huddles are meant to
be broken.

In Matthew 28:19–20, Jesus was breaking the huddle. The disciples were
enjoying the huddle and didn't want to go. They were comfortable. Jesus said,
"Go and make disciples." There is value in gathering, but we also must scatter.
There is a time and place to huddle. But just know that you will eventually
need to break the huddle. This is so God can use us to impact the world.

*Father, show me when it's time to break the huddle for kingdom work and
point me in the direction to go. Amen.*

AGAINST THE FLOW

You are a chosen people, a royal priesthood, a holy nation, God's special possession, that you may declare the praises of him who called you out of darkness into his wonderful light.

1 PETER 2:9

Every man feels the tension of fitting into the crowd or going with the flow. Some think peer pressure ends once you get past high school, but in some ways, pressure intensifies, and the stakes are usually higher. In fact, I feel more pressure to drink alcohol now than I did when I was in college. It's just part of the prevailing culture.

Following the crowd is easy because fitting in takes no effort. We instantly feel accepted and part of the group without struggle or tension. But the mob never strives for excellence; they drop their standards and ambition to the lowest common denominator.

Jesus expects more of us. He wants us to go against the flow. He wants us to act like His "special possession." He wants us to rise early and start our day in the Word while our friends soak up one more hour of sleep. He wants us to live with a sense of mission and passion to stand up to our culture. All great leaders of God swim upstream.

Daniel and his three friends were great examples of this. When the king made his decrees that violated their conscience, they resisted. They were protected, and God was magnified in the process.

We live with a different standard. We must be willing to go against the flow without compromise. Don't do what everybody else is doing. The godly life requires it.

Father, give me the courage I need to go against the flow. Amen.

DOG ON A LEASH

Put on all of God's armor so that you will be able to stand firm
against all strategies of the devil.

EPHESIANS 6:11 NLT

One time while I was in South Korea for a sports camp, I found a good running loop down back streets and trails. I began running in the dim light of the early morning, and then, out of nowhere, a dog charged at me. I practically leaped out of my shoes as I jumped away from the attacking dog. Fortunately, the dog made it only to the edge of the street and then stopped. For a moment, I wondered why he hadn't charged farther; then I realized the dog was on a leash.

The next morning, I was ready. I approached the same spot with confidence. But this time, my perspective was completely different. It was just a dog on a leash. I respected the dog, but I did not fear the dog like I had before.

It occurred to me that Satan is just like that dog. He is a dog on a leash. Unfortunately, many Christians respond to him like I did that first day with the dog. They are surprised by Satan, and they fear and worry how he is attacking and impacting their lives. We can't live our lives seeing how close we can get to Satan without getting bit. Instead of asking ourselves how close we can get to the line without sinning, we must ask how close we can get to the Lord.

Do you realize that Satan is a dog on a leash? Yes, respect his power but do not fear him.

Father, thank You for Your victory. Give me Your eyes so I can correctly see the Enemy's leash and not fear him. Amen.

SET THE STANDARD

Live a life worthy of the Lord and please him in every way:
bearing fruit in every good work, growing in the knowledge of God.
COLOSSIANS 1:10

Creating a standard to live up to helps us fulfill our potential and become everything we're made to be. It encompasses the beliefs, expectations, and behaviors that drive performance. Having a standard creates accountability and helps eliminate excuses, reject shortcuts, and avoid compromise. Following a standard for an abundant life means we please God, bear fruit in every good work, and grow in the knowledge of God. When we do that, we enjoy strength, power, endurance, and joy.

I have found it helpful to phrase the components of my standard as "I will" statements.

- Mind: I will ignore the noise. I will win the battle of the mind, crushing the lies of the Enemy that attempt to discourage. I will focus on what is true and right (Romans 12:1–2).
- Body: I will keep my temple pure. I will honor God by turning away from visual garbage and protecting my body from sexual sin (1 Corinthians 6:19–20).
- Spirit: I will keep my eyes on Jesus. I know I can accomplish nothing if I get disconnected or distracted from Him and His purposes (John 15).

These "I will" statements help me stay focused on who I want to be and how to behave. They form a standard I strive for and aspire to. What about you? What's your standard?

Father, help me raise the bar in all areas of my life and define my standard so I can live a life worthy of Your call. Amen.

THE LEADERSHIP SECRET

Oh, Lord GOD! You Yourself made the heavens and earth by Your great power and with Your outstretched arm. Nothing is too difficult for You!

JEREMIAH 32:17 HCSB

After more than thirty years of leading thousands of sport ministry leaders in over one hundred countries, I have learned three secrets of leadership.

1. Leaders have great self-awareness. In a survey, seventy-five members of the Stanford Graduate School of Business Advisory Council rated self-awareness as the most important capability for leaders to develop.[36] When a leader knows his natural skills, strengths, and spiritual gifts, he understands his leadership fingerprint and his weaknesses. Having self-awareness allows you to lead within your capabilities, surround yourself with others who carry different strengths, and rely on God to fill in the gaps.

2. Leaders don't hide weaknesses. Having self-awareness helps you be candid and upfront about your weaknesses. This forces you to depend on others. Identified weaknesses are a powerful thing when you embrace them. Lead with your strengths and lean on your weaknesses. When you try to do it on your own, you are preventing someone else from leading with his or her strengths. Be open about your weaknesses because they empower others.

3. Leaders realize failure is inevitable without God's intervention. Counting on others is one thing, but counting on God is a whole other thing. A quote attributed to F. B. Meyer says, "You never test the resources of God until you attempt the impossible." God loves to pour out His favor to leaders who do not deserve it, the ones who remain broken and humble under His mighty hand. Remember: failure is at the doorstep every day unless God steps in.

Father, bless me with self-awareness, reveal my weaknesses, and step in when I attempt the impossible. Amen.

---

36 Bill George et al., "Discovering Your Authentic Leadership," *Harvard Business Review* 85, no. 2 (February 2007): 131.

HOLD NOTHING BACK

Whatever you do, whether in word or deed, do it all in the name of the
Lord Jesus, giving thanks to God the Father through him.

COLOSSIANS 3:17

When my kids turn eighteen, I take them skydiving. I've already made the
leap with all three boys, and my daughter is next! Each time we read and sign
several pages of disclaimers and warnings. The final warning is a reminder
that we could die doing this. Each time, we've taken a deep breath, signed our
names, and boarded the tiny plane.

Once in the air, there's no turning back. We're all in. When the plane
reaches the full altitude, the door swings open, and one at a time, we step
onto a two-by-two-foot platform and fall forward out of the plane. It's both
terrifying and exhilarating.

We believe the skydiving experts know what they are doing. We believe
we will ultimately make it back to the ground safely. Holding nothing back
requires belief, faith, and action. It's been worth it every time.

In our spiritual lives, holding nothing back also requires taking a risk.
When you're pushed outside your comfort zone, your ability to control every
circumstance must go. Many things in life will fall outside your control, so get
used to it.

It can be challenging to be all in for Jesus, and it takes incredible strength.
It doesn't mean we lose our competitive edge; it's quite the opposite. Our
lives really matter. Our homes and communities need us to be men who hold
nothing back. When we believe deeply that Jesus gave His all to save us, we
will give our all to live for Him.

Father, help me hold nothing back as I live for You. Amen.

GOD-SIZED VISION

God can do anything, you know—far more than you could ever imagine or guess or request in your wildest dreams! He does it not by pushing us around but by working within us, his Spirit deeply and gently within us.

EPHESIANS 3:20–21 MSG

Every vision needs three key ingredients. If you want to know if your vision is a God-sized vision, not just a good vision, answer these three questions:

1. Is your vision too small? If your vision doesn't terrify you, it is too small. You need to step outside your comfort zone. A God-sized vision should be so huge you are bound to fail unless God steps in. How big is your vision? The first ingredient is holy fear.
2. Is your vision too narrow? If your vision doesn't include others, it is too narrow. Having a vision doesn't mean it's you against the world. A God-sized vision must include others. God will raise up a multitude to embrace and own your vision. The second ingredient of a God-sized vision is others.
3. Is your vision just a daydream? If your vision doesn't get done, it is just a daydream. Too many men talk about what they are going to do and never produce results. A God-sized vision always gets done. Take one step toward accomplishing the vision God birthed in your heart. The third ingredient of a God-vision is doing.

Don't let the pace of life, negative thinking, or fears kill your vision. Men, do whatever it takes to hear from God over the noise of life and pursue the vision He's planted in your soul. One person with a God-sized vision can change the world.

Father, give me a vision so big that I am bound to fail unless You step in. Amen.

MENTOR ME

You should imitate me,
just as I imitate Christ.

1 CORINTHIANS 11:1 NLT

CrossFit has inspired millions to test their personal limits and train in ways most thought impossible, regardless of age. My friend Dr. Landan Webster, a former college athlete and now a doctor of chiropractic, is one of those guys. He used his built-in competitiveness and trained alongside some incredibly fit athletes who pushed each other to be their best. But, in his own words, "I never had a mentor. I never gave anyone permission to truly coach me, evaluate me, or help me get to the next level."

When Landan chose mentors and gave them permission to push him, everything changed. He asked them to show and tell, critique everything, and fully engage. The mentors did all they could to get everything out of him. He needed their knowledge, motivation, encouragement, and belief to get it out. In the end, he achieved incredible goals that never would have been possible otherwise.

We are designed to do life together with other godly men. We need to find other men who are diligently following Christ and ask them to mentor us. The best mentors know our current condition and can see our future capabilities. And while they're not perfect, they willingly show us their flaws and failures to spur us on to get it right.

Father, help me find a godly mentor and be one to others. Amen.

THE POSITIVE FEW

Kind words heal and help;
cutting words wound and maim.
PROVERBS 15:4 MSG

They are rare and very hard to come by, but occasionally, you can spot one. There aren't too many, but once you identify them, they stick out. I'm talking about the Positive Few. You know—the people who have a way of making you feel special. They have an exceptional ability to bring refreshment and encouragement by breathing life into the ordinary.

The Positive Few can make you feel like Superman because they speak words of life—words drenched in hope—not words of death. They aren't just make-you-feel-good words but also we-believe-in-you words. What a difference! They see God's greatness in others. They inspire others. Their encouragement isn't fake but powerful, purpose-filled edification.

Unfortunately, the Negative Multitude are everywhere—a dime a dozen. They take chunks of flesh out of you every time you encounter them, and they drain the life out of you. They criticize, complain, whine, make excuses, and find faults. That is their natural style of communication. Their words are laced with destruction, and they spew poison on anyone who dares to listen. Their goal is to pull you down to their level of misery.

Are you one of the Positive Few or the Negative Multitude? When you walk into the room, do people run, or do they pump their hands into the air? Your words can unlock God's greatness in others. You need to be committed to infusing life into others through your intentional words of nourishment. Let people feast off your encouragement. Be one of the Positive Few.

Father, help me be a source of nourishment and encouragement to others, one of the Positive Few. Amen.

MAKE IT COUNT

"From everyone who has been given much, much will be required;
and from the one who has been entrusted with much,
even more will be expected."

LUKE 12:48 CSB

My friend's job is to train the best in the world to be even better. As a master trainer, she trains Olympic athletes to compete on the world's greatest athletic stage. Her goal is to see top athletes maximize their gifts and opportunities so they will experience the thrill of victory and not the agony of defeat. She wants every Olympic competitor to make his or her performance count.

One of the athletes she trained made Team USA for the 2012 Olympics. Within days of making the team, the athlete was relocated to the Olympic Training Center (OTC) in Colorado Springs, Colorado. At the OTC, the athlete must maximize everything they do every minute for the best outcome. The best athletes in the world understand the need to go all out to make it count.

With great opportunity comes great responsibility. In Luke 12:48, Jesus reminded us that from those who are given much, much is required. When God blesses us with a lot, we must be even more responsible with what we do with it. We are not blessed just for us but also for others. "Be careful how you live. Don't live like fools, but like those who are wise. Make the most of every opportunity in these evil days" (Ephesians 5:15–16 NLT).

Those who recognize the opportunities they've been given are most likely to make them count. Live in such a way that you count your days and make your days count.

Father, thank You for giving me this one life to live; help me make it count. Amen.

ARE YOU A POOR TALKER?

Do not let any unwholesome talk come out of your mouths,
but only what is helpful for building others up according to their needs,
that it may benefit those who listen.

EPHESIANS 4:29

If you breathe, you are guilty of poor talk. It doesn't matter the circumstance or situation; people love to engage in poor talk. We gravitate to negative, pessimistic, and hopeless communication. Unfortunately, poor talk is easy and familiar. We fill our conversations with *can't, won't,* and *never.* Misery loves company, so most people love to join in and add their share.

Poor talk comes from scarcity thinking. It is a lack-of mindset. We believe there is limited time, money, and human interaction. Not only does this kind of thinking paralyze us, but it also prevents us from celebrating others' successes. More for you means less for me. Instead, we need to realize God owns it all, and He has unlimited resources. When we believe this, we believe in abundance.

The apostle Paul instructed us in Ephesians not to let any unwholesome words come out of our mouths. Another way to say it is to let no "poor talk" come out of our mouths. Poor talk is worthless, bad, and rotten. It focuses on the past, not the future. In Colossians 4:6, Paul wrote, "Let your conversation be always full of grace, seasoned with salt, so that you may know how to answer everyone." God calls us to fill our words with humility, hope, and grace.

Can you imagine if all of us decided to eliminate poor talk? We would transform the world. Let's start today.

Father, help me eliminate poor talk from my vocabulary and help my words honor You and others. Amen.

KEEP HIS PACE

Since we live by the Spirit,
let us keep in step with the Spirit.

GALATIANS 5:25

As I endured another wave of triathletes swimming over the top of me, I was fighting to survive. The words of my friend who is a seasoned triathlete echoed in my mind: "Just run your race." But I had chosen to ignore this valuable advice, sprinted to the front with the strongest swimmers, and was completely out of gas just 200 meters into the swim. Unfortunately, I got caught up in the emotion of the event and was influenced by competition. I abandoned the coaching because I thought I could do it on my own. I paid a price. Even though I finished the race, it was a punishing day. I was beaten and exhausted.

This is true of life as well. When we decide to go on ahead of God and do things our way, we end up beaten and exhausted. Very few will finish strong. That's why so many families are suffering—we get derailed by distractions and comparisons. It's all a lie.

Jesus gave us simple instructions for how to keep His pace. In Matthew 11:29–30, He told us, "Take my yoke upon you. Let me teach you, because I am humble and gentle at heart, and you will find rest for your souls. For my yoke is easy to bear, and the burden I give you is light" (NLT). Run your race. Keep His pace. Stay in step with the Holy Spirit. Let Him lead you and teach you the race pace that works for you. In the end, you can trust His plan, enjoy His promises, and finish your race well.

Father, help me stay in step with Your Spirit and pace. Amen.

FIVE MINUTES

More than that, I also consider everything to be a loss in view
of the surpassing value of knowing Christ Jesus my Lord.
Because of Him I have suffered the loss of all things
and consider them filth, so that I may gain Christ.

PHILIPPIANS 3:8 HCSB

On July 25, 2003, a Ukrainian swimmer experienced five brief minutes of glory. He achieved his lifelong goal of setting a world record in the one-hundred-meter butterfly. He was pumped—celebrating and throwing his hands in the air. His joy, however, was short lived as his time in the spotlight disappeared just as quickly as it arrived. Andriy Serdinov's world record stood only until eighteen-year-old US swimmer Michael Phelps broke his record five minutes later. It happened so fast that Andriy could not even finish one interview about his incredible accomplishment.

Fame is like the wealth described in Proverbs 23:5: "Cast but a glance at riches, and they are gone, for they will surely sprout wings and fly off to the sky like an eagle." Often, as soon as fame is achieved, it is gone. As men, we strive to be the best, but we cannot hold on to our accomplishments. We must offer them to the Lord to be used for His glory. The world's glory is rubbish. It will all be destroyed. The only thing that will last is God's kingdom. Too many men would rather have five minutes of worldly fame than any amount of eternal glory. Let's seek first the kingdom of God. Don't keep the glory for yourself.

Father, Your kingdom is the only thing that will last. I pray I will bring You glory all the time. Amen.

WARRIOR MINDSET

"When you go out to war against your enemies and see horses, chariots, and an army larger than yours, do not be afraid of them, for the LORD your God, who brought you out of the land of Egypt, is with you."

DEUTERONOMY 20:1 CSB

When my boys were little, they would dress up in military camouflage, and I would take them through a mini boot camp, making them salute and "give me ten!" pushups. They loved it. They played Army all around the house and yard. Tiny soldiers were everywhere. We even painted their room camo, put up military nets, and hung model B-2 bombers from the ceiling. Over the years, their warrior mindsets showed up on athletic fields, in the classroom, and as they faced various obstacles and challenges.

After the death of Moses, God chose Joshua to lead His people into the promised land. This task must have seemed impossible. God knew Joshua would face fear, doubt, and a sense of inadequacy; that's why He breathed courage into Joshua's heart and mind. God reassured Joshua that He would be with him wherever he went. God knew Joshua would face incredible opposition. He knew there would be challenges that seemed insurmountable.

In our culture, men need to return to the warrior mindset with supernatural strength and courage. Courage isn't the absence of fear; it's acting in the face of fear. Life will bring adversity, and we need to be fully prepared and ready. It's time to take every thought captive and remind ourselves God is with us; nothing is impossible with Him. We must be intentional to train our minds to overcome adversity, challenges, and setbacks. It's time to be strong and courageous.

Father, give me a warrior mindset that is courageous in the face of adversity. Amen.

GO GENEROUS

"Give away your life; you'll find life given back, but not merely given back—given back with bonus and blessing. Giving, not getting, is the way. Generosity begets generosity."

LUKE 6:37–38 MSG

In 2019, I went to Romania to visit our staff and was reminded of what a generous heart looks like. I have known Daniel since 2009, but I had never visited him in Romania even though he had traveled to the United States several times. He had told me about his work over the past ten years with the Roma people—he was doing sports camps as outreach to the villages. It was life-changing to see the impact of his ministry firsthand as we traveled to a village to meet several of the families.

The kids came running into the snow-covered street to jump into Daniel's arms. They gathered around him to sing "Jesus Loves Me." Daniel was generous toward the least of these with his time and resources. Not just once but for years. Daniel understood that when we are generous, God multiplies our giving.

Generosity means "irrational giving." It is allowing God to take us to the next level of blessing those around us. It is moving from a mindset of "there is never enough" to "there is enough" and then to "there is more than enough." God is generous to us, so why can't we be generous back to God and others? Generous living is filled with sacrifice, surrender, blessing, and miracles. It is over-the-top, bet-the-farm, burn-the-boats living. I want to see God transform my heart into a generous heart, not just a giving heart. Giving is expected, but generosity is unexpected.

Father, teach me how to live generously every day. Amen.

REAL LOVE

Now these three remain: faith, hope, and love—
but the greatest of these is love.

1 CORINTHIANS 13:13 CSB

I was speaking to a large corporate audience about making a difference and leaving a mark. I challenged them with this simple question: "What's one word you want people to think of when they think of you?" The responses were what I expected—*driven, passionate, successful, strong, steady, leader, provider.* The word I hope marks my life is *love.*

Most men have a hard time with this because we are so confused about what *love* means and how to express it; we are often uncomfortable with emotions other than anger or frustration. We equate love with being soft; we'd rather be warriors and winners. We'd rather be tough than tender. We generally don't think *love* is a masculine word unless it's associated with physical pleasure. We are bombarded by images that look like love but are really just lust.

When Jesus was challenged to name the most important command, He said, "Love." And "There is no greater love than to lay down one's life for one's friends" (John 15:13 NLT). Love requires an incredible amount of sacrifice. It doesn't sound weak at all. It sounds strong.

Real love is not for the weak; it's for the strong. In fact, the Bible teaches we can have the gift of prophecy, display great faith, and even give everything to the poor, but without love, we are nothing and have nothing (1 Corinthians 13:2–3). Real love avoids harsh criticism, unreachable comparison, and hurtful condemnation. Love always wins. You simply can't lose when you love.

Father, make me into a man who has the courage to love with strength, honor, and kindness. Let my life be marked by love. Amen.

THE BENCH

Where can I go to escape Your Spirit?
Where can I flee from Your presence?
PSALM 139:7 HCSB

While I was on a trip out of town, I went on my morning run through a cemetery. Let's get this straight: I don't spend lots of time running through cemeteries. But one thing that grabbed my attention as I hit the path was the number of benches. There were a lot. Sitting and soaking in memories of those who have gone before us is important, and the benches provided the perfect opportunity. Unfortunately, we don't always reflect on the positive. The negative likes to creep up.

I recall a phrase my dad always said: "Sit, soak, and sour." Some people reflect and only remember the negative, dredging up the junk and garbage of the past.

The negative leads to sour.

The positive leads to soar.

It's essential to step away from what clutters our lives to reflect, but we need to focus our thoughts on God's goodness. When my focus shifts toward the blessings of God and not the burdens of this world, the joy of the Lord changes my perspective. When I take time to sit and soak in God's presence, I begin to soar, not sour.

Is there a bench in your life that creates space for you to sit and soak so that you can soar? Sit at the feet of Jesus and wait for Him to reveal insights and truth. Linger in His presence and find out what is on God's heart. Sitting is our discipline; soaking is our posture; soaring is our response.

Father, help me sit in Your presence, soak before You, and soar because of Your promises. Amen.

PLAY

A joyful heart is good medicine.

PROVERBS 17:22 CSB

One year for my son's birthday, we created a football field in our yard with stripes and everything. All his friends came over and put on flags. Then we divided up the teams. I was all-time quarterback. Just as the game started, it began to downpour. But instead of pausing the game and running for cover, we made it into the best flag football memory ever and turned our yard into a muddy mess. We still laugh about that today—many years later. The grass didn't last very long, but the memories will last a lifetime.

I believe God invented the entire idea of fun, play, laughter, and celebration. Jesus said, "I have come that they may have life, and have it to the full" (John 10:10). Full, abundant life is not meant just for the young. It's for everybody. Celebrations in Jesus' day were common. He performed his first miracle at a wedding. Something tells me that place was filled with fun.

I also believe God has a tremendous sense of humor. Just look at some of the wacky animals He created—they're funny. He even designed our bodies to respond to play by producing healthy hormones when we laugh called endorphins. Endorphins bring a sense of well-being, healing, and pain relief. Laughter decreases stress, boosts the immune system, lowers blood pressure, and is a natural antidepressant. That's good news.

Life can be stressful, but it doesn't have to be void of play. God made life to be a gift, not a grind. Men, make time to play.

Father, thank You for the gift of play. You invented the idea of fun and celebration. Bring me a spirit of laughter and joy. Amen.

THE GO PRINCIPLE

The LORD said to Abram: Go out from your land, your relatives,
and your father's house to the land that I will show you.

GENESIS 12:1 HCSB

In 2013, I was presented with one of the greatest opportunities to have a larger impact through my position with the Fellowship of Christian Athletes. However, it required me to step out of the familiar and into the unfamiliar. Up to that point, I had been serving with FCA for almost twenty-five years, focused on growing the ministry in the United States. FCA asked me to lead FCA International—which was out of my comfort zone.

After much prayer and counsel, God led me to live out the Go Principle: when we go, God will show! I accepted the role even though I didn't know what that meant. God put me in a situation where I had to pray, *God, if you don't show up, I am bound to fail*. I felt exactly like Abram in Genesis 12 when God asked him to simply *go*—without much explanation. God told Abram that when he went, God would show him more. We find out in Genesis 12:4 that Abram obeyed. He was living out the Go Principle. I did the same when I said yes to leading FCA's international ministry. Even though it was one of the hardest decisions I have ever made, it has been one of the most rewarding.

God simply says to go, and then He shows us the path once we start the journey. Are you going and allowing God to show you? Live out the Go Principle, starting today.

Father, I ask for big faith—the kind of faith that depends on You showing up. Teach me to go and trust You. Amen.

AUGUST

PRAY LIKE BIRDIE

Be joyful in hope,
patient in affliction,
faithful in prayer.

ROMANS 12:12

Birdie Pitts served Christ for all her ninety-two years on Earth. In 1990, she was my first official prayer warrior when I went into ministry. Little did I know at that time, however, that Birdie had actually started praying for me eleven years before that.

I was in eighth grade when I first met her grandson, Tim, at a summer camp in New York. When I returned from camp, I met Birdie, and she started to pray for me. I was her grandson's new best friend. Birdie prayed for Tim and me faithfully; she prayed for God to use us significantly. We're convinced her years of prayer shaped and transformed us. Tim became a youth pastor, and I joined the staff of the Fellowship of Christian Athletes. It was evidence of a powerful God and the faithful intercession of His saint Birdie. Prayer changes everything!

If she hadn't heard from me, Birdie would call to say, "I haven't received any prayer requests from you this month. The ladies are gathering tomorrow for prayer. You don't need prayer this month?" She truly kept me on my toes. Birdie was serious about prayer. She carved out time to call upon the Lord for others. She knew about prayers of strength and length. She wrestled with God, and doors opened.

I wonder how many people count on your prayers—not counting on what you can do for them but counting on how you can pray for them. Why not pray like Birdie?

Father, I want to impact others through my prayer life. Help me be consistent, persistent, specific, faithful, and prayerful. Amen.

STAY CLOSE TO JESUS

Draw near to God,
and he will draw near to you.
JAMES 4:8 CSB

For years now, a bunch of men in my neighborhood have gotten together to go cycling. One of the most important parts of riding and staying together is the distance between the bikes. Keeping the right distance prevents accidents, but more importantly, it keeps the riders together as they pick up speed. The first rider works harder because he encounters most of the wind resistance. The riders that follow have less resistance, and it's easier to keep the pace if they stay close enough. The optimal distance is less than twenty-four inches apart, depending on the group's speed. If you fall behind more than six to eight feet, you must work hard to hang on as the line picks up speed. The closer you stay, the better the ride. This same principle holds true in our lives. In my life, the closer I stay to Jesus, the easier it is to hear and see His instruction for daily decisions.

Both Enoch and Noah were close to God. Scripture tells us that "Enoch lived 365 years, walking in close fellowship with God" (Genesis 5:23–24 NLT) and that "Noah was a righteous man, the only blameless person living on earth at the time, and he walked in close fellowship with God" (Genesis 6:9 NLT). God used both men in mighty ways. He even saved humanity through Noah when He rescued Noah's family from the flood.

Stay close to God. Start the day seeking God. Take His wheel right from the start. When we come close to God, He comes close to us.

Father, help me be intentional and determined to stay close to Jesus. Amen.

CHOOSE YOUR TEAM WISELY

There are "friends" who destroy each other,
but a real friend sticks closer than a brother.

PROVERBS 18:24 NLT

In the movie *Miracle*, US Olympic Hockey Coach Herb Brooks had a classic line as he was selecting the 1980 team. He showed the proposed roster of players to his assistant coach, Craig Patrick, who was shocked at who made the list and even more surprised at who was left off. Coach Brooks responded, "I'm not looking for the best players, Craig. I'm looking for the right ones."[37] His team went on to beat the heavily favored Soviet Union, ultimately winning gold by defeating Finland in the final, 4–2. We always think the best team consists of the best players. However, the best team is about getting the right players.

When we are looking for life teammates, we might be tempted to look at others' outside talents and characteristics. God doesn't look at the outside. He looks at the heart. What's on the outside is obvious. But what's on the inside is harder to discern.

If you could assemble your own team, who would be on it? I am not talking about a sports team but your own team of godly friends who build you up when you're down, pick you up when you stumble, guide you when you're uncertain, and confront you when you're out-of-bounds. Who are the right teammates to ensure spiritual success? Who will be in your inner circle, walking with you through thick and thin, pouring out God's wisdom?

Father, surround me with the right people who have the right heart at the right time. Amen.

---

37   *Miracle*, directed by Gavin O'Conner (Burbank, CA: Buena Vista Pictures, 2004), 135 min.

GAME CHANGER

Everything that was a gain to me,
I have considered to be a loss because of Christ.

PHILIPPIANS 3:7 CSB

Everyone has at least one favorite game-changing sports moment. It's that one play during a game that changes everything. Momentum shifts, and the outcome alters. Sometimes the play doesn't only change the game, but it also impacts an athlete's entire career.

Spiritual game-changing moments have a greater impact. I had a spiritual game-changing moment on August 4, 2007. I was standing in front of a grave in Seoul, South Korea, at the burial site of someone I didn't even know. We were visiting the cemetery that honored the first Christian martyrs in Korea. Seeing all the missionaries' graves was a real spiritual gut check, but the grave that altered everything for me was the tombstone of a woman named Ruby Kendrick.

Ruby was a young missionary from Texas who had responded to the call to preach the gospel to the Korean people. She died at age twenty-four, only eight months after she arrived in Korea. Her death inspired twelve young women to take her place. This was the quote on her tombstone: "If I had a thousand lives to give, Korea should have them all."

Ruby was totally surrendered to the Lord's work. She sacrificed everything, even her own life, for the sake of the call. I thought, *If I had a thousand lives to give Christ, who or what would deserve them all?* I couldn't shake that question. How about you? If you had a thousand lives, who or what would deserve them?

Father, if I had a thousand lives to give, You deserve them all. Help me clearly see how to invest my life. Amen.

THE LIGHT

Your word is a lamp for my feet,
a light on my path.

PSALM 119:105

Several years ago in Buena Vista, Colorado, my family and I decided to tour some caves and experience the underground world. The guides told stories of people who had made it through and others who had died along the way. I started to feel a little claustrophobic. At one point, they took us to a "room" deep within the cave and far from any natural light; they described what real cavers would have experienced before the caves were converted for tours. For real cavers, if they lost their light, they lost their lives.

God's Word is a lamp to our feet and a light for our path. A lamp provides enough light for decisions and direction. Every day brings new challenges and choices, and we need to know how to navigate. The Bible helps us walk with confidence by revealing stumbling blocks to avoid. Just as a light helps us see ahead for decisions about our future, God's Word helps us discern our purpose and pick the right path. His Word helps eliminate anxiety and fear about the future. It gives us wisdom to trust that God has plans for us.

Darkness is the absence of light and, spiritually speaking, the absence of Jesus. Spend time with Jesus. Spend time in His Word daily. When we turn the light on each day, we discover truth and wisdom. When we lose our light, we lose our life.

Father, thank You for the Bible and for the life of Jesus. Give me the discipline to read Your Word daily and treat it as a light. Amen.

SHOUT-OUT DRILL

Do not withhold good from those who deserve it
when it's in your power to help them.
PROVERBS 3:27 NLT

Whenever I coach, I love to bring the players together after every practice and game to create an environment of encouragement with the shout-out drill. Regardless of how they played, we always start with the positive. We allow the players to speak words of life and refreshment into their teammates about what they saw during the practice or game. It only takes one or two minutes, but the dividends are priceless. The shout-out drill develops great team cohesion and chemistry. It also creates a culture of blessing.

Several years ago, while visiting a local ministry, I met at the front desk an older man who asked me how long I had been in ministry. I responded, "Almost thirty years."

From behind the desk, he jumped to his feet, grabbed my hand, and shouted out, "Wow, thirty years of faithfulness! Praise God! You have been impacting lives for thirty years. Thank you. God is using you. Keep serving well." I was speechless. He did the shout-out drill in the moment. And it blessed me and marked me. His words have fueled me for years, and I will never forget him.

We need to do the shout-out drill all the time—with our family, friends, teammates, and coworkers. It will create a culture of encouragement and blessing. Others will be blessed. You will be blessed. God will be blessed. That's a triple blessing!

Father, I never want to withhold good from those who deserve it. May my words encourage and bless others. Amen.

MOMENTUM

The simple believe anything,
but the prudent give thought to their steps.

PROVERBS 14:15

Many years ago, my boys and I decided to enter the grand prix pinewood derby car races at our church. We got the car kits, pulled out all the materials to make the cars, and set up a workshop in the garage. I read the directions carefully and made sure we met all the criteria for the design, size, and weight. The boys carefully placed their cars on the track, but heat after heat, not one of our cars crossed the finish line. They simply did not have enough momentum to maintain their speed and finish the race. It was a long and disappointing day.

We define *life momentum* as "movement toward or away from God's best." Positive momentum feels good because we have purpose, passion, and power. The greater the positive momentum, the easier it is to overcome challenges and obstacles. It makes big things seem small. Positive momentum is movement toward God's best.

Negative momentum feels bad because we feel more helpless, hopeless, and worthless. If I have negative momentum with my finances, I'm probably spending more than I have and can't get out of debt. The greater the negative momentum, the harder it is to overcome challenges. It makes small things seem big. Negative momentum takes you away from God's best.

Men can change the momentum of their homes, their communities, and their lives. Momentum is created and sustained through a positive attitude and consistent action under God's power. Small choices lead to big changes. The right actions done with the right attitude consistently over time will result in positive momentum. Keep moving toward God's best.

Father, I desire to have positive momentum—to be moving toward Your best in every area of my life. Amen.

PRAY 9:38

"Pray to the Lord who is in charge of the harvest;
ask him to send more workers into his fields."

MATTHEW 9:38 NLT

In 2019, I was gathering with hundreds of sports ministry leaders from ninety-five countries to partner, prepare, and plan. It was amazing to worship with men and women from around the world and hear what God was doing in their citics and communities. God touched my heart with a fresh perspective of new ways to engage, equip, and empower coaches and athletes around the world.

During the first morning of the conference, something strange happened. At 9:38 a.m., buzzing and vibrating, phone alarms went off throughout the room. Suddenly, the presenter paused and then said, "Let's pray for God to send more workers into the harvest." After a short but powerful prayer, the conference continued. All week, the same thing occurred at 9:38 a.m.

I eventually learned that everyone was praying the words of Matthew 9:38, and it took me a few days to connect the dots. The time was the same number as the verse we were praying. When I finally figured it out, I was fired up! What a simple yet strategic way to engage people in responding to the Lord's invitation to join Him by praying for more workers for kingdom work. I thought, *I can do this!*

Men, I challenge you to set your alarm for 9:38 a.m. or 9:38 p.m. When the alarm goes off, stop and pray the words in Matthew 9:38. Pray for God to send more workers into the fields.

Father, You are the Lord of the harvest, and You are the only one who calls workers into Your fields. Send more workers. Amen.

SHOW UP

*"Now, go. I am sending you to Pharaoh
to bring my people the Israelites out of Egypt."*

EXODUS 3:10

Sometimes the hardest thing is just to show up. Showing up is really all about relationships. It's about connections and conversations. It's also about doing what God is asking you to do and fulfilling His purpose and plans for your life. If you don't show up, you'll miss out.

Men have a tendency to withdraw, become passive, and isolate more over time. It's easier to stay on the sidelines, but you'll pay a high price for sitting it out. There is no substitute for your presence. God is imploring men to engage, to get involved, and to show up.

For four hundred years, God heard the cries of His people who suffered in slavery under the oppressive hand of the Egyptians. When God spoke to Moses at the burning bush, He asked Moses to show up on behalf of the Israelites and confront Pharaoh. All Moses really had to do was show up and deliver the message; God was going to do the rest. But Moses wanted nothing to do with it. He went passive and started to make excuses.

God had something big planned for Moses, yet Moses didn't want to show up for God. I believe men experience the same thing today—we hesitate to obey God and show up. The Enemy does not want us to follow God. Moses finally decided to show up, and God did miraculous things. Moses relied on God's power, and millions of people were delivered out of slavery and set free. Moses would have missed out had he not shown up. What about you?

Father, give me the courage to obey Your voice and show up today. Amen.

DON'T MISS IT

Look straight ahead, and fix your eyes on what lies before you.
Mark out a straight path for your feet; stay on the safe path.

PROVERBS 4:25–26 NLT

On my daily runs, I don't like to stop—for anything. However, one morning I saw a car crawling toward me. As I approached the car, I saw maps scattered all over the front seat. The lost, elderly man had every map known to mankind at his fingertips. His papers were his GPS—old school! He asked, "Can you help me?"

A little bothered that I had to stop, I said, "Sure." He asked where the Ritz Charles was located. Stunned, I pointed to a sign ten feet in front of his car that said Ritz Charles. He then drove two seconds to his destination.

On my run home, I started to think how crazy it was that he was right in front of his destination but didn't see it. The Lord quickly took my judgmental attitude toward the lost driver and shifted it toward me. I can so easily recognize it in others, but it is hard to see cluelessness in the mirror. The Lord whispered, *You are the directionally challenged driver. You don't get your head up and see where you are going, so you miss the ultimate destination.*

In life, we need to keep our heads up. Our win is fulfilling the calling God placed on our lives and being faithful—every day. It is keeping our eyes fixed on Jesus. We can't do that if our heads are down.

Father, I pray I will never miss whatever You call me toward. Help me see with Your eyes and feel with Your heart. Reveal Your plan and desire for my life. Amen.

STAND STRONG

Put on the full armor of God, so that when the day of evil comes, you may be able to stand your ground, and after you have done everything, to stand.

EPHESIANS 6:13

You build a man the same way you build a cathedral—from the ground up. In order for a man to stand, he needs a solid foundation of faith in Christ. Jesus is the embodiment of every godly characteristic. When we build our lives on Jesus and His Word, when we put His Word into practice, we can stand in the midst of everything life throws at us (Matthew 7:24–27). Too many men have a shaky spiritual foundation or no foundation at all. This leads to compromising, taking shortcuts, and making excuses.

Daniel and his buddies Hananiah, Mishael, and Azariah serve as great role models for how to stand strong under incredible pressure.

- In Daniel 1, the young men refused to violate their consciences by eating food from the king's table offered to idols. They chose God's ways and were rewarded with incredible health.
- In Daniel 3, Shadrach, Meshach, and Abednego (renamed by King Nebuchadnezzar) refused to bow and worship false gods even with the threat of certain death in the blazing furnace. God protected and delivered them from the fire.
- In Daniel 6, Daniel refused to stop devotion to God in prayer and was thrown into the lions' den. God shut the mouths of the lions and rescued Daniel.

As men, we must stand strong. We need to be willing to stand against the evil that threatens our hearts and homes and stand with those who are defenseless—the least, the last, and the lost. Let's stand for the love, compassion, and grace of Jesus.

Father, help me stand strong under pressure. Amen.

THE GREATEST UPSET

"No word from God will ever fail."

LUKE 1:37

One of my all-time favorite upsets was when the USA Hockey Team beat the Soviets in the 1980 Olympic Games. No matter how impossible the odds might seem, the underdog can still shock the world and win.

That's what happened back on August 12, 1919, when a powerful horse named Man o' War suffered the only loss of his storied career. My grandpa had a framed print of that legendary horse on one of the walls at his old farmhouse in central New York. The name of the horse who beat him was Upset. And while the horse may not be the origin of the meaning of *upset*, it certainly solidified it in our family's language. It describes when the underdog beats the favorite.

Upsets don't just happen in sports; they happen in all aspects of life. The Bible is full of examples of when the impossible turned possible. It's as if God wants to remind us that when all hope seems lost, when the obstacles seem too big to move, when adversity seems too hard to overcome, nothing will be impossible with Him. He wants us to expect the upset and look for it with anticipation.

It's easy to get discouraged by what we see going on all around us and be tempted to give up. But God is urging us to hang on to faith, to grab hold of more courage, to fix our eyes on Jesus, and to stop focusing on our circumstances. And while our external conditions may not change or be magically fixed, our internal condition can be transformed to peace.

Father, help me look for the upset when things seem impossible. Amen.

HONOR GUARD

"Shall I then go to my house to eat and drink, and to lie with my wife?
As you live, and as your soul lives, I will not do this thing."

2 SAMUEL 11:11 NKJV

Known for his courage and loyalty, Uriah was a valiant warrior in King David's army. David, unfortunately, allowed temptation to cloud his judgment and had an affair with Uriah's wife, Bathsheba, when Uriah was at war. When David discovered Bathsheba's pregnancy, he planned to cover up his sin by bringing Uriah back from the front lines to sleep with his wife.

Despite having the opportunity to be with his wife, Uriah chose to sleep at the door of the king's house, showing loyalty to his fellow soldiers who were still on the battlefield. When David questioned Uriah's decision, Uriah responded with devotion to his brothers and duty to the nation: "The ark, Israel, and Judah are dwelling in tents, and my master Joab and his soldiers are camping in the open field. How can I enter my house to eat and drink and sleep with my wife? As surely as you live and by your life, I will not do this!" (2 Samuel 11:11 CSB).

Honor is in short supply today, and we often justify moral compromises for personal gain or pleasure. Honor involves holding ourselves to a higher standard. It means respecting our commitments, responsibilities, and relationships—even when it requires personal sacrifice. True honor extends beyond our immediate circle to the bigger picture. We have a duty to represent Jesus with integrity. The reputation of Christ is at stake. Our families, communities, and nation depend on us to be men of honor.

Father, make me a man of honor who faithfully does the right thing. Amen.

THE ENEMY OF TODAY

Worry weighs a person down.

PROVERBS 12:25 NLT

Today we are facing an enemy that will destroy mankind. Throughout history, we have encountered disease and sickness that ravage families, friends, and community; however, there is a greater danger that threatens to kill us from the inside out. It attacks our minds and controls our behavior. We begin to listen to the lies we tell ourselves instead of speaking the truth. This enemy is called worry.

Corrie ten Boom, the author and speaker who helped hundreds of Jews escape the Holocaust during World War II, was spot on when she wrote, "Worry does not empty tomorrow of its sorrow, it empties today of its strength."[38]

Worry is the lack of absolute faith that God is in control. Worry is a great enemy, and it attacks everything. Unfortunately, we sometimes believe worry will actually help and protect us from danger. We try to give worry value, but justifying an unhealthy emotion is unwise. Worry is wrong every single time. When we worry, we get stuck in the future and stop focusing on today. Instead of winning the day, we worry about tomorrow.

Worry always asks, "What if?" This question can plague us and keep us from living our lives with purpose. *What if I get sick? What if I lose my job? What if my business fails? What if the results come back positive? What if I lose my friend?* Worry…worry…worry.

Where there is worry and anxiety, there is a lack of faith and trust. There is a strong relationship between them. Faith and trust will bring peace and joy. Remember that we're on the team that wins the day. We don't need to worry. God is in control.

Father, forgive me for the times I worry about things I can't control. Release me from worry and anxiety. Amen.

---

38   Corrie ten Boom, *Clippings from My Notebook* (Nashville, TN: Thomas Nelson, 1982), 33.

THE CHASE

My eyes are fixed on you, Sovereign LORD.
PSALM 141:8

An old Chinese proverb warns, "If you chase two rabbits, both will escape." I've watched my dogs try this, and whenever two rabbits are on the scene, I know their pursuit is hopeless. In contrast, the hawk is a skilled hunter and goes after only one at a time with tremendous success. Focus and single-minded determination are important.

The psalmist realized the power of focus—his was knowing and serving Christ. He knew a divided heart and mind would hinder his spiritual growth and effectiveness in serving God's kingdom. He understood that looking back at past mistakes or trying to chase after multiple goals would only slow him down.

This life is full of distractions, and it's easy to become entangled in the pursuit of worldly desires and lose sight of our ultimate purpose. We might find ourselves chasing after success, wealth, recognition, or pleasure, often at the expense of things that matter most. When we seek to please God and follow His purpose for our lives, our priorities become clear. We must forget the past—release the weight of guilt, regrets, and failures—and press on toward the goal for the prize of the upward call of God in Christ Jesus.

Single-minded focus on Christ enables us to stay the course. When we align our hearts with God's will, we experience a sense of purpose and fulfillment that worldly pursuits can never provide. Keep your eyes fixed on Jesus, the author and perfecter of faith.

Father, keep me focused on one thing at a time among the things that matter most. Amen.

TURN IT OFF

Too much talk leads to sin.
Be sensible and keep your mouth shut.
PROVERBS 10:19 NLT

We live in a wordy world. Most of us are plugged in and tethered to words and noise all the time. Especially right now—it feels like we get a constant stream of twenty-four seven news. Our ears, eyes, minds, and hearts are constantly filled with opinions, ideas, and insights. We talk, blab, and make noise all the time; we are constantly filling the air with our words. If it is not our own words, we fill it with other voices appearing on TV and in podcasts, videos, music, and more. Our minds get jammed with noise, which leads us to believe silence is for the weak and soft.

Our world is noisy because we are wordy.

Silence is golden. Silence is a discipline we need to pull from the shelf, dust off, and put into action. We need to pursue silence because it doesn't happen on its own. Silence is a lost spiritual discipline for a follower of Christ. We can redeem our time by seeking silence. Others may not value our pursuit of it, and many may equate our silence to indifference or idleness. However, silence purifies the soul. Silence brings focus, simplicity, and clarity.

God speaks and reveals His heart to us in silence. We need to protect the fire within us from our wordy world. Let's turn it off and tune in to God's still, small voice. This is a voice that we discover when we are silent.

Father, forgive me for filling my life with the wordy world. I want to make time for silence and solitude. Give me a listening ear so I can hear Your still, small voice. Amen.

EAT THE FROG

Sluggards do not plow in season;
so at harvest time they look but find nothing.

PROVERBS 20:4

In his book *Eat That Frog!*, renowned author Brian Tracy encourages us to tackle our most challenging tasks first thing in the morning, akin to eating the biggest and ugliest frog first. Instead of postponing or dreading the difficult tasks, we should face them head-on, prioritizing them in our schedules. By addressing the most significant challenges early in the day, we can avoid the drain of mental and emotional energy that comes with prolonged procrastination and get a sense of accomplishment and momentum for the rest of the day.

But first, we must identify the "frogs" in our lives—the tasks or responsibilities that we tend to procrastinate or avoid. It could be tackling a challenging project at work, addressing unresolved conflicts in relationships, or taking steps toward personal growth and self-improvement. We must take intentional and consistent action toward our goals and not get distracted by little things that won't move us forward.

In Proverbs 20:4, the one who procrastinates misses out on opportunities and faces the negative outcomes of delayed action. There's nothing so fatiguing as an uncompleted task. It serves as a reminder to be diligent and proactive in our endeavors, taking timely and purposeful steps toward our goals.

As we apply eat-the-frog principles in our lives, let's cultivate a heart and mindset of discipline and hard work. It takes disciplined action to tackle the most important things first because it's often easier to check the box of something simpler. But don't give in—be disciplined. Eat the frog.

Father, give me the discipline to tackle the most challenging thing first. Amen.

KEEP IT SIMPLE

Do not swear—not by heaven or by earth or by anything else.
All you need to say is a simple "Yes" or "No."

JAMES 5:12

Two of the all-time greatest coaches in history were Red Auerbach and Vince Lombardi. Red coached the Boston Celtics in the 1950s and '60s, and Vince had tremendous success with the Green Bay Packers. One of the amazing things about these coaches was their commitment to keeping it simple. They didn't have elaborate offensive and defensive schemes, but instead they ran only a few plays. The key was that the players executed those plays to perfection. The Boston Celtics won every NBA championship from 1959 to 1966. And Vince had the Super Bowl trophy named after him.

The principle of keeping it simple is also a very effective strategy for life. We often get so bogged down with complexity, but solutions are really quite simple. We need to strive for simplicity. Complexity happens naturally. But keeping things simple takes work. In the end, it's worth it because you perform better and enjoy life more.

James 5 advises against making elaborate oaths or promises but, instead, tells us to strive for straightforward honesty and integrity. Letting our "Yes" be yes and our "No" be no reflects simplicity and sincerity. This type of simple communication prevents unnecessary nonsense and gives people confidence that you mean what you say. "Keep it simple" is an easy mantra that serves as a reminder not to make things more complicated than they need to be. It helps you eliminate clutter and confusion that inhibit peak performance.

Father, help me simplify so I can unclutter my mind and environment and perform at my best. Amen.

CONSUMED TO SERVE

Do you have the gift of helping others? Do it with all the strength and energy that God supplies. Then everything you do will bring glory to God through Jesus Christ. All glory and power to him forever and ever! Amen.

1 Peter 4:11 nlt

Are you consumed to serve? Is there a consuming fire that burns in you to serve others around you who are hurting? Do you realize the ultimate purpose of serving is to glorify Christ?

Pastor Rick Warren said, "We serve God by serving others. The world defines greatness in terms of power, possessions, prestige, and position… In our self-serving culture with its me-first mentality, acting like a servant is not a popular concept."[39] As men, we struggle with the me-first mentality. We buy into the lie that we are better than others because of our giftedness and accomplishments.

When serving, we need to have intentionality, intensity, and intimacy. The passion for serving must come from the heart. Samuel Chadwick said it best: "Spirit-filled souls are ablaze for God. They love with a love that glows. They believe with a faith that kindles. They serve with a devotion that consumes. They hate sin with fierceness that burns. They rejoice with a joy that radiates. Love is perfected in the Fire of God."[40]

We need to be radical about serving. Can you imagine if all men got passionate about serving their families, communities, friends, and coworkers? Why shouldn't that revolution begin with us?

Father, I confess that serving is hard. I struggle with a me-first mentality. Help me see ways I can serve others. Amen.

39   Rick Warren, "First-Person: How Real Servants Act," Baptist Press, March 17, 2005, https://www.baptistpress.com.

40   Samuel Chadwick, *The Way to Pentecost* (Berne, IN: Light and Hope Publications, 1937), 41–42.

PUSH

"Lord, if it's you," Peter replied,
"tell me to come to you on the water."
MATTHEW 14:28

Baby eagles need a push to leave their nests and soar into the sky. In the wild, when eaglets are ready to take their first flight, the mother eagle begins to remove the soft and comfortable materials from the nest, leaving only thorns and sharp objects. This change creates a discomfort that encourages the eaglets to venture out and explore the unknown. As the eaglets attempt to return to the comfortable nest, the mother eagle does not allow it. Instead, she gently pushes them off the edge, forcing them to flap their wings and learn to fly. This process may be frightening and challenging for the eaglets, but it is necessary for their growth and survival.

We often find ourselves in familiar situations that keep us in our comfort zones. However, staying in these zones can hold us back. We need that push, that discomfort, to break free from safety and take risks to pursue our dreams and aspirations.

Peter got a "push" from Jesus when He said to get out of the boat and walk on the water. It was a risk, but Peter did it and experienced something miraculous, even if for a few seconds. We must be willing to make mistakes and learn from them. Each flight, each attempt, brings us closer to our goals, and over time, we gain confidence.

The push we need can come in various forms: a new opportunity, a life-changing event, or even a setback. Embracing these pushes and stepping out allows us to discover our true potential, develop new skills, and experience personal growth.

Father, give me that push I need to step outside my comfort zones and attempt great things for You. Amen.

ONLY 48 PERCENT

You're going to find that there will be times when people will have no stomach for solid teaching, but will fill up on spiritual junk food— catchy opinions that tickle their fancy. They'll turn their backs on truth and chase mirages.

2 TIMOTHY 4:3–5 MSG

A study by the Cultural Research Center found that evangelical Christians are almost as likely to reject absolute moral truth (46 percent) as to accept it (48 percent).[41] It is sad but not surprising. I knew it wouldn't be high, but I didn't expect it to be that low.

Truth has become relative because people think it depends on the situation. But even in the world of sports, many truths cannot be relative (e.g., wins and losses). Imagine if every athlete used a different metric to decide who won— one by score, one by hustle, one by the best fans, and so on. It would be chaos! Fortunately (or unfortunately), the scoreboard determines who wins. Life without truths, absolutes, and boundaries leads to chaos.

Psalm 31:5 says the Lord is the "God of truth" (CSB). God is our standard. The Bible isn't just filled with truth, it is *the* truth. Many of us embrace absolute truth (Jesus Christ), but we find it hard to apply His truth to others. However, God wants to use us in others' lives, and helping them understand His truth can set them free.

We must hold fast to the truth and not compromise under any circumstance. "Buy truth, and do not sell it; buy wisdom, instruction, and understanding" (Proverbs 23:23 ESV). Are you part of the 48 percent? Do not sell out. We need to stand for truth.

Father, I know You are the truth. Help me have a clear head and pure heart so I do not compromise the truth. Amen.

---

41   Tracy Munsil, "A Nation Unmoored—CRC Study Shows Americans Reject Moral Truth Rooted in God's Word," Arizona Christian University, May 19, 2020, https://www.arizonachristian.edu.

FOR THE TEAM

May the God who gives endurance and encouragement give you
the same attitude of mind toward each other that Christ Jesus had,
so that with one mind and one voice you may glorify the God
and Father of our Lord Jesus Christ.

ROMANS 15:5–6

One of the things I have always liked about Notre Dame football is the fact the players don't have their names on the back of their jerseys. There is a sense that when you play for this school, you are part of something far bigger than yourself. The school boasts decades of historic and legendary coaches, players, and miraculous wins.

No one player is more important than the team. It takes commitment, sacrifice, and a relentless pursuit of excellence from every single person in the locker room—from the water boys to the head coach, from the athletic trainers to the quarterback. To truly perform at their best, they need each other. Our mission as disciple makers requires the same type of total team effort.

No individual believer is more important than any other in the body of Christ. We are part of a team that has been built on the shoulders of great men and women who sacrificed their very lives for the sake of the gospel. The disciples were beheaded, stoned to death, and crucified for their faith. We are living in their legacy, part of this spiritual team. The body of Christ is most effective and influential when we pull in the same direction and are more concerned with God's glory rather than our own.

Father, help me remember I am part of Your body, the family of God, and I am here for Your glory, not my own. Amen.

REAL GUTS

"I know, my God, that you test the heart and are pleased with integrity.
All these things I have given willingly and with honest intent."

1 CHRONICLES 29:17

Legendary Hall of Fame basketball coach John Wooden once said, "A leader's most powerful ally is his or her own example. There is hypocrisy to the phrase 'Do as I say, not as I do.' I refused to make demands on my boys that I wasn't willing to live out in my own life."

Too often as men, we desire to live a life we haven't committed to in our hearts. What I mean is that we desire for our external life—the life that everyone sees, our successes and accomplishments—to be greater than our internal life—the life no one sees, our thoughts and desires.

The Hebrew word for "integrity" is *tom*, which means "completeness."[42] No cracks or gaps. It means there should be no difference between our public and private lives. God wants every aspect of our lives to be rock-solid and filled with integrity. Chuck Swindoll said, "You want to shock the world? Start here…demonstrating the guts to do what's right when no one is looking. It takes real guts to stand strong with integrity in a culture weakened by hypocrisy. Start today."[43]

Integrity starts with a deep-rooted, abiding walk with Christ. It means being honest and truthful, even when it is hard. It's about living a life of transparency and authenticity. Remember: If we have integrity, nothing else matters. If we don't have integrity, nothing else matters. Real men have real guts and live with integrity.

Father, I long for You to be pleased with my integrity. Help me live completely for You. Amen.

---

42   James Strong, *Strong's Expanded Exhaustive Concordance of the Bible*, Hb. 8537.

43   Charles R. Swindoll, "A Battle for Integrity," Insight for Living Ministries, June 15, 2009, https://insight.org.

BLIND SPOTS

Who can discern their own errors?
Forgive my hidden faults.

PSALM 19:12

The *American Idol* talent search is a wildly entertaining process. They invite ordinary Americans to audition and display their undiscovered singing abilities. While some of the auditions are amazing, the majority shown on TV are absolutely awful. But what makes this process most troubling is that every single person genuinely believes he or she can sing with the best of the best; they just haven't gotten their big break! And the worst singers often say, "All my friends tell me how great I sing."

This is a great picture of what's commonly referred to as *blind spots*. We all have them—things we can't see in ourselves. Flaws that prevent us from seeing the truth about ourselves. Like the contestants, we can't see when our character is out of tune.

God will sometimes use other people to expose our blind spots. He does this for our ultimate benefit. Nathan did this for David, and Jesus did this for the Pharisees. But God is also always available to help us if we ask.

Maybe we think we're encouraging, but we're really very critical of others. Maybe others think we're devoted to God, but we spend very little time in prayer and reading the Bible. I don't know your blind spots, but trust me, you have them, just like I do. We all need to humbly ask God, and sometimes a trusted friend, to bring them to light so we can change.

Father, please reveal the blind spots in my character and conduct so I can address them with humility and action. Amen.

ATTITUDE OF HUMILITY

Make your own attitude that of Christ Jesus.

PHILIPPIANS 2:5 HCSB

At the beginning of every sports season, thousands of coaches, athletes, and teams gather to discuss their goals in order to get everyone on the same page. They passionately share their goals, plans, and expectations and write them down with anticipation and excitement. It's an experience filled with energy, hope, and optimism. Most likely, you have experienced this many times.

But it only takes a few defeats, injuries, or disappointments for the positive energy and optimism we felt at the beginning of the season to fall to the tests and challenges of reality. The goals that we committed to with such hope and enthusiasm are likely in the garbage can; we find ourselves simply trying to survive the season.

You might not be jumping into a new sports season, but you are part of many teams as a man of God: your family, work, church, and community—to name a few. You may start off with high hopes, but problems, tragedies, and conflicts have the potential to blow up these teams. We can't control outcomes or results, but we can control our attitude every single time.

Chuck Swindoll reminded us that "life is 10 percent what happens to you and 90 percent how you react."[44] Paul exhorted the Philippians—and us—to have the same attitude as Christ, which is an attitude of humility. "He humbled himself by becoming obedient to the point of death—even to death on a cross" (Philippians 2:8 CSB). Decide to have an attitude of humility—no matter what. God can use us greatly if we have an attitude like Christ Jesus.

Father, develop in me an attitude of humility so I can glorify You in every situation. Amen.

---

44   Charles R. Swindoll, *Life Is 10% What Happens to You and 90% How You React* (Nashville, TN: Nelson Books, 2023), ix.

HE HAS YOUR BACK

He will command his angels concerning you
to guard you in all your ways.

PSALM 91:11

It has been said that life is not a playground; it's a battleground. And if you
spend any time reading the Old Testament, you will realize our God is a
righteous warrior. Most of the battles happen in the unseen world of angels
and demons and then play out in the physical world that we see. God gives us
the assistance of angels in the heavenly realm to guard us.

God gives us very clear instruction on how to be prepared for the battle.
He lists six important weapons that make up our spiritual armor. All six—the
belt of truth, the breastplate of righteousness, the shoes of peace, the shield of
faith, the helmet of salvation, and the sword of the Spirit—protect you from
the front. Not one piece of armor provides protection for your back.

In fact, Paul instructed us in Philippians 3:13 to "[forget] what is behind
and [strain] toward what is ahead." Paul told us to never look back. There's no
need. God has your back. He gives us no armor for our back because He has
it covered. When we live according to the Spirit, when we're right with God,
when we confess our sins, we have nothing to fear.

Ask NFL Hall of Famer Peyton Manning how important his left tackle was.
He literally could drop back in the pocket and never worry about getting hit
from behind. He could keep his vision down field to attack the defense. When
you have that assurance, that confidence, you can perform at the highest levels.

Rest assured: God has your back!

*Father, thank You for protecting me from things I can't see and having my
back. Amen.*

$10 MILLION TONGUE

Sometimes it praises our Lord and Father,
and sometimes it curses those who have been made in the image of God.

JAMES 3:9 NLT

Carson Palmer, the Heisman Trophy winner and 2003 number one NFL Draft pick, signed a $49 million, six-year contract with the Cincinnati Bengals. A total of $10 million of the deal was his signing bonus. However, that $10 million wasn't attached to his great throwing arm, quarterback intelligence, or play calling. It was attached to his tongue and whether he would say anything negative about his new team, coaches, or management. Basically, it was a loyalty pledge guaranteeing he would not be critical. If he ripped into his team, he lost the cash. That is quite an incentive for keeping talk positive and encouraging.

In the heat of battle, it is difficult to keep our tongues from slipping. After someone has wronged us, it is easy to lash out. God desires for us not only to keep our mouths from cursing but also to abstain from being critical.

When the pressure comes, we speak what is in our hearts. If you squeeze a toothpaste tube, what comes out? Toothpaste. When you get squeezed, what comes out? Criticism or godliness? You might not get paid $10 million for a Christlike tongue, but your Savior will be glorified. That's worth more than any amount of money.

Father, teach me how to encourage others. Cleanse my heart of any bitterness, criticism, or anger I might carry toward others so I can glorify You, even when I'm squeezed. Amen.

TRAINING

Train yourself to be godly. For physical training is of some value,
but godliness has value for all things, holding promise for both
the present life and the life to come.

1 TIMOTHY 4:7–8

I love the fact that Paul drew a comparison between physical and spiritual training. But we often either completely discount the benefits of physical training or miss the fact that we should actually engage in spiritual training. Neither of these responses is correct. Clearly, spiritual training in godliness is superior to physical training. Eventually, our bodies are going to wear out; thankfully, we'll each receive a new, incorruptible body in heaven. But that doesn't mean we shouldn't take care of what God has entrusted to us—including our bodies.

In fact, we are called to love God with all our mind and strength. Our physical condition will have a direct impact on our thinking, moods, energy, and strength. Proper nutrition and exercise also help us prevent disease. For those who understand how important it is to be physically healthy, we often miss the fact that we need to train spiritually. We need a plan. And we need to sacrifice time, effort, and energy to get stronger in our relationship with God. It's time to do whatever it takes to renew our minds, hear from God, and combat the influence of flesh and the world.

For some of us, if we trained physically like we do spiritually, we'd be morbidly obese. For others, if we trained spiritually like we do physically, we'd be missionaries.

It's time to start training as though we're preparing for an Ironman. We need to put in the hours and the miles necessary to win—pray, read, and worship.

Father, help me take my spiritual and physical training seriously. Amen.

HUMBLED AND HEALED

Naaman was commander of the army of the king of Aram.
He was a great man in the sight of his master and highly regarded…
He was a valiant soldier, but he had leprosy…
Elisha sent a messenger to say to him, "Go, wash yourself."

2 KINGS 5:1, 10

Naaman was a great commander and valiant soldier, but his pride almost prevented his healing. His desire for Elisha to simply "wave his hand over" his leprosy and heal him (v. 11) without having to disrobe and expose the extent of his illness is the evidence. Naaman, as a high-ranking military commander, likely had a strong sense of pride. The idea of disrobing and exposing his leprosy in front of others, even a prophet like Elisha, would have been humiliating. Like many of us, Naaman wanted to cover and avoid revealing his weakness to others.

He may have been looking for a quick and easy solution. He wanted a miraculous healing that required minimal effort or personal discomfort. He's not the only one. A lot of us have a tendency to seek easy solutions, even when facing significant challenges.

Our pride can get in the way of the healing God wants to perform in our lives. It can be a barrier that prevents reconciliation in relationships, physical healing, or even emotional healing. We must be willing to expose our pain in order to experience the healing touch of God. Covering up or hiding the truth never works.

Father, don't let me cover up or hide my weakness. Instead give me the humility I need to be healed. Amen.

RISKY PRAYER

I want the men in every place to pray,
lifting up holy hands without anger or argument.
1 TIMOTHY 2:8 HCSB

An outside source was trying to convince players that big-time college sports were exploiting them. The instigators encouraged players from both teams to protest the game. Everyone was anticipating a conflict, but what people didn't expect, including the seventy-four thousand fans watching, was some risky prayer.

This 1986 historic football game became one of the greatest between number three Oklahoma and number five Nebraska. Oklahoma's running back Spencer Tillman and Nebraska's Stan Parker decided to do the unthinkable. They led several of their teammates to midfield prior to the opening kickoff. The crowd watched in awe as they knelt to pray, holding hands at the fifty-yard line in Lincoln, Nebraska. It was risky prayer.

We now see prayer after games all the time. It has almost become a tradition. But when was the last time you saw pregame prayer at the center of the field or court? Players coming together as competitors, not enemies, who desire to help one another play their best? It would be a way of showing everyone that God comes first, not last.

How many times have you ended something like an activity, task, project, or game and said, "Okay, now let's ask God to bless this"? Instead, we should say, "Before we even start, let's pray and ask God to be at the center of everything we do." Risky prayer is when you start with prayer, not end with prayer. It is praying instead of protesting. Bending a knee, not raising a fist.

Father, I ask for wisdom to know when to pray, even when it takes me out of my comfort zone and gets risky. Amen.

SELFLESS SERVING

Serve wholeheartedly, as if you were serving the Lord, not people.

EPHESIANS 6:7

Think about the people who have impacted your life the most. Were they individuals who focused solely on their own success, or were they people who selflessly served and uplifted others? It is often those who give generously, without seeking attention, who leave the most significant impact.

Craig was one of those individuals in my life. He was my high school youth group volunteer who never spoke up front or led meetings, but he was the guy who invested in me and many others behind the scenes. He showed up at my house to lift weights, go for a run, and pray with me. He loved, cared for, and served me. No one witnessed him making the investment that impacted my life.

As men, we often strive to be in the spotlight and get the recognition; however, it's important to remember the power of serving selflessly. Serving others is not a sign of weakness. When we choose to put others before ourselves, we tap into a wellspring of fulfillment. True greatness lies in how we use our gifts and talents to bless the lives of those around us. Jesus set the ultimate example of selflessness. He washed the feet of His disciples, healed the sick, and gave His life for others. Use your gifts to serve your family, friends, colleagues, and community wholeheartedly. Lend a listening ear, offer a helping hand, or pray for a specific need. Remember: serving others is not just an act of kindness; it is also an act of worship.

Father, teach me to find joy and fulfillment in putting the needs of others before my own. Amen.

SEPTEMBER

I GOT THIS?

"Take the staff, and you and your brother Aaron gather the assembly together. Speak to that rock before their eyes and it will pour out its water. You will bring water out of the rock for the community so they and their livestock can drink."

NUMBERS 20:8

As men, one of our greatest weaknesses is that we rely on our own strength. Moses gave us a great example of how we fall into this trap. When God first asked Moses to step up and set the Israelites free, Moses was timid and lacked confidence in his ability to speak boldly. But over time, Moses saw God use him to do miraculous things, and he grew in confidence.

So when God told him to "speak to that rock" to bring water to His people as they wandered in the desert on the way to the promised land, Moses made a mistake by relying on himself. Moses basically said, "I got this," as he struck the rock twice with his staff instead of obeying and depending on God's power. The entire nation paid the price.

When we are too confident, we lose dependence on God. We start to believe we don't really need Him, and we try to do everything on our own. We begin trusting in ourselves instead of trusting God to work.

There are two keys to making sure a strength remains a strength: balance and blessing. When we are self-aware and accountable, our strengths will be a blessing. When we aren't, they become a burden. The gifts and strengths God has given us are designed for us to give away to bless others.

Father, make each gift and ability You have given me a blessing to others. Amen.

WHATEVER IT TAKES

"You will seek Me and find Me
when you search for Me with all your heart."
JEREMIAH 29:13 HCSB

My grandfather Pop showed me what it meant to be hungry spiritually, even to the very end. I had a lasting encounter with him right before he died. I went to visit Pop when I was in college. It was his seventy-ninth year of life, one month before he passed away. As we talked in his living room, I noticed an interesting array of things on his end table. Three things in particular intrigued me. The first was a large-print Bible. The second, a magnifying glass. The third, a tape recorder. I knew his eyesight had been failing for years, which accounted for the first two things. But the tape recorder puzzled me.

Out of curiosity, I asked him about it. His answer astonished me. "This is where I meet God every morning, and I need the magnifying glass to read my Bible. And unfortunately, by the end of the day, I sometimes forget what the Lord taught me from His Word that morning, so I decided that if I read the Bible *and* listened to it on tape, I'd double my chance of remembering it."

My grandfather was hungry until the very end, and he was willing to do whatever it took to feed that hunger. What about you? Do you have a hungry heart for the Lord? Are you willing to do whatever it takes to satisfy it?

Father, I am hungry for You. Help me do whatever it takes to feed my spiritual hunger. Amen.

THE PELOTON

Just as a body, though one, has many parts,
but all its many parts form one body, so it is with Christ.

1 CORINTHIANS 12:12

The Tour de France is considered the Super Bowl of cycling and is arguably one of the most physically, mentally, and spiritually demanding events in all of sports. For twenty-one stages in just twenty-three days, 180 of the most highly conditioned athletes ride twenty-two hundred miles through some of the most beautiful countryside and grueling mountains in the world. Winning the Tour without the sacrifice and cooperation of your teammates is impossible. The team leader depends on the strengths of each teammate. Everybody takes their turn at the front. Some riders bring food and water to the leaders. Others set the pace out front to try to break their opponents.

But the peloton is the secret. Peloton power is that large mass of riders working together to conserve energy. The reduction in wind resistance is dramatic; riders can save up to 40 percent of their energy. If any teammate falls off the back of the peloton, it's very common to see a rider or two go back and work to help them rejoin the group. And at the end of the stage, the riders have far more energy for the next day.

We are better together. We are designed to work together as a team, to bear one another's burdens, and to push each other to do great things. When we are united by the love of Jesus and our mission to share His truth with others, we accomplish much more than we could on our own.

Father, thank You for designing each of us with unique gifts and talents to bring to Your team. I know we are better together. Amen.

RABBIT'S FOOT

*Jesus told them a story showing that it was necessary
for them to pray consistently and never quit.*

LUKE 18:1–3 MSG

When I was playing professional lacrosse, I was the only Christian on my team. I was outspoken about my faith during my four years of playing, and I never had another player share with me about their faith in Jesus. I felt God placed me on the team to be a light. Because I was the token Christian player, my teammates designated me to do the team prayer. Usually, if it was a big game, I would have a player say something like this, "Pray a *good* one, Dan. This is a huge game!" The mentality was that my good prayer would lead us to victory; a bad prayer would lead to defeat.

For good luck, some people believe in carrying a rabbit's foot. In the same way, some people think of prayer like a rabbit's foot. But prayer is not a rabbit's foot nor a good luck charm. Prayer is a battle.

Paul challenged us in 1 Thessalonians 5:17 to pray without ceasing. Oswald Chambers said, "Prayer is not an exercise, it is the life."[45] Constant, ongoing, continual, pervasive prayer is tough work. Prayer is digging below the surface so God can reveal His character to us. Don't ask God for His hand of blessing but ask God to reveal Himself to you. Pray that you will know Him better every day. Pray for Him to shine His light through you. Pray you will feel His pleasure as you go about your day. Pray for protection and safety for everyone around you.

Jesus, I know I have treated prayer like a rabbit's foot. Please forgive me. Help me go deeper when I seek Your face in prayer. Amen.

---

45   Oswald Chambers, "Think as Jesus Taught," My Utmost for His Highest (website), May 26 devotion, https://utmost.org.

SPECIAL OPS

The LORD is a warrior;
the LORD is his name.

EXODUS 15:3

The United States Special Operations Forces (SOF) have a warrior mindset. They are the most highly trained, disciplined, capable, mission-driven people in the world. They serve in many capacities all around the world to fight for and defend freedom. The SOF people are most familiar with are the Navy SEALs, but every branch of the military has them. They enter the most dangerous circumstances and complete the most extreme missions. Knowing this helps me sleep better at night.

These warriors are strong and courageous. I love their focus, determination, and discipline. I'm challenged by their mental toughness and their internal voices that must say, *I will never back down, give in, or give up.*

God encourages us to be prepared and take on a warrior mindset. Our thoughts determine how we feel, and that drives what we do. Here are three principles of a warrior mindset we can model in our own lives:

1. Refuse to make excuses. Remove negative thinking and replace it with what's possible. Take responsibility for what you can do and stop complaining about what you can't (2 Corinthians 10:5).
2. Revel in the toughest circumstances. Anticipate challenges and obstacles. Be willing to enter the "crucible" so you can be refined, tested, and proven. In adversity, warriors say, "I'm made for this!" (John 16:33).
3. Recover from setbacks. When something goes wrong, a warrior says, "What can I do to fix it?" Quickly put disappointments behind you and move forward. Keep your eyes on Jesus. Forget the past and stay focused on the finish line (Philippians 3:13–14).

Father, help me refuse to make excuses, revel in tough circumstances, and recover from setbacks. Amen.

BUILD OTHERS UP

The words of the reckless pierce like swords,
but the tongue of the wise brings healing.

PROVERBS 12:18

As the words floated off the end of my tongue, I realized I blew it. I did it again. I spoke negative words toward others. It is so easy for me to become the cut-down king. It doesn't take much. Plus, others usually laugh. But my reckless words can cut. They pierce like a sword and cause damage. Being someone who cuts down is not my desire. I want to be a man who builds up others.

God desires for us to build up one another instead of cutting others down. It takes effort, and you need to be intentional. It does not come naturally for many of us, especially when we tend to be sarcastic. But when we make a change and intentionally stop cutting people down, it is awesome. It blesses so many. People need strokes, not pokes.

A friend of mine once said that everyone in the world is underencouraged, and I agree. Truett Cathy, founder of Chick-fil-A, nailed it when he said, "How do you know if someone needs encouragement? If they are breathing!"[46] Ask the Lord to show you ways to encourage friends, family members, and even people you do not know. Be a man of God who builds others up by speaking words that bring healing, hope, and blessing.

Father, I have cut others down way too much. Today, I make a commitment to stop and to build them up. May my words heal and not damage. Amen.

---

46   Chick-fil-A, "Truett Cathy was fond of saying," Facebook, September 8, 2015, https://www.facebook.com.

ELEPHANTS

"Pardon me, my lord," Gideon replied, "but how can I save Israel?
My clan is the weakest in Manasseh, and I am the least in my family."

JUDGES 6:15

Elephants are some of the biggest, most powerful, most intelligent animals on the planet. And in certain parts of Asia, farmers still use elephants to do much of the heavy labor. Some countries even hold elephant festivals to celebrate their strength and intelligence. These festivals always end with a tug-of-war between one elephant and one hundred men, and—you guessed it—the elephant always wins!

But amazingly, the only thing elephant owners in Asia have to do to control an elephant is tie a rope to its right hind leg and a small wooden post in the ground. That's it! The elephant won't move, even though the wooden post and rope to an elephant are like a toothpick and dental floss to you and me. This is because when the elephants are young, they experience something called learned helplessness.

Owners tie a strong rope around a young elephant's hind leg and tether it to stakes driven into the ground. Initially, a young elephant struggles and tries to break free. However, as the elephant repeatedly attempts to escape but fails, it eventually learns that its efforts are futile. Over time, the elephant develops a mindset of helplessness and stops trying to escape, even when it becomes stronger and can easily break free.

We can be a lot like those elephants. We have great strength inside us, but we struggle to remove the invisible barriers and limitations in our minds. We let doubts or fears and negative, destructive thinking keep us from reaching our full potential. Real transformation comes through the renewing of our minds. We must change the way we think and refocus on what's possible with God.

Father, help me focus on what's possible and reject learned helplessness. Amen.

WE OR ME?

Be devoted to one another in love.
Honor one another above yourselves.

ROMANS 12:10

At the end of the movie *The Greatest Game Ever Played*, a gripping scene depicts what winning is all about. Based on a true story, the movie tells of twenty-year-old golfer Francis Ouimet, who won the 1913 US Open (an event he had caddied before) with a ten-year-old caddie named Eddie. After accomplishing this unthinkable feat by sinking the winning playoff putt on the eighteenth hole, Francis yelled to Eddie, "We did it! We did it!" Francis played the round of his life, but he understood he won because of the help and encouragement of his caddie.[47]

This scene captured my heart, and I was convicted because I am embarrassed to say I would have yelled, "I did it. I did it." I was reminded that *we* is more powerful than *me*. God desires for us to pick up our cross daily and follow Him. We must die to self every day. Those are hard words, tough words. To be crucified daily means to empty ourselves and look after not only our own interests but also the interests of others. It is not I who lives but Christ within me. It is a daily battle of dying to self.

God can use us best when we sacrifice our own interests. When we devote ourselves to one another in love and honor one another above ourselves, we value *we* over *me*. We need to be reminded that we win together. What will it be for you? *We* or *me*?

Father, I talk too much about my own accomplishments. Help me go from me *to* we. *Amen.*

---

47   *The Greatest Game Ever Played*, directed by Bill Paxton (Burbank, CA: Buena Vista Pictures, 2005), 120 min.

FIVE-HOUR ENERGY

Whoever claims to live in him
must live as Jesus did.

1 JOHN 2:6

There's a 5-Hour Energy commercial that shows a man accomplishing great tasks because of a tiny energy drink. In five hours, this man played a round of golf, read a book while learning to play guitar, ran a 10K while knitting a sweater, parachuted from a plane, and became a ping-pong master while recording his debut album. Obviously, this example is an exaggeration of what you can get done after drinking the energy drink. But it demonstrates the power of focus and energy. If you were to set aside five hours this week for your spiritual growth, how much could you get done? What kind of change might that bring to your life? How could you maximize your time to energize and transform your life?

One thing I've discovered is that I tend to do what I enjoy. Three things I've come to enjoy that help me grow spiritually are reading through books in the Bible, listening to praise music, and reading a men's devotional. There are lots of other options, but this works for me. Find what works for you. I've also discovered that being rested is a key component of my spiritual growth. Waking up refreshed from regular sleep helps me start my day motivated.

Whatever you pick, stick to it and carve out time on a daily basis. Shoot for five hours of spiritual energy this week and get ready to grow. Remember: disciplined action leads to progress, and progress is the name of the game.

Father, help me be diligent in my spiritual training program so I can grow into the person You've made me to be. Energize me to live for You. Amen.

EXTREME MAKEOVER

Do not lie to one another, since you have put off the old self with
its practices and have put on the new self. You are being renewed in
knowledge according to the image of your Creator.

COLOSSIANS 3:9–10 HCSB

I loved watching the TV show *Extreme Makeover: Home Edition*. Each
episode featured a family who faced a hardship, so a team of workers came
in and completely remodeled their home. The show should be called *Extreme
Transformation* because they identified a huge need and transformed it. When
they finished, they did the great reveal by moving a large bus parked in front
of the house. The homeowners would jump with joy. Never did I see them say,
"That is exactly what I thought you would do." No, their expressions said it all.
They were blown away. It was hard not to tear up at their responses.

I wish this same thing would occur in our lives. We could call it *Extreme
Makeover: Man Edition*. We could bring in a team of experts to fix our
problems. At the end, we'd just say, "Move that bus!" and a newly transformed
man would be standing there. If only it were that easy. Transformation takes a
lot of work, but it's possible. If it's done right, the change first happens on the
inside, not the outside. It happens in the heart, soul, and mind.

In Romans 12, Paul said we can either be a conformer or a transformer.
Conforming involves changing only our behavior. Transforming involves
changing our heart and mind as well. Christ desires to do some heavy-duty
work in your life. Are you willing to let Him in and begin that transformation?
What are you waiting for?

*Father, I want an extreme makeover in my life. Do Your work and make me
more like Christ. Amen.*

RUN INTO THE FIRE

"I only know that in every city the Holy Spirit warns me
that prison and hardships are facing me."

ACTS 20:23

The images from September 11, 2001, are still pretty vivid in my mind. Most people who are old enough to remember know exactly where they were when they heard the news that terrorists flew planes into the Twin Towers. What sticks out most in my mind is the video footage of heroic police officers and firefighters running toward the Towers as thousands ran away in fear. In the face of chaos, they ran into the buildings on a mission to save lives.

Paul was like an old-time firefighter. He expected to face danger and hardship everywhere he went. He went into "burning buildings" on a mission to save lives. And since he expected to experience opposition, he was ready for it and persevered.

Life is not easy. It's full of challenges and heartbreaks. The Holy Spirit warned Paul, and Jesus told us to expect tough times. But He also told us to be courageous in the face of adversity and to trust Him. The battle is the Lord's, and it's won and lost by those willing to rely on the power of God. Jesus said, "In this world you will have trouble. But take heart! I have overcome the world" (John 16:33). And better still, He told us we can experience peace right in the middle of chaos.

We, like the firefighters on 9/11, are called to rescue. May God give you the courage for whatever you're facing today.

Father, prepare me to face my fires head-on and give me the courage to run in and help save others. Amen.

GET YOUR FACE IN THE BOOK

God means what he says. What he says goes. His powerful Word is sharp as
a surgeon's scalpel, cutting through everything, whether doubt or defense,
laying us open to listen and obey.

HEBREWS 4:12–13 MSG

While playing on a summer lacrosse team in 1994, I met a college student
named Shane. During his time on the team, God got hold of his heart, and
I remember being with him when he asked Jesus to be the Savior and Lord
of his life. Pursuing discipleship, I asked Shane if we could start meeting for
breakfast. It was a joy to see him grow over a several-month period. Then, one
day, everything changed.

He showed up before I got there—which was a first—and he already had
his coffee. He was waiting for me with a big grin on his face. Before I could
even sit down, Shane said loudly so I and others in the restaurant could hear,
"I figured it out!" Before my bottom could hit my seat, Shane was practically
over the table with his Bible wide open. Leaning over, he got right in my face
and literally started slapping the pages of his open Bible. Shane said these
exact words: "I realized this week that if I do not get my face in the Book, I am
dead meat! *I gotta get my face in the Book!*"

His words marked me. No options. Just one goal—get my face in the
Book every day. I saw it transform Shane's life firsthand. I have experienced it
transform my life. Will it transform yours?

*Jesus, I want to be transformed and experience victorious living by getting my
face in Your Book every day. Amen.*

FLASHING LIGHTS

Whoever still won't obey after being warned many times
will suddenly be destroyed. Nothing can save them.

PROVERBS 29:1 NIRV

One of the cool things about where we live in Colorado is that trains go through the middle of Old Town. Some people get annoyed by it because it can slow you down if you are in a hurry. But I love the charm.

A few weeks ago, I was driving through town and had to abruptly stop as the train track arms with flashing red lights came down to warn of the oncoming train. I must have been distracted, but thankfully I saw the lights and stopped just before it was too late. The lights protected me from a catastrophic collision.

In the Bible, God sets up flashing lights, or principles, designed to protect us from harm. But I believe it's also wise to put flashing lights in place that warn us of destructive situations in advance. Flashing lights are personal standards of behavior that prevent disaster and promote life. They might be different for everyone, but they help us stay far from sin and decisions we'll regret.

God uses flashing lights for several reasons:

- To wake us up. Sometimes we don't realize the decisions we're making could lead to sin.
- To keep us on track. Choosing detours that lead to destruction creates delays and robs us of the relationship with God that He desires.
- To prevent a disaster for us and others around us. Our choices always affect more than just us. Somebody else can get hurt.

Pay attention to God's flashing lights that warn you of danger and keep you on the path that leads to life.

Father, show me the flashing lights that are protecting me from sin and promoting life. Amen.

FINDING GREATNESS

"A disciple is not above his teacher,
but everyone who is fully trained will be like his teacher."

LUKE 6:40 HCSB

Not many people know who Bertoldo di Giovanni was. However, most people know Michelangelo. He became one of the greatest sculptors of all time. In his book *A Call to Excellence*, Gary Inrig told the story of how, at age fourteen, Michelangelo became Bertoldo's student because Bertoldo saw greatness in him. Bertoldo was wise enough to realize that people with enormous talent are often tempted to do the minimum rather than be disciplined and put in the work to become great.

One day in the studio, Michelangelo was working on a sculpture far easier than he was capable of, and Bertoldo realized his student was not doing his best. So Bertoldo grabbed a hammer, smashed the work into hundreds of pieces, and shouted, "Michelangelo, talent is cheap; dedication is costly!"[48]

We can always recognize greatness, but often we don't know the story behind the greatness. There is always someone who sees greatness in others before they become great. Bertoldo saw greatness in Michelangelo before he saw it in himself. Michelangelo became Bertoldo's disciple, and he dedicated himself to Bertoldo's guidance.

Are we finding greatness in others? Are we tapping someone on the shoulder and investing in them so they can be everything God created them to be? In Luke 6:40, Jesus imparted a profound lesson on discipleship and reminded us that discipleship is a lifelong journey of growth and transformation. Through the power of the Holy Spirit, we can train, mentor, and disciple other men to become more Christlike each day.

There is a younger generation longing for us to tap them on the shoulder and develop greatness.

Father, I want to give of myself and invest in the next generation. Show me whom I need to reach out to and ask them to start the journey. Amen.

---

48   Gary Inrig, *A Call to Excellence* (Wheaton, IL: Victor, 1985), 102.

ASK

You do not have because you do not ask God.

JAMES 4:2

When I went to my parents and said, "Can I ask you a question?" they always responded, "It never hurts to ask!" I quickly learned that asking didn't mean I would always get a yes, but it was still important to ask.

In the movie *Evan Almighty*, Morgan Freeman plays the character of God. In one scene, Freeman is having a conversation with Evan's wife and says, "If someone prays for patience, do you think God gives them patience, or does He give them the opportunity to be patient? If they prayed for courage, does God give them courage, or does He give them opportunities to be courageous? If someone prayed for their family to be closer, do you think God zaps them with warm, fuzzy feelings, or does He give them opportunities to love each other?"[49]

It is a powerful scene. Fortunately, God loves us too much to give us everything we want at the very moment we want it. Instead of fixing our circumstances instantly, He often puts us on a journey to develop something in us and not just to fix something for us.

We often want the answer to be easy, comfortable, and safe. We want God to give us what we ask for. "Can you just fix my problems? Can I just wake up in the morning with everything going my way?" Even though our questions may sometimes seem silly, God says to always ask. When we get in the habit of going to God for little things, we eventually trust Him for the bigger, more meaningful things. He always knows what's best for us and doesn't want us to settle for less. So remember: always ask.

Father, help me never stop asking and trusting You for answers. Amen.

---

49   *Evan Almighty*, directed by Tom Shadyac (Universal City, CA: Universal Pictures, 2007), 96 min.

FOR THE GLORY

Whether you eat or drink, or whatever you do,
do everything for God's glory.

1 CORINTHIANS 10:31 HCSB

I live for the glory. Not any kind of glory but for the real stuff. The kind I am talking about is not the everyday, ordinary glory that you can get from people or things. Instead, it is for God's glory. As men, it is easy to get caught up in receiving glory because it is always coming from so many sources.

Paul reminded us in 1 Corinthians 10:31 that whatever we do, it must be "for God's glory." And an easy way for me to remember this simple truth is to break down the acronym FOR into three areas: focus, obey, and reflect.

1. Focus: Our focus determines our destination. When I focus on myself, my eyes are down. When I focus on Jesus Christ, my eyes are up. Hebrews 12:2 encourages us to keep our eyes on Jesus. When we focus on Jesus, all glory goes to Him—not us. Are your eyes fixed on Jesus?

2. Obey: God desires for us to discover what pleases Him. If we love Him, we will obey His Word. When my kids were young, we had a rule called First-Time Listening. If I had to ask them to do something twice, that meant they weren't obeying. God said to me, *Do you listen to Me the way you expect your kids to listen to you?* What about you? Are you obeying His voice?

3. Reflect: We either soak up the glory God deserves or reflect the glory back onto Him. Imagine there's a mirror over your head so when Jesus looks down, He sees Himself. Are you reflecting or absorbing?

Father, I want to give You all the glory. Help me focus, obey, and reflect. Amen.

STRENGTH FOR TWO

"Be strong and courageous.
Do not be afraid or terrified because of them,
for the LORD your God goes with you;
he will never leave you nor forsake you."

DEUTERONOMY 31:6

In Greek mythology, a hero is believed to have strength for two. In other words, to be heroic, you had to thrive on your own *and* help someone else thrive. Superheroes have the physical and moral strength to help others.

Spartan Racing inspires me when I see those who are strong helping those who are struggling. I've seen racers literally carrying other competitors and helping them clear obstacles. Will you have the strength for two? And what are you willing to do to get ready? What will you go through to be strong enough in mind, body, and spirit to help others when the time comes?

Here are three keys:

1. Push beyond your normal limits. To increase capacity, you must be stretched and tested. If it doesn't challenge you, it will never change you.
2. See pain as your friend. We all have to stop seeing pain as something to avoid and instead start using it to our advantage. Let God turn your pain into progress.
3. Face your fears. We have two choices when dealing with fear. We can forget everything and run, or we can face everything and rise.

Heroes have the strength for two. We need men who are morally strong. We need men unwilling to cut corners or compromise, physically strong men who can help others in need. We need emotionally strong men who can refresh and encourage those who are down and out. Will you have strength for two?

Father, help me develop the strength for two as I protect, provide, and preside. Amen.

GAP-FREE LIVING

He is a shield to those who walk in integrity.

PROVERBS 2:7 NASB

There is a story from the French Revolution that tells of a man who was seen running after a mob. As he moved quickly into danger, somebody screamed, "Stop! Stop! Don't follow that mob!"

He continued to sprint toward the mob, calling back, "I have to follow them! I'm their leader!"

It's funny how often things don't appear to be the way they actually are. This happens a lot with our spiritual lives. We often live differently from what we try to convey to others. This, however, goes directly against our calling to live lives of integrity. Our being and doing should line up.

Here are the big questions for us: What would our lives look like if our inside became our outside? What would it look like for our private lives to become public? Having integrity means we are whole and undivided; it means there are no gaps between what we believe and how we live.

The tension in our lives is the gap between the outside and the inside, the public and the private, what they see and what we know. Living with gaps will not bring life change; it will bring inner torment. God doesn't want there to be any gaps in us. Gap-free living is hard but worth it. It moves us from bondage to freedom, from dark to light, from hurt to healing. When you pursue authenticity rather than duplicity, everybody wins—God, others, and you!

Father, help me pursue integrity and eliminate every gap. Amen.

I THINK I CAN

Since, then, you have been raised with Christ, set your hearts on things above, where Christ is, seated at the right hand of God. Set your minds on things above, not on earthly things.

COLOSSIANS 3:1–2

Have you ever heard, "If you think you can or think you can't, you're right"? Our patterns of thinking eventually determine our destination. If I think I can't do something, my motivation to try or train is diminished. We see this all the time. We sabotage our efforts with negative thinking. We ultimately fail because we forgot to train our brain. On the other hand, if I think I can do something, I line up my time, energy, and resources behind getting it done. The likelihood of success is amplified. My ability to overcome obstacles and challenges is enhanced because I believe it can be done. I simply will not accept failure.

The greatest athletes in the world all have incredible physical capacity—they have strength, endurance, and flexibility. But what separates them from the rest is the way they think. They've developed mental toughness over time. They reject negative, self-defeating thinking and replace it with belief and faith. They replace problems with solutions and what can't be done with what can. They teach their brains to overcome their emotions and to beat back the demons of defeat.

But this is not the power of positive thinking. Instead, this is the power of transformed thinking. It's about being "transformed by the renewing of your mind" (Romans 12:2). Stop dwelling on the negative lies from the Enemy and start dwelling on the truth of God's Word.

Father, teach me to win the battle of the mind. Help me remove destructive thoughts that keep me from being my best. Amen.

GIVE UP

This is how we know what love is: Jesus Christ laid down his life for us.
And we ought to lay down our lives for our brothers and sisters.

1 JOHN 3:16

Just give up. Yes, it is counterintuitive, but there is incredible power in giving up. In fact, it should become a daily practice. You probably think I'm crazy. But I'm not talking about giving up as in quitting. I'm talking about giving up our rights and control, surrendering them to the Lord. You see, God hates the quitting kind of giving up, but He loves the surrender kind of giving up. He wants us to give up our lives for the sake of His kingdom.

Oswald Chambers wrote, "Every time I insist upon my rights, I hurt the Son of God…The disciple realises that it is his Lord's honour that is at stake in his life, not his own honour."[50] Jesus gave us the perfect example of laying down His life on the cross, and we should lay down our lives as living sacrifices—not just for Jesus but also for others. We might freely lay down our lives for our Savior, but we often kick and scream when we have to sacrifice for other people.

Paul said in Romans 12 that we must become a living sacrifice. Dead sacrifices don't crawl off the altar like living ones do. Our tendency is to make every excuse for why we should not give up and surrender. But it's time to stop. It's time to give up. Surrender and see what God will do with your life today. You will become a channel for God's greatest work.

Father, I ask for the power to give up. I don't want to be a quitter but a surrenderer who desires to do Your will. Amen.

---

50   Oswald Chambers, "The Account with Persecution," My Utmost for His Highest (website), July 14 devotion, https://utmost.org.

NEVER QUIT

As for you, brothers and sisters,
never tire of doing what is good.

2 THESSALONIANS 3:13

You've probably seen the T-shirt that reads, "Pain is temporary. Quitting lasts a lifetime." It's been a reminder for me that when the going gets tough, the tough get going. If you start, you finish. Period.

I've experienced plenty of times when I've wanted to quit, to give in to the pain and suffering or disappointment. But then I remember that I need the power and presence of God—especially in the hardest moments. My never-quit attitude was tested on a thirty-seven-mile bike ride in the mountains of Colorado. Others had warned me of the relentless climbs, and at sixteen miles in, I grew weary. I played mental games and even prayed the Lord's Prayer a few times. But the climbing just kept coming. Finally, with a long, uphill road in front of me, I decided to get off the bike and take a break. By "take a break," I mean "quit." Sure, I finished the ride, but I gave up before reaching the summit.

Grit helps you not quit. Forging mental toughness and grit requires challenges that push your limits. We may never experience the full power of God until we step way out of our comfort zone. Scripture tells us we are made to do good works that God has prepared in advance for us. Sometimes doing good deeds is a thankless effort, especially if we are doing things behind the scenes and don't get recognized for them. But we need grit so we never quit doing what is good.

Father, help me develop grit so I never quit. Help me rely on Your power and presence in the toughest times so I can finish strong. Amen.

GOT WISDOM?

Real wisdom, God's wisdom, begins with a holy life and is characterized
by getting along with others. It is gentle and reasonable, overflowing with
mercy and blessings, not hot one day and cold the next, not two-faced.

JAMES 3:17–18 MSG

I once read about a coach who told a player who received four Fs and one D
on his report card, "Son, looks to me like you're spending too much time on
one subject." That kind of wisdom will get you in trouble. Too often wisdom
is thought of as just "smarts," but it is much more than that. Knowledge is
knowing, but wisdom is knowing when to use it.

Wisdom is essential, a nonnegotiable in today's world. So many men
disqualify themselves because of poor choices. It is always the right time to
do the right thing, but if you do not know what to do, then you get in trouble.
James explains there is a difference between wisdom from God and wisdom
from the world. We show our wisdom through our daily walk, but we must do
it with humility.

When we get rid of the junk in our hearts like envy and selfishness, we
create space for wisdom to fill it. If we pursue wisdom, God will produce a
great harvest in and through us.

*Father, help me pursue wisdom at all costs. You say if anyone lacks wisdom,
they should ask for it. I'm asking for wisdom today. Amen.*

FRIENDS AND FUTURE

The righteous choose their friends carefully,
but the way of the wicked leads them astray.

PROVERBS 12:26

In almost every major professional and collegiate sport, athletes get in trouble during the offseason when they leave the team environment of high expectations, focus, and accountability to reconnect with their "old friends." Headlines are full of athletes who engage in foolish behavior when the spotlight is off them.

Proverbs teaches over and over about the importance of choosing the right friends. Whom we spend our time with will either make us better or lead us into trouble. Two great principles in Proverbs deal with friendships: be a good friend and find wise friends.

To attract faithful friends, you must become the type of friend you want to be around. If you want trustworthy friends, be trustworthy and honest. If you want friends who are growing in their relationships with Christ, focus on growing spiritually as well. If you don't want friends who gossip, don't gossip.

Here are three simple questions to ask to figure out if your friends are wise:

1. Do they follow Jesus?
2. Do they do the right thing?
3. Do they make others better?

These are litmus-test questions for assembling your inner circle.

I've heard it said, "Show me your friends, and I'll show you your future." So examine your five closest friends. Are they making wise decisions? Do they make you better? Are you doing the same for them? Remember that friends will shape your future.

Father, help me be a trustworthy, faithful friend. Lead me to an inner circle of friends who love You and make wise decisions. Amen.

HIT THE STAY BUTTON

I sent messengers to them with this reply:
"I am carrying on a great project and cannot go down.
Why should the work stop while I leave it and go down to you?"
NEHEMIAH 6:3

Staples, the office supply store, had a funny ad about hitting the "easy button," and suddenly, ordering office products became easy. I actually have an easy button on my desk that doesn't work anymore because I used it so much. I think the batteries died.

I love the easy button, but I think a better button would be a "stay button." So many of us want the next big thing and aren't willing to hunker in for the long haul. The heroes of the faith understood the power of staying. Joseph, Daniel, David, Paul, and Stephen were just a few. God honored and blessed them for their unwavering resolve and commitment not to start over.

When you hit the stay button, you choose to stay put when it seems like a smarter idea to pack up. You choose to trust God although it seems far easier to do something else—something that promises bigger, greater, and better opportunities. Little do we know that God has already begun a great work in us, right where we are; we often just don't recognize it.

Nehemiah was an incredible leader who rebuilt the Jerusalem wall in fifty-two days. He hit the stay button over and over. Men approached him and told him to stop five times. They tried to discourage him. But each time, he simply replied, "I am carrying on a great project and cannot go down."

Let's hit the stay button because God is doing a great work.

Father, help me fully understand I am doing a great work and cannot come down. Amen.

CHALLENGE FLAG

Brothers and sisters, if someone is caught in a sin,
you who live by the Spirit should restore that person gently.
But watch yourselves, or you also may be tempted.

GALATIANS 6:1

In the NFL, a coach can throw a challenge flag, and the referees must stop and review the film to make sure they got the call right. It gives the referees a chance to get it right if they were wrong. Making the right call "after further review" often affects the outcome of a game and, potentially, the success of a season.

In 2 Samuel 12, the Lord sent Nathan to David, and Nathan threw the challenge flag. He told David a hypothetical story that was very similar to what David had sinfully done with Bathsheba that resulted in the death of her husband Uriah. After David heard the story, "[he] burned with anger against the man and said to Nathan, 'As surely as the LORD lives, the man who did this must die! He must pay for that lamb four times over, because he did such a thing and had no pity.' Then Nathan said to David, 'You are the man!'" (2 Samuel 12:5–7).

The challenge flag was thrown, and David was confronted with his own sin. It broke him, and he returned to God in confession and repentance. It restored his soul.

Challenge flags aren't for us to throw at others—unless they give us permission. But we are to give them to an inner circle of friends, trusting they will throw the flag to challenge our attitude and actions when necessary.

Father, help me find men I can trust with a challenge flag so they can help me get it right in life and expose my sin. I want to reflect Christ. Amen.

LINGER LONGER

You will show me the way of life, granting me the joy of your presence and the pleasures of living with you forever.

PSALM 16:11 NLT

For a long time, I approached my devotions as something to get done. I had a conquer-it attitude. It went something like this: *I rise. I read. I am done! Now I can get on with the day.* I was simply checking the box. My mindset toward devotion time was that it was like taking medicine or eating spinach, something I must do instead of something I longed to do.

My mindset has changed over the years. I used to think my devotions were all about me—what I got out of them and how much I needed them. Yes, I do desperately need them, but now I realize God longs for me to be with Him. The Lord delights when I sit at His feet each day and linger in His presence. Stepping away from all the stuff that clutters my life so I can be consumed by His love is now nonnegotiable.

Lingering longer allows us to hear God's voice. He will always use our time with Him for His work. But we need to stop the rushing, drop to our knees or fall on our face, and soak in His glorious presence. Sit at the feet of God and wait for Him to speak. We need to shut it down and listen to the Holy Spirit instead of filling our time with words. Linger in His presence and find out what is on God's heart. This is hard to do, but it's essential. Extend your time with the Savior and enjoy His presence!

Father, help me soak in Your presence. I worship You with all my heart, mind, soul, and strength. Amen.

THE WATERBOY

"Whoever wants to become great among you must be your servant, and whoever wants to be first must be slave of all. For even the Son of Man did not come to be served, but to serve, and to give his life as a ransom for many."

MARK 10:43–45

Waterboys often run onto the field to squirt water into the mouths of thirsty competitors. Competitors perform better if they are well hydrated. Even though it's a small job, it's important. Waterboys never take a shot, run a race, or score a goal, but they serve.

Jesus never views those who play a seemingly small role as unimportant. He never looked down on those who served behind the scenes or did the jobs nobody else wanted. In fact, He said the least among us will be the greatest. Those we consider great will only be great in God's eyes if they serve like a waterboy.

In Mark 9, the disciples were arguing with each other about who was the greatest. So Jesus called them over and confronted them, saying, "Anyone who wants to be first must be the very last, and the servant of all" (v. 35). Jesus is the ultimate waterboy. He washed His disciples' feet. It was an example of genuine love. Jesus came to serve out of the position of humility, not to sit in the place of honor. He didn't seek status; He served. Those we think are least important God considers most important.

We say all the time that we want to be more like Jesus. Serving out of humility produces greatness. There is no other road. If you want to be great, you must serve.

Father, help me find specific ways to serve and draw others to You. Amen.

OLD SCHOOL LOYALTY

I desire loyalty and not sacrifice,
the knowledge of God rather than burnt offerings.
HOSEA 6:6 HCSB

Loyalty is essential. When you get down to it, loyalty is priceless. It is unswerving, unshakable faithfulness at all times. However, it seems that loyalty has become a thing of the past. Very old school. It may be something our parents value, but it is not a part of our vocabulary. Loyalty is imperative in all areas of our lives. Author Napoleon Hill wrote, "Lack of loyalty is one of the major causes of failure in every walk of life."[51]

Loyalty might be old school, but it needs to become new school. Men need to rediscover this lost characteristic. To make loyalty a part of your life, you need to remember three things:

1. Give loyalty to get loyalty. In 1 Chronicles 12:33, David's soldiers fought with undivided loyalty. David was totally loyal to his soldiers, so in battle, they gave it back. It starts with you. God desires for you to give your loyalty to others first. Remember that loyalty is all or none.
2. Don't be disloyal to others. In Mark 14:18, Jesus told His twelve disciples that one would betray Him. Ask God to help you never be disloyal, no matter what.
3. Place your loyalty in Jesus Christ. If you love God, it will be hard to be disloyal to others. Try it. Love God with all your heart, then go out and be disloyal. It isn't possible. If there is a conflict of loyalty, obey Jesus first—at all costs, even if it hurts.

Father, teach me how to have unswerving, unshakable loyalty. And most importantly, I want to be loyal to You alone. Amen.

---

51   Napoleon Hill, *Think and Grow Rich* (New York: Ballantine Books, 1983), 88.

TOXIC WORDS

The soothing tongue is a tree of life,
but a perverse tongue crushes the spirit.

PROVERBS 15:4

I took my son to a lacrosse game at a local college, and we sat on the turf just off the playing field. There were families with little kids and college students all around us. As we were enjoying the game, three college-age guys started having a conversation loud enough for everyone within twenty yards to hear. Every other word seemed to be a swear word. We were all getting more and more uncomfortable. After a few minutes, I finally said, "Hey guys, do you mind cutting the profanity? There are lots of kids around, and we're all trying to enjoy the game." They semi-apologized and stopped the nonsense.

Profanity is the new norm. It has spread like a wildfire and become acceptable in every corner of the culture. But toxic words can be both what we say and what we think.

Words have the power of life and death. Reckless words pierce like a sword. Harsh words stir up conflict. Criticism can crush our spirits. But sometimes the harshest words are the words we think in our heads and say to ourselves—words like *I can't*, *I'm not good enough*, and *It'll never work*. We call that stinkin' thinkin'. Over time, negative and defeated thinking spreads and takes over. Toxic words say a lot about who you are, and they also determine the direction of your life. So be careful what you say and think because it will affect who you are and what you do.

Father, I want to be clean and refreshed by You. Please forgive me for the toxic words I have said and thought. Amen.

MEN SACRIFICE

"Whoever wants to save their life will lose it,
but whoever loses their life for me will find it."
MATTHEW 16:25

A lot of men are still acting like boys, failing to launch. They stay in the adolescence phase until they are almost thirty, stuck playing video games, living at home with their parents, and delaying their God-ordained roles and responsibilities. The world is suffering because of it.

There is a big difference between men and boys, and one way we can measure it is in the gap between sacrifice and selfishness. God needs men to step up and take up the mantle of living a sacrificial life. There is no greater love than to lay down your life for another. In fact, many men are willing to die for those they love. That is the protector inside us. But we can demonstrate an even greater love when we live a life of sacrifice for others.

Laying aside your own selfish desires for the blessing and benefit of someone else is a high calling. And it is evidence that a boy has become a man. When we are selfish, we choose our feelings over responsibilities. We do what we want instead of what we should or must do. Sacrificing means we put aside our own desires for others. We become a living sacrifice. And while leisure and adventure are great parts of life, men know that making a real contribution is part of our purpose. It feels good to sacrifice for others.

Father, help me step up to my responsibilities as a man and sacrifice for others. Amen.

OCTOBER

THE NEW FOUR-LETTER WORD

Anyone who meets a testing challenge head-on and manages to stick it out is mighty fortunate. For such persons loyally in love with God, the reward is life and more life.

JAMES 1:12 MSG

Several years ago, the football team at the Oscoda Area High School in Michigan canceled the last five games of the season as a result of going 0–4 and not having scored a single point. I know going winless and scoreless has a sting to it, but my heart hurts thinking that someone gave up on a group of athletes. I guess they had never heard the famous Winston Churchill quote that says, "Never give in, never, never, never, never—in nothing, great or small, large or petty—never give in."[52] As a great leader, Churchill advised people not to quit.

The new four-letter word is *quit*.

Quitting is something that has permeated our society and regretfully become a core value for many. People quit without giving the repercussions another thought. However, I believe we need to remove the word from our vocabulary. Not only do I see it as a curse word, but it's also a curse to all who live by it.

Christ did not quit on the cross. Paul did not give up preaching the gospel when he was thrown into jail. Daniel did not stop praying when he was trapped in the lions' den. It is easy to give up when it gets tough. However, when it gets tough and we press on, God is glorified. Our goal is to keep our eyes fixed on Jesus so we finish strong.

Father, help me when things get tough. Fill me with Your Holy Spirit so others see You in times of trouble. Amen.

52   Winston Churchill, "Never Give In, Never, Never, Never, 1941," America's National Churchill Museum (website), accessed November 18, 2023, https://www.nationalchurchillmuseum.org.

IS IT IN YOU?

You are not controlled by your sinful nature.
You are controlled by the Spirit if you have the Spirit of God living in you.
ROMANS 8:9 NLT

I love watching the Gatorade commercials that show athletes giving their all to either train or compete, and the neon green or orange sports drink is pouring out of them as they sweat. The commercials always end with the tagline, "Is it in you?" The implication is that, somehow, this drink will make you perform better on the field. Do you have what it takes to be a champion? Is it in you?

Scripture tells us the Spirit of God, the very essence of Christ, is in you and me. The same Spirit that raised Jesus from the dead comes to dwell in us when we believe. And this isn't some kind of temporary thing. When you give your heart to Jesus, the Holy Spirit breathes life into your spirit. He literally brings you back from the dead—spiritually that is. Sin brings death, but the Spirit brings life. And the really cool thing is that the Spirit gives you power. Power to choose God's road over the road of sin. Power to perform better in life. He makes you a champion over sin.

Every day you're given a choice: Will you be led by the sinful nature, or will you be led by the Spirit of the living God? When you choose God's way, it will be obvious to everyone that there is something different about you. But it won't be Gatorade—it will be Christ.

Father, help me surrender to the instruction and direction of the Holy Spirit in me. Amen.

ENGAGE GOD

"Seek first the kingdom of God and His righteousness,
and all these things will be provided for you."
MATTHEW 6:33 HCSB

Coach Buckley's football practices were brutal. I was only eleven, but I still remember them to be grueling, agonizing, and dreadful. The trademark practices had tons of running and repetitive drills, all without scrimmaging. Many players wouldn't make it through the practices without losing their lunch, and many of them quit. Even my best friend left the team; his parents pulled him. Although the sacrifice was great, the return was sweet. We earned a perfect season; no team even scored on us. The Braddock Road Sharks brought fear to all eleven-year-olds who dared to play football.

Our practices were not marked by complexity but by simplicity. Drills, drills, and more drills. We went over the basics in every practice. Coach Buckley stressed the fundamentals of the game and of each position. Those were the keys to our success.

If fundamentals are the key to success on sports teams, then what are the fundamentals of being on God's team? What are the basics our head coach, Jesus Christ, wants us to focus on?

Engage God, no matter what.

In Matthew 6:33, Jesus shared the key to success. Basically, He said the first thing—the most important thing, the only thing—is to seek the Father. Jesus modeled this as He engaged His Father every day. It was not optional. It was a must. If you want clarity and spiritual success in your life, start with the Word of God. Focus on the spiritual fundamentals.

Father, I ask You to make my relationship with You plain and simple. Teach me the simplicity of picking up Your Word and engaging You daily. Amen.

MIND GAMES

You were taught, with regard to your former way of life, to put off your old
self, which is being corrupted by its deceitful desires; to be made new in
the attitude of your minds.

EPHESIANS 4:22–23

Yogi Berra once said, "Baseball is 90 percent mental. The other half is
physical."[53] While Yogi's math might be a little off, he is right on target with the
importance of training the mind.

After completing the Civil War Century ride, a grueling 105-mile bicycle
ride through the mountains of Maryland and Pennsylvania, I was reminded of
the importance of both physical and mental preparation. It was a perfect day
for riding, and I felt great physically, but I had never ridden beyond 50 miles.
Although I regularly ride the hills, I was not prepared for the long, steep,
8-mile climbs throughout the day.

At the 70-mile mark, I started to cramp up—first in my calves. I began
to "superhydrate" to attempt to prevent the inevitable. At 85 miles, I saw
other riders on the side of the road, suffering from cramps and rubbing their
legs so they could finish the ride. My cramping started to get far worse with
every climb. I had been praying silently for miles, but now my prayers were
audible. I am certain that my mental dependence on God throughout the race
overcame my physical difficulties as I finished.

Our Creator knows the power of the mind more than anyone. He even goes
so far as to say that if we want to be different, if we want to be exceptional, if
we want to follow Him even when life gets tough, it all begins in our mind.

*Father, renew my mind so I can live a life pleasing to You and overcome
hardships. Amen.*

---

53   Victor Mather and Katie Rogers, "Behind the Yogi-isms: Those Said and Unsaid," *New York Times*,
September 23, 2015, https://www.nytimes.com.

TWO OUNCES OF POWER

In the same way, the tongue is a small thing that makes grand speeches.
But a tiny spark can set a great forest on fire.

JAMES 3:5 NLT

When I was sixteen years old, I felt confident and acted cocky. I had a full-blown ego that caused me to think I could do or say anything I wanted, but that all came crashing down one afternoon during a disagreement with my mother. I can't even remember what the argument was about, but I do remember what I said that ended the discussion. I am thankful for a godly mom who forgave me, and we now look back at that encounter as a defining moment in our relationship.

It has been said that the tongue weighs practically nothing, yet very few people can contain its power. The average human tongue weighs only two ounces, but it is considered one of the strongest muscles in the body. The tongue is a tough worker—helping mix food, form letters and sounds, and filter out germs.

Most men struggle with their mouths. The book of James compares the tongue to fire because of the potential damage it can inflict. It's interesting how James associates the tongue to fire and not to water. A small glass of water wouldn't likely start a flood, but one small careless spark can destroy thousands of acres. James warns us that the tongue can pollute our whole body. Ask God to control your tongue by purifying your heart. Understand that your words will either bring healing or hurt, blessings or burdens, truth or torture.

Father, I want my words to bring life and deliver Your truth. May I use these two ounces of power for Your glory. Amen.

FOLLOW THE LEADER

Be imitators of God,
as dearly loved children.

EPHESIANS 5:1 CSB

Follow the leader is a copycat game in which people in a group try to imitate the actions of the leader and the person in the middle tries to figure out who the leader is. The person who is "it" must identify the leader—the one person whom everyone else is copying.

On fields, in boardrooms, and in homes all over the world, people are following leaders. They are watching what they do, hearing what they say, and watching how they react under stress. They are learning habits and beliefs. And like it or not, they are not only taking notes but also following.

Every one of us has influence. How we live is likely to have a big impact on those who are watching, for better or worse. Paul told us in Ephesians 4 and 5 to be imitators of God. We're to follow our leader and do what He did. Jesus told us in Luke 9:23, "If anyone wants to come with Me, he must deny himself, take up his cross daily, and follow Me" (HCSB). As we follow Christ, others follow our example. Following God changes the way we think. He replaces our negativity and pessimism with possibility and belief. Making excuses and blaming others becomes a thing of the past. He changes the words we speak. He replaces words that tear down with words that build up. He changes the things we do.

Ultimately, Jesus completes His transformation process as we follow Him. And those who follow us will never be the same.

Father, help me live in such a way that I'm worth imitating because I'm imitating You. Amen.

IT'S NOT ABOUT YOU

*Everything they do is done for people to see…The greatest among you will
be your servant. For those who exalt themselves will be humbled,
and those who humble themselves will be exalted.*

MATTHEW 23:5, 11–12

Every man I know wants to be the best. Being good is good, but being best is
better. We want to go from good to great in every aspect of life. We must be
number one no matter what we are doing. Nobody remembers the loser. We
engage in the relentless pursuit of excellence.

"I must be the best me" is a principle I believe and live daily. In Luke 12:48,
Jesus told us, "Even more will be expected of the one who has been entrusted
with more" (HCSB). No matter what gifts you've received, you must desire to
be faithful and maximize them. It is essential that we are lifelong learners who
desire to grow and develop.

We are made for others. We receive so we can give to others. We are loved
so we can love others. We are blessed so we can bless others. Our purpose is to
serve and bless. When we pass on what God has given to us, the blessing flows
through us. We are meant to be a river, not a pond.

When Jesus is our center, we take our eyes off ourselves, and we become
willing to invest in others. Serve. Sacrifice. Give. Love. If we pursue Christ
in an effort to become more like Him, we make others better. And this only
happens because of Jesus in us.

Are you intentionally taking others under your wing to pour out what God
has poured in? This is what God has called us to do. Men of impact have a
three-word job description: make others better!

*Father, I desire to make others better. Teach me Your ways so I can help, bless,
and encourage. Amen.*

LIFE CHANGERS

I am convinced that neither death nor life, neither angels nor demons, neither the present nor the future, nor any powers, neither height nor depth, nor anything else in all creation, will be able to separate us from the love of God.

ROMANS 8:38–39

My two oldest boys were eagerly awaiting the start of the lacrosse season. They had both been starters on their championship team the previous year, and they couldn't wait to defend the title. They had spent hours in the gym preparing, getting stronger, and improving speed and quickness. They were familiar with pain and sacrifice.

During the first game, my sophomore son won the face-off, and his team scored first. After the second face-off, he got a return pass near the crease and scored, but he was hit after the shot and braced his fall with his right hand, breaking his wrist. As his mom took him to the hospital for X-rays, my senior broke his wrist diving to keep a ball in play near the sideline. Within ten minutes, both boys had broken their wrists and were out.

Life-changing moments happen all the time—for better or worse. Sometimes life changes are unexpected and out of our control; sometimes they are a result of small decisions we've made. In all these things, we are more than conquerors through Him who loved us. No life-changing adversity or blessing can separate us from the love of Christ. Neither our present circumstances nor things that are on the way can change God's love for us. Not the mountaintop of success and favor or the valley of adversity and disappointment. God is there for it all.

Father, help me see every life-changing moment as an opportunity to grow. Amen.

POWER UP

God has not given us a spirit of fear and timidity,
but of power, love, and self-discipline.

2 TIMOTHY 1:7 NLT

It's all about power these days. We have PowerBars, Powerade, power play, power training, and power ratings. Bigger, faster, and stronger is the battle cry. But God's game plan is different—He wants us to have spiritual power. This is not what the world offers, but it's the kind of power that comes only from God. We can tap into this power by remembering what POWER stands for:

- P—Pursue Purity: Men must pursue purity in all things. Sexual purity is essential because purity paves the way to intimacy in all relationships. In 1 Corinthians 6:18, Paul warned us to "flee from sexual immorality" (ESV). Run, sprint, flee!
- O—Obey the Call: God places a call or a mission in each of us. The question is not whether you are called to do God's work but whether you will respond to the call God has on your life.
- W—Worship Daily: Worshiping God is like breathing. It's mandatory. Seek God constantly. Pursue Him with everything you have. He will never disappoint you.
- E—Engage Others: Great friends are like rare, expensive diamonds— hard to find but once you do find them, they have great value. Surround yourself with people who want the best for you.
- R—Reject Apathy: An apathetic spirit is the I-don't-care attitude. Don't take the easy way out. Every moment counts. So ask the Lord for the courage to be bold and maximize every moment.

What kind of man do you want to be? Choose to be a man of power!

Father, I want to be a man of power. Mark my life with purity, a calling, worship, great friends, and a spirit of courage. Amen.

GRIP IT AND RIP IT

What, then, shall we say in response to these things?
If God is for us, who can be against us?

ROMANS 8:31

A good friend of mine helped me play my best round of golf with two pieces of advice: play to my strengths and play with absolute freedom and confidence. He said if I were tentative, I would never enjoy the game. That day I approached the ball and said to myself, *Grip it and rip it!* When an athlete lacks confidence, plays timidly, or is not willing to take risks, he doesn't perform at his best. When you play not to lose, you lose.

Peter was the original "grip it and rip it" disciple; he was a spiritual risk-taker. He had a heart and passion for Jesus even before he understood who Jesus was. He wanted to do great things and was willing to make mistakes. Peter was the only one who took the risk to join Jesus on the water. He would never forget what he was capable of when he obeyed the voice of God. When we boldly take risks as God fills us and leads us, God does the miraculous in and through us.

But Peter wasn't a moral risk-taker—living close to sin or taking immoral or unethical chances; that would never be acceptable. Instead, he took risks that stretched his own faith, put what he believed to the test, and required God to show up in miraculous ways. What about you? Are you ready to grip it and rip it today—living all out for Jesus?

Father, take away my fear of failure and empower me to grip it and rip it as I take risks for You. Amen.

NEVER TOO LATE

He called out to the LORD: "Lord GOD, please remember me.
Strengthen me, God, just once more."

JUDGES 16:28 HCSB

Professional golfer Blayne Barber had finally qualified for the PGA Tour. It was a dream come true. However, a week after playing in the tournament that qualified him, he couldn't get a leaf out of his mind. In the second round of the tournament, he had accidentally brushed a leaf in the bunker on the thirteenth hole. This is an infraction because it could potentially make your shot easier, so Barber marked his scorecard with a one-shot penalty for the infraction. Later that night, he learned it was a two-shot penalty. He played the final two rounds, but a week later, he didn't have peace because he believed he had signed an incorrect scorecard that noted only a one-shot penalty, so he did the right thing. He disqualified himself, which cost him a spot on the PGA Tour.

It's never too late to do the right thing. When we have to go back and correct something, it's usually hard and involves sacrifice. Messing with the past is difficult and complicated. God loves it when we go back, correct our mistake, and make it right. There is no time limit on doing the right thing. It's hard but right, painful but powerful.

In the Bible, we read about Samson starting out well in life, but he got into a heap of trouble by making some bad decisions. However, even Samson realized it wasn't too late to make things right. At the end of his life, he called upon the Lord and did the right thing.

Whether it is days, weeks, months, or years, we need to do the right thing no matter the cost.

Father, I know it is never too late to do the right thing. Give me the courage to do it. Amen.

BECOMING PROTECTORS

"Greater love has no one than this:
to lay down one's life for one's friends."

JOHN 15:13

There is no better feeling for a young boy than for him to know his dad is there to protect him. It's not uncommon to hear boys telling one another, "Oh yeah? Well, my dad is stronger than your dad." Just thinking about that makes me smile. It gives boys confidence and assurance to know that their dad won't let anything bad happen to them.

Many times when my kids were young and I was away traveling, they all ended up in one big bed with their mom so they'd feel safer. But as they got older, I entrusted the oldest boys to take care of their mom and ensure the house was locked up and secure. I was giving them a taste of additional responsibility and setting the expectation that they would act as protectors in my absence.

Boys need protection, whereas when they grow up into men, they become the protectors. Men are designed to be protectors, whether in families, friendships, or communities. This responsibility mirrors the sacrificial love Christ displayed by giving His life for us. Jesus said in John 15:13, "Greater love has no one than this: to lay down one's life for one's friends." True men courageously stand in the gap, defending those in need and fostering an environment of safety and security. Men need to be aware that evil exists and be ready to handle the threats. Ultimately, a protector is willing to lay down his life to protect others.

Father, help me step up and protect my family and loved ones. Amen.

SAME OLD, SAME OLD

"You have heard it. Observe it all. Will you not acknowledge it?
From now on I will announce new things to you,
hidden things that you have not known."

ISAIAH 48:6 HCSB

As a frequent traveler, I am in and out of airports and hotels all the time, which means I also use many different restrooms. On one trip, I began to run out of patience as I kept waving my hands to turn on the water, but no water came out. After about thirty seconds, I thought the sink was broken. When I started to move to the next sink, I noticed a handle on top of the faucet. Busted.

I laughed all the way to my plane until God reminded me, *You do the same thing with Me.* Busted again. Most often, I expect God to show up exactly like He did in previous occasions. Not only do I expect it, but I often want it the same way too. Approaching God with an attitude of familiarity never works.

Jesus did not act in the same way twice, from sharing the gift of salvation to working miracles. Author and pastor E. M. Bounds insightfully wrote, "God does not repeat Himself…He has not one pattern for every child."[54] His healings ranged from "Get up, take your mat, and go home" to "Go wash in the pool." Maybe it was His way of ensuring people didn't put Him in a box. No formulas allowed. Don't we love to package our "God encounters" and export them to whoever will listen? Even worse—we personally approach Jesus with familiarity and commonplace attitudes. Approach the God of the universe with a freshness today. No more same old, same old. Today is a new day.

Father, help me not to expect You to show up the same way twice. Amen.

---

54   E. M. Bounds, *The Essentials of Prayer* (Grand Rapids, MI: Baker, 1979), 48.

GIVERS

Each of you should give what you have decided in your heart to give,
not reluctantly or under compulsion, for God loves a cheerful giver.

2 CORINTHIANS 9:7

The world encourages self-preservation and accumulation, but God calls us to embody a different spirit—a spirit of generosity. Men are givers, not takers. Our purpose extends beyond personal gain. We need to demonstrate a heart of generosity, seeking to bless others through our actions, resources, and time. The example of Jesus, who gave His life as a sacrificial offering, reminds us of the call to selflessness and serving others. As men, we are called to lead with a spirit of giving, imitating Christ's sacrificial love.

Sowing and reaping are related. If you sow sparingly, you reap sparingly. Just as a farmer who sows few seeds will yield a small harvest, those who give little will receive little. On the other hand, those who sow generously will reap a bountiful harvest. Our generosity must come from the heart, not out of compulsion. God delights in a cheerful giver—someone who gives willingly and joyfully. This speaks to the importance of aligning our motivations with God's heart of generosity. When we give with joy, we reflect the nature of our heavenly Father.

God's promises are unwavering and unchanging. Not only is He capable of blessing us, but He is also eager to do so. God's blessings aren't just limited to material provision. They extend to every aspect of our lives. When we align our hearts with His, our capacity to do good works, to bless others, and to impact the world multiplies. Generosity reflects our character and dependence on God's provision.

Father, give me a heart of generosity to bless others as You have blessed me.
Amen.

STARVING THE SPIRIT

Everything that goes into a life of pleasing God has been miraculously
given to us by getting to know, personally and intimately,
the One who invited us to God.

2 PETER 1:3–4 MSG

It was just a matter of time. My kids had a pet rabbit for many years with one
responsibility: feed the rabbit. At first, they took great care of it; however, over
the years, as their commitment to activities increased and life got busier, it
became difficult for them to find time to feed the rabbit. I covered for them
occasionally but reminded them it was their job. The rabbit became sick. The
kids didn't mean to neglect it, but when you don't feed a rabbit, it suffers harm.

Life lessons hurt. I was mad, and the kids were crushed. The lesson of this
story is that when you stop doing the things you need to do, destructive results
are inevitable. As I thought about my kids' mistake, the Lord said, *Dan, you
do the same thing. You know you should feed your soul with the Word of God.
When you don't, you starve Me because my Spirit lives inside you.*

I don't want to starve the living God who dwells in me, but when I don't
carve out daily time for Him, I starve Him. We need to make sure we don't
crowd out, squeeze out, or starve out Jesus. Today, do something that only
you can do. Do whatever it takes to get spiritually healthy. Pray, read, study,
meditate, share, fellowship, memorize. Men, your future depends on it.

*Father, I want to get serious about my spiritual health. I don't want to be a
weak, starving, malnourished son of God. Amen.*

ETERNAL PERSPECTIVE

We fix our eyes not on what is seen, but on what is unseen,
since what is seen is temporary, but what is unseen is eternal.

2 CORINTHIANS 4:18

When we are young, it can seem like time is standing still. But as we get older, time seems to fly by. We often wonder where all the years have gone. I've heard it said that "the days can be long, but the years are short." I've found this to be true. Sometimes our current successes or challenges can consume our attention as we keep our noses to the grindstone. Sometimes the here and now takes on an importance it was never intended to have. But it's easy to get consumed by the urgent stuff we must do right now. And that's not all bad. Addressing circumstances of life is necessary, and investing our time and attention into things that matter most—like relationships, serving, and blessing others—is also part of our purpose.

As we mature, our perspective changes. We become eternally focused, much less worried about the temporal. While boys may chase after fleeting pleasures and momentary achievements, men recognize the impermanence of worldly pursuits. True men fix their eyes on eternal values by investing in relationships, character, and spiritual growth. Their decisions are guided by a desire to build God's kingdom here and now. They plan to leave a legacy that will last beyond their earthly years. This eternal perspective helps us care about what God cares about. It also allows us to put challenges, suffering, and setbacks into proper context, understanding that our difficulties are fleeting compared to the eternal joy and reward awaiting us.

Father, give me an eternal perspective and help me invest my time in what truly matters. Amen.

CUT OFF THE SOURCE

Submit yourselves, then, to God.
Resist the devil, and he will flee from you.

JAMES 4:7

During the American Revolutionary War, on October 6, 1781, forces under George Washington cut off the British soldiers from their supply lines. Running out of ammunition and suffering high casualties, the British army, under General Cornwallis, was forced to seek a truce and cease-fire to negotiate his army's surrender on October 19. They simply no longer had the food, fuel, or firepower necessary to attack. This victory led directly to America's independence.

In the midst of life's battles, we, too, must act to resist the Enemy and sever the source of negativity and doubts that hinder our progress. The devil is a liar and an accuser; he is the source of all negativity. He relentlessly attacks us with fiery darts to create doubt and discouragement. By resisting the devil, you actively cut off the supply lines of negativity and doubts, and he will flee from you. Ultimately, this will result in victory.

Just as Washington's army cut off the supply lines to the British troops, deliberately cutting off the Enemy's attempts to create fear weakens his grip of doubt in your life. If you cut off the Enemy's ability to bother you by taking those thoughts captive and choosing to dwell on positive and edifying thoughts, you create a mental environment that fosters faith, hope, and resilience.

Negativity and doubts often arise from external influences such as negative news, toxic relationships, or self-limiting beliefs. We must cut off these sources that drain our energy and hinder our progress and walk in the power of the Holy Spirit.

Father, grant me the discernment to identify and cut off the sources of negativity and doubts in my life. Amen.

THE BLESSING OF PAIN

All this is for your benefit, so that the grace that is reaching more and more people may cause thanksgiving to overflow to the glory of God.

2 CORINTHIANS 4:15

Have you ever wondered why God allows pain and suffering? Life sure would be easier without those two pieces. But I'm not sure it would always be better. When my wife was diagnosed with cancer, that ushered in pain and suffering. But it also brought the healing of wounds she didn't know she had and burdens she didn't know she was carrying and the ability to bless thousands more who were on the same journey.

The apostle Paul knew that in the end, no matter what he experienced, it would be worth it. Pain can be a blessing with the right perspective. We want the blessing but not the pain. We enjoy God's promises, but if we're looking for a pain-free, problem-free life, we've chosen the wrong path.

While it's true we're His children and heirs to the kingdom, we're also called to share in Christ's sufferings (Philippians 3:9–11). God never wastes our pain; it is never without a purpose. And God always works all things together for the good of those who love Him. This promise helps us endure the longest days, the toughest challenges, and the hardest disappointments. God needs to do more in us so He can move through us. God walks with us in our pain to make us mature and complete, lacking in nothing. Pain, while uncomfortable at the time, may be exactly what we need to be transformed into the likeness of Christ.

Father, let me see pain as a blessing with purpose so I become more like Jesus and make a bigger difference. Amen.

PHYSICAL ANCHORS

Buy truth, and do not sell it.
Get wisdom, instruction, and understanding.
PROVERBS 23:23 NASB

When I played sports as a kid, the parents would pull up their cars and shine their headlights on their field when practice ran late. We loved seeing the car lights light up the field.

As men, we need to *see* the light—not the car lights but the light that deals with our physical bodies. If we don't, we'll be in the dark. The acronym SEE stands for "sleep, eat, and exercise." These three daily physical anchors are essential for every man:

1. How much sleep do I need? Since the physical affects the spiritual and emotional, if you do not get enough sleep, you'll be hurting other areas of your life. Psalm 127:1–2 states, "It's useless to rise early and go to bed late, and work your worried fingers to the bone. Don't you know he enjoys giving rest to those he loves?" (MSG).
2. How do I view food? I love food, but I must remember God created food not only to enjoy but also to fuel the body. I won't put bad fuel in my car, so why would I put bad fuel in my body? Before we put something into our mouths, we need to ask if it will honor Him.
3. How am I training? Exercise is tough. Staying physically fit is hard, and it never becomes natural. God wants us to keep our "engines" tuned up at all times.

God cares about your sleep, eating, and exercise. Let's get wisdom, discipline, and understanding and put these three physical anchors into place.

Father, I realize You created me in Your image. Help me sleep, eat, and exercise so I can glorify You with my body. Amen.

CONTRIBUTE

If anyone does not provide for his relatives, and especially for members of his household, he has denied the faith and is worse than an unbeliever.

1 TIMOTHY 5:8 ESV

Manual labor can be very satisfying. There's just something about working with your hands and producing something of value. It's also great when you can see the results of your labor. When I was a boy, my brother and I started a paper route and rode our bikes around the neighborhood delivering papers. On the weekends, we stuffed all the ad inserts in the weekend edition and lugged those around door to door.

As we got older, we spent our summers working construction as "grunts." That meant we did all the work the more skilled builders didn't want to do. Who could blame them? But there was a special satisfaction in driving dump trucks, delivering materials, keeping construction sites clean, and bracing basements. We would get home exhausted, but we were satisfied.

Men are contributors, not consumers. Boys are often consumed by their desires and instant gratification, while men are driven by a higher purpose. Men are diligent and hardworking, recognizing their responsibility to contribute positively to their families, communities, and the world around them. This echoes the biblical principle of stewardship, in which God entrusts his servants with talents to multiply and manage for His glory.

Working hard and making a positive contribution no matter the job is a mark of a man, but it starts when men are boys. Learning to contribute instead of letting others do the work is part of the job. It's a surefire way to provide for your family and develop strength of character along the way.

Father, I commit my efforts to making a contribution. Amen.

THE RIGHT RACE

"I count my life of no value to myself, so that I may finish my course and the ministry I received from the Lord Jesus, to testify to the gospel of God's grace."

ACTS 20:24 HCSB

The first race I ever ran was a marathon. I quickly learned there are four key aspects to every race, and they all relate to the spiritual life:

1. The race is against the competition. There were thousands of competitors I wanted to beat who also wanted to beat me. In the same way, when we run the race for Christ, we have three main competitors: the world, the flesh, and the devil. Each one wants to prevent us from crossing the finish line.

2. The race is against the clock. The clock at every mile marker was a constant reminder that the race was coming to an end. Christ says since you have one life, you should make it count.

3. The race is for the prize. I received a medallion suspended by a ribbon for completing the marathon. Not much of a prize. But as Christians, our prize is heaven and a life with God suspended from eternity.

4. The race is for the praise. It was awesome as hundreds of people cheered for me as I finally crossed the finish line, but it won't compare to one day hearing these words from Jesus: "Well done, good and faithful servant."

When I was growing up, my pastor would always ask the question, "Are you running the right race or the rat race?" Then he reminded us that even if you win the rat race, you are still a rat. Let's run the right race by fixing our eyes on Jesus.

Father, I want to run the right race and finish the course. Amen.

STAY PURE

How can a young person stay on the path of purity?
By living according to your word.

Psalm 119:9

Purity has been under direct assault more than almost anything else in our culture. Access to moral filth has reached an epidemic of availability. If you read the stats of how many men, including Christian leaders and people of faith, are trapped by pornography and other elicit material, it can be demoralizing.

But this behavior is not acceptable for men of God. The Enemy is working overtime to destroy the minds and hearts of men and get us to compromise our moral standards. He baits us on social media and every form of entertainment, and he tempts us with immoral images. Today, even some elementary schools are exposing children to immorality. This is unacceptable.

I believe there is a resurgence of men who want to live pure lives. We know the devil lies as he attempts to destroy us from the inside out. It's time for a new type of man to arise, a man of honor who refuses to compromise and instead keeps his eyes and heart pure. The only way to do this is by guarding your heart according to God's Word. Seek God with your whole heart and do not deviate from His instruction because it always leads to life. Get into the Word today. Refuse to let moral filth compromise you. Stay pure.

Father, guard my mind and heart. Guide me into a pure way of life according to Your Word. Amen.

YOU OWE ME

Before his downfall a person's heart is proud,
but humility comes before honor.
PROVERBS 18:12 CSB

It appears the world has been overtaken with the somebody-owes-me-something attitude. The bottom line is that we have become entitled. We believe we deserve something because of who we are. Somehow, we think everyone owes us and that we owe nothing in return.

Entitlement affects everyone, including you and me. The sin of entitlement is very dangerous. Satan will trick us into thinking we have certain rights. If Satan can make the sin of entitlement look like normal behavior and not so evil, then he can get a major foothold in our lives. It is a subtle sin that most wouldn't even call sin. It's one that others see in us but we rarely see in ourselves.

Today's culture breeds entitlement thinking even in the church. Supposedly, if we have our daily devotions, go to church, and help the old lady across the street, God should bless our lives. We think God owes us for all we are doing for Him.

When we can accept that faith in Christ grants us the greatest entitlement of all, "to be called children of God," then that is what truly becomes sufficient. Entitlement doesn't have to mark us. When we are clothed with humility, we will not fall to the sin of entitlement. Remember that nobody owes you anything. You are nothing without Christ.

Father, I ask for a heart filled with humility. Forgive me for the times I felt like somebody owed me something. Cleanse me of the sin of entitlement. Amen.

FOLLOW THE PLAN

All Scripture is God-breathed and is useful for teaching,
rebuking, correcting and training in righteousness.

2 TIMOTHY 3:16

Every NFL coach puts together a game plan that positions the team to win. There is an offensive game plan designed to put points on the board and a defensive game plan designed to stop the opposition.

God has given us a game plan for life; it's called the Bible. It's the definitive book about how to live. The Word brings a change of heart and a change of behavior. The Bible offers us both an offensive and defensive game plan. On offense, it teaches us how to love, serve, encourage, and forgive. It instructs us how to be generous, speak words of life, build relationships, handle money, and even get back on track. We're taught how to share our faith, pray, and engage in the supernatural battle. On defense, Scripture teaches us how to flee from temptation, get out of compromising situations, and combat the Enemy's attempts to discourage, defeat, divide, and destroy. Above all else, we learn how to guard our hearts.

Get to know God's game plan. In the Bible, He's given us everything we need for life and godliness. We must study the plan in order to know the plays. When we know the plan, we can defeat our opponent. If you want to win, you need to follow the plan.

Father, I believe Your Word, the Bible, is my game plan for life. Help me know it and live it out. Amen.

TEN PRINCIPLES OF SERVING

"If I, your Lord and Teacher, have washed your feet, you also ought to wash one another's feet. For I have given you an example that you also should do just as I have done for you."

JOHN 13:14–15 HCSB

Jesus did the unthinkable. He redefined leadership as serving. He gave us a clear example and said we should do the same. Over the years, I have picked up ten serving principles that help me serve others:

1. Serving is love, not duty. Serving should be a natural overflow, not a manufactured effort. Serving is born out of desire, not drudgery.
2. Serving is relationships, not projects. Are you more focused on accomplishing something or blessing someone?
3. Serving is about others, not self. Self-denial is the core of serving. You can't be a servant if you're full of yourself.
4. Serving is costly, not convenient. Sacrifice is always a key ingredient.
5. Serving is stewardship, not ownership. Do you try to control how you help people? We don't own the blessing of serving. God does.
6. Serving is private, not public. When we serve, humility should consume us. Serving doesn't seek recognition.
7. Serving is about the heart, not hands. Serving is an inside job. You can't serve with a critical and insecure heart.
8. Serving is about God, not man. We need God's heart. Don't use God but be used by God for His purposes.
9. Serving is opportunity, not obligation. Joy is a by-product of serving. It is hard, not easy.
10. Serving is not optional—period! Jesus gave us an example. We must serve.

Father, I want to follow Your example and be a servant. Teach me Your ways. Amen.

POSSIBLE

"With man this is impossible, but not with God;
all things are possible with God."

MARK 10:27

Athletic apparel company Adidas had a campaign that said, "Impossible is nothing." I had to reread it to let its simple message sink in. This statement is referring to a mindset. It's a way of thinking. It's an approach to training, competition, and life that requires a different way of looking at the challenges we will face—the unbeatable opponent, the unreachable achievement, the unattainable goal.

I believe the single biggest obstacle we must overcome is a lack of belief. Maybe you have a tough relationship or a persistent problem you just can't solve. You have failed so many times in your quest to reach your goals that you truly don't believe it can happen.

I get the feeling this is exactly what Jesus confronted in Mark 9. A father brought to Jesus his boy, who was controlled by an evil spirit. The spirit made him deaf and mute and continually tried to kill him, throwing him into fire or water. You get the feeling this dad was worn out. So when he asked Jesus if He could do anything to help, Jesus responded, "If you can?" Are you serious? "Everything is possible for him who believes." Then the father responded, "I do believe! Help me overcome my unbelief!" (vv. 23–24).

Sometimes we get stuck believing something can't happen for us. Then we make God very small and our problems very big. Our circumstances choke out our faith. The most important part of Mark 10:27 is the final two words: "with God." Nothing is impossible *with God*. What is impossible for man is possible with God.

Father, help me believe that with You, nothing is impossible. Amen.

WHAT'S YOUR GO-TO?

He often withdrew to deserted places and prayed.
LUKE 5:16 HCSB

When the lacrosse game was on the line and the team needed a goal, I went to my go-to move: the inside roll dodge. It was the move I practiced thousands of times and executed in competition with great success. Every athlete has their go-to move.

If this is true for the sports world, it is especially true for the spiritual world. What is your go-to move that allows you to be your best for Christ? My friend and leadership expert Dan Webster shared with me three spiritual go-to moves that can help you maximize your impact for Christ:

1. Go-To Place: Where do you go every day to connect with God? My go-to place is the desk my grandfather gave me while I was in college. The desk has become my spiritual gym where I work out every day to produce spiritual sweat. Where is your go-to place? Find one and get there every day.
2. Go-To Passage: What passage gives you the greatest comfort and hope, direction and guidance? What verses revive your soul? We all need a fresh go-to passage. What verses are you chewing on daily?
3. Go-To Person: Everybody needs at least one go-to person who will show up at your doorstep if you call them at 3:00 a.m. So many people I know have gone down in flames because they did not have someone to do life with.

Allow these three spiritual go-to moves to impact your life and others.

Father, I ask for You to show me the right place to meet, Scripture passage for direction, and person to do life with. Amen.

BREAKTHROUGH

"Do not remember the past events,
pay no attention to things of old."
ISAIAH 43:18 HCSB

On October 28, 2008, I witnessed a breakthrough moment in Nashville, Tennessee. At the official World Hamburger Eating Championship, eating machine Joey "Jaws" Chestnut crushed the legend Takeru "Tsunami" Kobayashi by inhaling a world-record 103 hamburgers in eight minutes. It was a breakthrough moment for Jaws, and he continued to defeat everyone in every competition for many years since then. Have you ever witnessed or experienced a sports play that became a breakthrough moment? Most likely it was more significant than mine.

Breakthrough is a great word that is often used in sports. For an athlete, any play they make that changes the course of a game is usually called a breakthrough play. For a team, a breakthrough game is one that changes the course of their season.

One thing I do know: breakthrough moments are game changers. Breakthroughs can even define and shape a legacy. Imagine a breakthrough in the spiritual realm. Spiritual breakthrough can be defined as going from the ordinary to the extraordinary. We need to identify specific obstacles and barriers that are keeping us from spiritual breakthrough and ask God to remove them.

Spiritual breakthrough happens when we serve others unconditionally, allow the eyes of our hearts to be opened, see in the spiritual realm, experience tears of confession, rely on Christ alone, make decisions that are full of faith and bathed in prayer, serve Christ with reckless abandon, have passionate and contagious faith, and see God transform our lives and the lives of others.

Are you ready for a spiritual breakthrough?

Father, I long for spiritual breakthrough in my life. Amen.

UNLEASH THE POWER

"Where two or three gather together as my followers,
I am there among them."
MATTHEW 18:20 NLT

All three Britton kids played lacrosse at Liberty University, and it was truly a blessing to see them all attend the same school. I loved watching hundreds of games over a six-year period, but the best part happened after the games. At Liberty, every sports team goes to the center of the field or court to pray—win or lose. Also, they invite the other team to join. Every time, either part or all the other team joined in.

It always blew me away when teams united arm in arm to pray together. They were tapping into a powerful spiritual principle: prayer unleashes God's power. It changes us, and it changes the way we look at circumstances. The post-game prayer usually lasted less than a minute, but it made a lasting impact.

Prayer has a way of putting things into perspective. It resets the heart, makes things clear, and eliminates noise. Prayer can stretch us because of where we pray. When we do it in public, we have to check our hearts and make sure we are not praying for personal gain or attention. The religious leaders in the Bible were notorious for praying in public so everyone could see how spiritual they were. And Jesus let them have it. God-honoring prayer is when God gets the glory; prideful prayer is when we get the glory. How might the world change if we all prayed for His glory and not ours?

Father, unleash the power of prayer through me. Whether in public or private, help me be obedient to pray so You alone get the glory. Amen.

LAUGHTER

When the LORD restored the fortunes of Zion, we were like those who dreamed. Our mouths were filled with laughter, our tongues with songs of joy. Then it was said among the nations, "The LORD has done great things for them."

PSALM 126:1–2

Laughter and joy are not just fleeting moments of happiness. They are also gifts from God. Psalm 126:1–2 beautifully illustrates how our laughter and joy can be a testament to the great things God has done for us.

Laughter relieves stress. Life can be challenging, filled with pressures from work, family, and personal struggles. When we laugh, our bodies release endorphins—the body's natural feel-good chemicals. These endorphins not only lift our mood but also reduce the stress hormones that can negatively impact our health. Laughter becomes a means of trusting in God's sovereignty over our circumstances. Proverbs 17:22 reminds us, "A cheerful heart is good medicine."

Laughter builds better relationships. Laughter is a universal language that breaks down barriers and fosters connections. Sharing a hearty laugh with friends or family strengthens the bonds of love and unity. Laughter is not only an expression of joy but also a tool for building community. Ecclesiastes 3:4 tells us there is "a time to laugh" because God designed us to find joy in one another's company.

Laughter attracts people to Jesus. When we embrace joy and laughter, we testify to the goodness and faithfulness of our heavenly Father. Psalm 126:2 proclaims that our joyous laughter can declare God's great deeds among the nations. Let's remember that our joy does not depend on circumstances but on our unshakable faith in God's love and promises.

Father, help me laugh freely and regularly. Amen.

BURN PLOWS, KILL COWS

Elisha left him and went back. He took his yoke of oxen and slaughtered them. He burned the plowing equipment to cook the meat and gave it to the people, and they ate. Then he set out to follow Elijah and became his servant.

1 KINGS 19:21

Elisha was chosen to follow in Elijah's prophetic footsteps. He was a farmer, so when he burned the plows and killed the cows, he was literally and figuratively leaving everything behind. This was a demonstration of a wholehearted commitment to God, leaving behind the past and dedicating himself to His calling. It's a reminder that following God often requires us to abandon the safety of our comfort zones.

Burning the plows means leaving our comfort zones, just as Elisha did. He left behind the security of his livelihood to follow God's call through Elijah. Following God requires trust in God's guidance and a willingness to let go of control. Elisha's act of killing the cows and burning his plowing equipment symbolized breaking attachments to his past life. We may need to let go of past sins, regrets, or negative influences that hold us back from fully following God. And we may need to leave our source of security and certain provisions too.

Elisha's response to Elijah's call was an immediate and wholehearted commitment. It left no plan B. He didn't look back; he followed Elijah without hesitation. Burning the plows in our lives means fully embracing God's call, whatever that may be. It's about dedicating ourselves to His service, allowing Him to lead and direct our steps, and being willing to follow wherever He leads.

Father, help me let go of plan B and be completely obedient to Your calling in my life. Amen.

NOVEMBER

THE GREATEST FINISHER

Not only so, but we also glory in our sufferings, because we know that
suffering produces perseverance; perseverance, character;
and character, hope.

ROMANS 5:3–4

My son Jake decided he needed a big challenge, so he chose to complete an Ironman competition. That's a 2.4-mile swim, 112-mile bike ride, and a 26.2-mile marathon to finish. The hardest part isn't the start; it's not even the finish. The hardest part comes around mile twenty-one of the marathon—when your body is fatigued, your mind is weary, and the finish line seems far away. You feel like giving up. But winning is found in finishing.

Anybody can start well when energy and motivation are high, but not everybody can finish strong when fatigue sets in and the voices in your head tell you to call it quits. Each day starts with a new motivation and resolve to make the right choices but often ends with excuses and failure.

Jesus became the ultimate finisher when He obediently went to the cross to forgive our sins and reconcile us, by grace through faith, to God the Father. And even today, He works in us to finish the work He began. He is the author and finisher of our faith.

There are three key things that will help you finish strong:

1. Self-Talk: Finishers know words have power. They flood their minds with positive thinking, optimism, and belief.
2. Raving Fans: Finishers have people cheering them on with encouragement. Then they can overcome obstacles and setbacks.
3. Clear Vision: Finishers keep the finish line in sight. When the motive is big enough, they find a way.

Keeping our eyes on Jesus is guaranteed to keep us on track to finish.

Father, help me keep my eyes on You and overcome every challenge, disappointment, and obstacle. Amen.

STICKS AND STONES

"The things that come out of a person's mouth come from the heart,
and these defile them."

MATTHEW 15:18

Words are a powerful thing. Even though we've all heard that sticks and stones can break our bones but words can never hurt us—we all know this isn't true. We've all experienced pain from what others have said to us; we can often remember hurtful or discouraging words literally decades later.

God tells us the words we speak are an overflow of what's in our heart. So no matter what we say—whether encouragement or praise, cursing or criticism, life or death—our words are a reflection of our heart. This can be convicting because profanity is increasingly acceptable in our culture, but it's not befitting a follower of Christ.

A small bit in the mouth of a horse controls the direction of the horse. A small rudder on a ship controls the direction of the ship. Our words—spoken and written—control the direction of our life. The bit, the rudder, and our tongue must be controlled. When the farmer controls the horse, it can plow a field. When the captain controls the ship, it can deliver great cargo. When we control our tongue, we can bring life to those around us.

We shouldn't praise God and then put down others. We shouldn't cheer on our favorite team and then criticize each other. We shouldn't read God's Word then turn around and gossip about our friends. Let's pay attention to the words we speak. Our words are powerful, and their effect can be widespread and lasting.

Father, help me be quick to listen, slow to speak, and slow to become angry so I can control the words I speak. Amen.

TRAIN YOUR BRAIN

"He was a murderer from the beginning, not holding to the truth,
for there is no truth in him. When he lies, he speaks his native language,
for he is a liar and the father of lies."

JOHN 8:44

I was in the gym and saw this message on a T-shirt: "Don't believe everything you think." I quickly realized the real battle is in my mind. My thoughts affect how I feel, my feelings affect what I do and how I do it, and those things affect everything in my life.

In life we have an adversary, the devil, who makes accusations and tells lies. He loves to get inside our heads and get us off our game. The problem comes when we don't take these lies captive, when we let them play over and over in our head, and when we finally start to believe them. *I'm not good enough. I could never do that. It's never going to change.*

Our patterns of thinking eventually determine our destination. If I think I can't do something, I create a self-fulfilling prophecy and self-sabotage. On the other hand, if I think I can do something, I line up all my time, energy, and resources behind getting it done. My ability to overcome obstacles and challenges is enhanced because I believe it can be done. But this is not the power of positive thinking. Instead, this is the power of transformed thinking. It's about not believing the lies and cleaning up the junk. This is where you win or lose the game of life: in your mind. If you truly want a transformed life, train your brain. Until then, don't believe everything you think.

Father, help me train my brain to think like You think and live a transformed life. Amen.

BLOCKER OR BUILDER?

Let's agree to use all our energy in getting along with each other. Help others with encouraging words; don't drag them down by finding fault.

ROMANS 14:19–21 MSG

Coach Scott was a great offensive line football coach. When I was a ten-year-old aspiring right guard, he taught me the basics to being a great blocker: elbows up and out with hands tucked in. It was the old school way to block, which didn't involve using hands.

Blockers are everywhere in life—at our jobs, in our homes, and at our churches. Elbows up and out, they try their hardest to prevent others from getting around them. It's hard to be around them and serve under them because they're selfish, prideful, controlling people. All of us have a blocker mindset to some degree. That's why we should constantly examine our own hearts for the blocker mentality.

There are ten ways blockers lead and treat others:

1. Blockers keep others from reaching their potential.
2. Blockers cannot celebrate the success of others.
3. Blockers look at life through the "me" lens, not the "we" lens.
4. Blockers criticize easily and can't praise others.
5. Blockers use the power given to them to advance themselves not others.
6. Blockers fear that others will get credit for their accomplishments.
7. Blockers are threatened by people who are more gifted.
8. Blockers are insecure in who they are and in their giftedness.
9. Blockers do not recognize themselves as preventers.
10. Blockers lead out of fear, pride, and control.

Instead of being blockers, let's be builders. We can assist others in reaching their potential. Christ wants us to serve, bless, praise, encourage, and love.

Father, it's so easy for me to be a blocker, but I desire to be a builder. Help me break out of my blocker attitude. Amen.

TRASH DAY

Get rid of all bitterness, rage, anger, harsh words, and slander,
as well as all types of evil behavior.

EPHESIANS 4:31 NLT

In 1986, Philadelphia municipal workers went on strike. Trash began to pile up around the city—beer bottles, produce, rotting food, you name it. The city hired a contractor who incinerated the garbage, toxic materials and all, and loaded the poisonous ash onto a ship called *Pelicano*. It moved from harbor to harbor looking for someone to take the toxic ash, but port after port turned them away. No one wanted the garbage.

Trash has a way of entering and accumulating in our lives every day. It can come in through social media, YouTube videos, Netflix series, politics, and the news. Even things like negativity and bad attitudes can pile up. Sometimes we contain it and take it to the curb. Every now and then, we forget, and it overflows and begins to stink.

We have the choice to allow or not allow negative things to accumulate in our lives. Just because there's trash on the incoming ship doesn't mean we have to accept it. Every day we get to decide what goes straight to the trash, how long we keep it, and when it gets rolled to the curb. Trash day is a daily decision. And the best decision of all may be to never let trash make its way into your home and life. Take authority over your heart, the port of entry into your life, and say no to the trash arriving at your doorstep.

Father, help me make every day trash day and refuse the garbage that shows up at my door. Amen.

POWER OF THE CIRCLE

Ruth replied, "Don't ask me to leave you and turn back.
Wherever you go, I will go; wherever you live, I will live.
Your people will be my people, and your God will be my God."

RUTH 1:16 NLT

Recently I saw cyclists wearing matching jerseys with *FOG* in large block letters on their backs. As I got closer, smaller print revealed what the acronym stood for: "fast old guys." I laughed. Yes, they were old, and yes, they looked fast. But when I've thought about this more, I've come to believe that what we need is Faithful Old Guys, not Fast Old Guys. We need examples of men who have been faithful in their walk with Jesus Christ year after year.

Are you willing to do whatever it takes to finish faithfully? The "win" is to live well, finish well, and die well—to be faithful to the end. Very few followers of Christ finish well without doing something really stupid.

We need to invest our time in personal relationships and build trust. We need to move from sitting and listening to walking and growing. Circles are better than rows, and connecting is better than listening. Transformation happens most effectively when we are in circles, not rows. Circles give us opportunities to connect personally with others and take comfort that we are not alone no matter what we are going through. We gain wisdom from others' life experiences as we seek God together in community.

Ruth was committed to go with Naomi. Ruth said, "Wherever you go, I will go." Naomi could count on Ruth because they were in a circle together. She was willing to journey with her friend—through trials, tests, blessings, and victories. God desires us to experience life together.

Father, give me a desire to stay connected and be a part of a circle. Amen.

I'VE BEEN WATCHING

The fun and games are over. Get serious, really serious. Get down on your
knees before the Master; it's the only way you'll get on your feet.

JAMES 4:7–10 MSG

A close friend who has known me for twenty years approached me with a
surprising question. "I've been watching you closely for the past year, and you
have changed. I see transformation in your life. What are you doing?" I was
totally humbled and deeply thankful someone noticed I had changed.

The change was a tribute to the power of God's transforming work. After
explaining to my friend about a renewed, serious, daily commitment to my
spiritual disciplines of reading, studying, and praying, he asked for more
details. He said, "Whatever it takes, I want to do it in order to experience
God's transformation in my life too." I encouraged him that the key was
becoming more like the Lord Jesus Christ, not just learning more about Him.

As my friend and I continued talking over a period of several months,
he developed his own spiritual disciplines, and sure enough, the Lord began
transforming him. He said he had never experienced God's presence and
power in his life like that.

Within all of us, there is a deep desire to strengthen our relationship with
Jesus. How are you responding to that longing? For me, I want my spiritual life
to be fiery, not feeble; powerful, not pathetic. Are you willing to do whatever it
takes to press in and pursue the Almighty so you can have a transformational
relationship with your Savior?

*Father, take me deeper in my walk. Reveal the depths of transformation that
are possible in my own life. Amen.*

GROW UP

When I was a child, I spoke as a child, I understood as a child,
I thought as a child; but when I became a man, I put away childish things.

1 CORINTHIANS 13:11 NKJV

Kids are generally controlled by their feelings and what they want at any given moment. You see it all the time when two siblings want the same toy or when they don't get their way. Chaos erupts. Kids are also driven by their dreams, and they are very good at using their imaginations. A healthy childhood has plenty of time for play, creativity, and fun times. Some of my fondest childhood memories involve exploring the woods or spending time with friends.

But there comes a time when boys need to take responsibility for their words, actions, and how they spend their time. They can't always just do what they love to do. They can't be driven by their feelings, but instead, they need to learn to control and harness them for the greater good.

In a culture that often promotes emotionalism, where we are told to act on what we feel and say whatever comes to mind, Christians must hold a higher standard of rationality and truth. True manhood involves embracing facts over fleeting emotions and making decisions based on God's Word rather than shifting feelings. The Bible serves as the ultimate source of wisdom and guidance, guiding men to lead with discernment and clarity. The book of Proverbs grounds men in wisdom for righteous living. It's important that all of us evaluate our thoughts and words and move on from childish things. That doesn't mean you can't have fun, but it's time to grow up.

Father, help me step into my calling as a man with wisdom and understanding. Amen.

BUILD. HEAL. ENCOURAGE.

Keep your mouth free of perversity;
keep corrupt talk far from your lips.
PROVERBS 4:24

It's easy to underestimate the influence of our words. But our words have the power of life and death. Our words can breathe life into weary souls or bring death through discouragement and negativity. And they are an indication of what's going on inside us.

Proverbs 16:24 reminds us that "gracious words are a honeycomb, sweet to the soul and healing to the bones." Many times, careless words wound and hurt others. But God wants our words to bring healing to a hurting world.

In Ephesians 4:29, Paul encouraged us to build others up. "Do not let any unwholesome talk come out of your mouths, but only what is helpful for building others up according to their needs, that it may benefit those who listen." Our words should be constructive, tailored to the needs of others, and aimed at building them up. Our conversations can benefit and encourage those who hear them.

In 1 Thessalonians 5:11, Paul challenged us to encourage and breathe life into others. "Encourage one another and build each other up, just as in fact you are doing." Our speech should be a source of strength and inspiration to those around us.

Our words can bring life, healing, and encouragement to others. They can build up and provide grace to those in our sphere of influence. Let's be intentional about using our words to reflect the love and grace of Christ, making a positive difference in the lives of those we encounter.

Father, help me control the words I speak so I build, heal, and encourage. Amen.

100 PERCENT

"The eyes of the LORD range throughout the earth to strengthen those whose hearts are fully committed to him."

2 CHRONICLES 16:9

I bought a lifetime bumper-to-bumper warranty on my Jeep because I planned on keeping it and didn't want to be out of pocket on major repairs. Jeep wasn't used to someone taking advantage of their commitment, so they dispatched an inspector to confirm my repair. The visit was designed to find a way to nullify the contract, which they did. Buried deep in the agreement was a clause that said it was void if any modifications were made. I had put on larger tires, and Jeep used that to deny the claim and cancel the agreement.

It can be challenging to find anyone who is fully committed to anything anymore. But for a man of God, commitment is the name of the game. We should never look for an escape clause or a way out. Instead, we should be 100 percent—all in.

It turns out that God is looking for men who are 100 percent committed to Him. He chooses people for important tasks when He knows their hearts are fully devoted. David was selected to be king over all his brothers for this very reason.

Our full allegiance is to God. We are committed to love what He loves and live a life of sacrifice. It means we are committed to

- purity by protecting our eyes and our hearts from moral filth,
- fidelity by contending for our marriages, and
- purpose by building the kingdom of Christ through evangelism and discipleship.

When you give your all, you align yourself with God's purpose, and His presence will be with you every step of the way.

Father, count me in as someone whose heart is fully committed to You. Amen.

WHITE KNUCKLES

A man without self-control is like a city broken into and left without walls.
PROVERBS 25:28 ESV

When a crisis hits, we respond one of three ways: fight, flight, or freeze. Worry, anxiety, and insecurity can replace peace, joy, and patience. We desperately hold on to what we have instead of surrendering it. When we grip tightly to things we can't control, we quickly get white knuckles.

In the Bible, King Saul was a white-knuckle leader. He gripped his power. Nobody was going to take it from him, even if it meant giving up his life. David, the young warrior, was the new hero. The people sung a new, popular song about him: "Saul has killed his thousands, but David his tens of thousands" (1 Samuel 21:11 CSB). Saul did the math: he was losing his power and fame. Saul gripped his kingship with everything he had, but it was being ripped from his white knuckles, not by David but by God.

Imagine if Saul had embraced God's plan and invested in David as a young leader. It would have been one of the best biblical examples of mentoring. Instead, a horrific circumstance occurred, and Saul tried to kill David.

When we control things, we get white knuckles. We hold on to our position, our people, our programs, our paychecks, and our perks. Releasing is difficult. It is natural to hold on to things and unnatural to give them away. Corrie ten Boom's words cut me to the core: "I have learned in my years on earth to hold everything loosely because when I hold things tightly, God has to pry my fingers away. And that hurts."[55]

Men, no more white knuckles. Live a life committed to giving up control and giving away power. Trust God. Trust others. And watch God work.

Father, reveal when I have white knuckles. Teach me how to let go and trust Your ways. Amen.

---

55   Corrie ten Boom, *Clippings from My Notebook* (Nashville, TN: Thomas Nelson, 1982), 2–3.

VALOR

The angel of the LORD appeared to him and said to him,
"The LORD is with you, O mighty man of valor."

JUDGES 6:12 ESV

Valor is heroic courage, boldness, and determination in the face of great danger or battle. It's marked by strength and honor and emotional and mental fortitude.

Gideon was a man whom God called a "mighty man of valor." When the angel of the Lord appeared to Gideon, the first thing he addressed was Gideon's identity. Despite Gideon's initial doubts and fears, God saw the potential for courage and strength within him. We are never defined by our weaknesses but by the God who equips us with valor. Our valor comes from God's presence and promises.

In every challenge and uncertainty we face, we have the assurance of God's presence, which empowers us to stand strong and resolute. Gideon's response to God's call revealed his humility and recognition of his own inadequacy. Yet God's response was not focused on Gideon's limitations but on the strength God would provide.

In today's culture, there are dozens of ways we must stand up for righteousness. We cannot shrink back in fear or weakness. We must contend for truth and defend what is good and right. We must act to protect our children from being exposed to offensive material and ideologies. We must contend for our marriages and families.

Our call to valor extends beyond physical battles; it involves spiritual warfare as well. Ephesians 6:12 says we wrestle not against flesh and blood but against spiritual forces. Our courage in standing for righteousness, truth, and justice is a reflection of our commitment to God's kingdom.

Father, help me advance with a spirit of valor to defeat the schemes of the Enemy. Amen.

HOW'S YOUR HEART?

"I will give you a new heart, and I will put a new spirit in you. I will take
out your stony, stubborn heart and give you a tender, responsive heart."

Ezekiel 36:26 nlt

Every time I see my good friend Ron, he always asks me the same question. It
cuts through all the fluff and hits me in the gut. I should be ready for it, but it
always takes me by surprise. He doesn't ask the typical, "How are you doing?"
Instead, he asks, "How's your heart?"

Usually when someone asks, "How are you doing?" it is easy to simply
reply, "Good. How are you?" Unfortunately, many times when I'm asked how
I'm doing, I take the easy route by faking it, and I tell people what I think
they want to hear regardless of how I actually feel. However, Ron's question
demands a better response.

Instead of taking a risk and being transparent and real, we often play it safe
and cover things up. We must look our best, live our best, be our best, and
perform our best. On the inside, we might be dying with problems, conflicts,
or struggles, but we are still expected to keep going. Over time, this leads to
a hard, cold heart. What a blessing to know that God has replaced my stony,
stubborn heart with a tender, responsive heart.

We need to stop faking it and get real. There is hope, and transparency is
possible. It is found in pursuing wholeness of soul and letting the love of Jesus
invade our hearts. This brings the healing that we desperately need. So how's
your heart?

*Father, give me a tender, responsive heart. Invade my heart because I want to
be real, whole, and complete. Amen.*

ENTHUSIASM

We rebuilt the wall till all of it reached half its height,
for the people worked with all their heart.

NEHEMIAH 4:6

Have you ever noticed how enthusiasm can fuel your actions and drive you to accomplish incredible things? Enthusiasm isn't just about energy and excitement; it's also about being filled with God's Spirit, energy, zeal, and passion. Enthusiasm is like a fire that burns within, motivating us to give our best in whatever we do.

In Nehemiah's time, the people were rebuilding the wall of Jerusalem, facing opposition and intimidation. Yet they worked with all their hearts or, in other words, with enthusiasm. Their dedication and passion were evident, and it fueled their progress.

When we approach our work, relationships, and service to God with enthusiasm, we tap into the energy and zeal that come from being filled with God's Spirit. Enthusiasm is not something we manufacture on our own. It's a result of being filled with God's Spirit. When we invite God's presence into our lives, we experience a renewed sense of purpose and passion.

Our enthusiasm doesn't just affect us; it also influences those around us. Approaching our responsibilities with enthusiasm can inspire and motivate others to do the same. It creates a positive ripple effect in our families, workplaces, and communities. Just as Nehemiah faced opposition but pressed on, our enthusiasm can give us and others the endurance needed to overcome obstacles.

We desperately need to be filled with the Spirit of God if we are to work with passion and purpose. Even the smallest tasks can be meaningful when we keep this perspective. Enthusiasm keeps us motivated through the menial and mundane parts of life.

Father, keep my enthusiasm tank full as I work with all my heart. Amen.

A NEW THING

I am about to do something new. See, I have already begun!
Do you not see it? I will make a pathway through the wilderness.
I will create rivers in the dry wasteland.

ISAIAH 43:19 NLT

Forbes reported that only 38 percent of people have a worldview that says, "Change is good, even if (or especially if) it means leaving our comfort zone."[56] The other 62 percent "don't like to leave their comfort zone or do so only occasionally."[57] Most people love to hunker down and stay put. A quote often attributed to Mark Twain nails it: "I'm in favor of progress; it's change I don't like."

Sometimes we can choose change, and other times change is forced upon us. Either way, change has a huge impact on every area of our lives. I have realized we can respond to change in three different ways:

1. Head Down: Change leads to pain and regret. We go dark and shut down. Over time it turns into discouragement and disappointment.
2. Head Spinning: Change overwhelms us and creates chaos. This leads to distraction and doubt.
3. Head Up: Change challenges us. We respond with determination and decisiveness.

Let's embrace change and realize these key ideas:

- God is always doing something new.
- God is always working.
- We need to keep our head up to see it.

Let's find our determination and decisiveness. God is the waymaker, and He is doing a new thing. Imagine if every man of God looked through the lens of Isaiah 43:19. Do you see God doing a new thing? Have you embraced it? Don't miss God's work that He is doing God's way.

Father, I believe You are doing a new thing, and I want to see You doing Your work in Your way. Amen.

---

56   Mark Murphy, "The Big Reason Why Some People Are Terrified of Change (While Others Love It)," *Forbes*, August 14, 2016, https://www.forbes.com.

57   Murphy, "Some People Are Terrified of Change."

GO OUT SWINGING

"If we are thrown into the blazing furnace, the God we serve is able to deliver us from it, and he will deliver us from Your Majesty's hand. But even if he does not…we will not serve your gods or worship the image of gold you have set up."

DANIEL 3:17–18

Years ago, my wife was diagnosed with cancer and given a not-so-promising prognosis. In fact, if you were a betting man, you would have passed on this one. But with God, nothing is impossible for those who believe, so we chose to remain optimistic and trust God. But every single time we went to the hospital, the news seemed to get worse. So much so that I actually asked the head doctor before our visit if he could lead with some positive or hopeful news, even if he had to make it up. He agreed.

At the same time, a friend of mine suggested I begin to prepare for the worst. He counseled that I should get my ducks in a row and prepare mentally and emotionally for the likely result. I decided to take the advice and give it a try. After just five days, I was depressed, so I scrapped that idea.

In that moment I decided we were going to go out swinging. I would never resign myself to defeat just to soften the blow. Instead, I decided to remain optimistic and fight like crazy. Fourteen years later, we are still winning, and we keep swinging. This was the same attitude of Daniel and his three friends. Their situations looked bleak, but instead of becoming resigned to defeat, they declared victory and trusted in God. What about you?

Father, give me a fighter's spirit and unwavering trust in You. Amen.

WELCOME TO LEADERSHIP

You should keep a clear mind in every situation. Don't be afraid of
suffering for the Lord. Work at telling others the Good News,
and fully carry out the ministry God has given you.

2 TIMOTHY 4:5 NLT

Within twenty-four hours of being in Ukraine, I was done. I had experienced a long day of travel, spent time training leaders, was trying to keep up with numerous schedule changes, and was still adjusting to a new time zone. My original plan had been thrown out the window, and I was on the struggle bus. That's when Andriy, our FCA Ukraine director at the time, turned to me and said, "Welcome to leadership!"

Now, years later, my team uses that phrase when there are changes, conflicts, and messes. When things don't go as planned and schedules get changed, we simply say, "Welcome to leadership!" Now we laugh about it, but when Andriy first said that to me, I wasn't laughing.

In 2 Timothy 4:5, Paul wrote to Timothy to prepare him for ministry. Throughout the entire book, he encouraged Timothy to be diligent, strong, and alert. He shared transparently about real, up-close leadership. Paul said leadership is

- refreshment and discouragement,
- highlights and lowlights, and
- blessings and burdens.

This was Paul's "Welcome to leadership" letter to Timothy. Two verses later, he defined the win for Timothy: "I have fought the good fight, I have finished the race, and I have remained faithful" (v. 7 NLT). Leading is hard, but it's not impossible.

Men, welcome to leadership. God is calling us to step up and carry out the mission He has given us.

Father, give me a clear mind and pure heart to endure hardships as a leader. Amen.

VIRTUE

The fruit of the Spirit is love, joy, peace, patience, kindness, goodness, faithfulness, gentleness, self-control; against such things there is no law.

GALATIANS 5:22–23 ESV

Benjamin Franklin, a Founding Father of the United States, was known for his commitment to self-improvement and moral virtues. He recognized the importance of character and virtuous living. He developed a plan for self-improvement, focusing on thirteen virtues he believed led to a more fulfilling and impactful life. These virtues included temperance, silence, order, resolution, frugality, sincerity, justice, moderation, cleanliness, tranquility, chastity, humility, and industry. Franklin's commitment to these virtues was rooted in his desire for personal growth and excellence. He believed cultivating these virtues would lead to a life well lived and would contribute to his success in various areas. His intentional pursuit of virtue exemplifies the biblical principle in Galatians 5:22–23. By working to develop virtues, our lives will bear much fruit.

As men of faith, our commitment to virtue goes beyond personal excellence; it's an expression of our devotion to God. Virtues such as integrity, humility, kindness, and self-discipline align with the teachings of Christ. They enable us to reflect His character in our interactions with others and in our daily choices.

While Benjamin Franklin's pursuit of virtue is commendable, our ultimate example of virtue is found in Jesus Christ. He embodied all virtues perfectly and calls us to follow in His footsteps. His sacrificial love, humility, and moral integrity provide the foundation for our pursuit.

By focusing on character development, we change from the inside out. Let's strive to be men of integrity, character, and virtue—living in alignment with the teachings of Scripture and the example of our Savior, Jesus Christ.

Father, help me focus on developing into a man of virtue to reflect Christ in all I do. Amen.

THE POWER OF WITH

*Let us think of ways to motivate one another
to acts of love and good works.*

HEBREWS 10:24 NLT

One day, Ron, a great friend of mine for over twenty years, invited me to read the book of Proverbs with him for the upcoming month. "Would you like to do the Wisdom Challenge and partner with me by going through Proverbs together?" Ron asked.

I had taken on some Proverbs challenges where I read a chapter of Proverbs each day for a month and greatly benefited from this exercise; however, I had never done it with someone. For thirty-one straight days, we texted each other every day what God revealed to us. We encouraged and commented on one another's insights. I was blown away by the significance of going through Proverbs with someone versus by myself. The big surprise wasn't necessarily what I was gleaning from Proverbs but the dynamic interaction with Ron through a couple of texts each morning. The interaction was life-changing.

At the end of the month, Ron encouraged me to invite someone else to do the Wisdom Challenge. So the following month, I decided to do it with my son, Elijah. Spending thirty-one straight days in God's Word with my son and hearing how God was speaking to him was something I will never forget.

Life's graveyard is filled with the good intentions that went nowhere because someone thought they didn't need others on the journey. Let's commit to do life with others.

Father, I commit to walking with the wise so I can become wise. Amen.

GOING, GOING...GONE

*Come now, you who say, "Today or tomorrow we will travel...
and do business..." You don't even know what tomorrow will bring—
what your life will be! For you are like smoke that appears for a little while,
then vanishes.*

JAMES 4:13–14 HCSB

On November 21, 2006, five-time Olympic champion Ian Thorpe retired from competitive swimming at the age of twenty-four. He said breaking records "wasn't as inspiring as it should have been."[58] As a teenager, Ian splashed into the swimming scene and set thirteen world records between 1999 and 2002; he then became an international star after dominating at the Sydney Olympics.

It didn't take long for Ian to realize success isn't all it's cracked up to be. Medals, titles, records, and accomplishments didn't last long. The fans went home. Ian was left with an empty feeling—even after breaking world records. Hype never lasts, and it's never enough to satisfy. Compared to eternity, life on earth is like a couple of seconds.

As a young man, Ian realized something: blink and all those achievements are gone. If your focus is on the seen, you'll hold on to things too tightly and live a hard life. If your focus is on the unseen, you'll hold things lightly, and you will live free. In the book of James, the apostle reminded us that life is a vapor, a mist. Going, going...gone. That's our life on earth.

Men, set your minds on things above. Don't let what is temporary weigh you down. Live free.

Father, I want to hold lightly to anything in the here and now. Help me dwell on what's eternal, not what is external. Amen.

---

58   Christopher Clarey, "Ian Thorpe, Australian Hero, Throws in the Towel," *New York Times*, November 21, 2006, https://www.nytimes.com.

DEFENSE

"No weapon forged against you will prevail, and you will refute every tongue that accuses you. This is the heritage of the servants of the LORD, and this is their vindication from me," declares the LORD.

ISAIAH 54:17

A friend of mine recently had a former employee make all kinds of accusations of impropriety and fraud. The truth was clear, and while my friend believed it would come to nothing, it still was tempting to go on the defense. In a world filled with accusations and lies, we have a promise from God—a promise of divine defense and vindication. Isaiah 54:17 reminds us that no weapon formed against us will ultimately succeed. It's hard to believe this at times, and we often strike back. But God's way is better.

God is our ultimate protector. He shields us from the weapons formed against us, whether they are physical, emotional, verbal, or spiritual. When we face opposition or attacks, God stands as our defender.

Accusations and slander can be damaging. But as we walk in the power of the Holy Spirit, God promises divine vindication. When we are falsely accused or unjustly treated, we can trust that God will bring justice in His time. Others will recognize our integrity and faithfulness. Our faith in God's promises strengthens us to face accusations and lies with confidence. We can trust God is in control, working for our good, and defending us against every attack.

God's defense doesn't mean we won't face challenges or opposition. It means that, with God on our side, we can stand firm and resilient, knowing His truth and justice will prevail.

Father, I trust that You will defend me against the false accusations and lies of the Enemy. Amen.

DEFINING *COMPETITION*

> "'Love the Lord your God with all your heart and with all your soul
> and with all your strength and with all your mind';
> and, 'Love your neighbor as yourself.'"
>
> LUKE 10:27

After fifty years of competing as a coach and athlete in multiple sports, I have realized people define *competition* differently. I have had coaches scream in my face, "Let's go out there and kill them! Let's destroy them!" Others say, "Let's go out there and play our best!" It's all over the map.

Over the years, I have learned there are two possible definitions of *competition*. One is to defeat an opponent in score, skill, or combat. The other considers the Latin word for "competition," which is *competere*. The root word *com* means "with," not "against." So this other definition means "to walk alongside of." I imagine two or more people working together to bring another along or to partner together.

The second definition introduces a vastly different way to compete, a way that sounds more like loving our neighbor. We could define the Christian view of competition as elevating each other's involvement to higher levels of participation, skill development, and effectiveness for the glory of God.

As men, we compete in every area of our lives from business to social to family. So when we compete, we should sense and feel God's pleasure in us. When we desire to come alongside our competition and see them improve by releasing our abilities for God's glory, we are competing God's way. Becoming Christlike while we compete is our win. If we are willing to redefine *competition*, we become Jesus' hands and feet to our opponent.

Father, help me be someone who understands how to love others, even my competitors. I want to become more like Jesus every day. Amen.

CALL UP

One of the young men answered, "Behold, I have seen a son of Jesse the Bethlehemite, who is skillful in playing, a man of valor, a man of war, prudent in speech, and a man of good presence, and the LORD is with him."

1 SAMUEL 16:18 ESV

A close friend has been an NFL coach for almost thirty years, and one thing he's great at is evaluating talent. He can work a player out on the field like all the rest, but even better, he has a sense for what makes that player tick from the inside out. That's a gift, and it's made him not only successful but also a significant part of his players' lives.

Whenever I read the story of how God chose David, it makes me realize God is one of the greatest talent scouts in history. He sees things others don't. In fact, he's looking for things others aren't. We look at the obvious like physical stature, strength, presence, and personality. But God looks past all that and sees the intangibles—inner toughness, resilience, character, and wisdom.

Anyone can get good at measuring someone based on the externals, but the real talent is seeing the internals. This is particularly important for us as men because we need to call out things we see inside others we are discipling, mentoring, or in accountability with. Our job is to tune our hearts so we can see as God sees. Those around us need us to pay attention to the heart behind the habits, the purpose inside the potential, and to call up people to a higher standard that they are capable of attaining.

Father, help me see the best in others and call them up to live that standard. Amen.

THANKSGIVING POWER

*One of them, seeing that he was healed, returned and, with a loud voice,
gave glory to God. He fell facedown at His feet, thanking Him.
And he was a Samaritan.*

LUKE 17:15–16 HCSB

After every practice and every game, Jessie, a lacrosse player I coached, would approach me before leaving the field and utter one small but powerful sentence: "Thank you, Coach!" During the entire two years she played on my lacrosse team, she never missed a single day of saying those three powerful words. Jessie understood the value of gratitude, and she wanted to make sure I knew she did not take a single practice or game for granted. Not only did Jessie have an attitude of thanksgiving, but she also put it into action. The power of thanksgiving is in the action.

In Luke 17, out of the ten lepers healed by Jesus, only one man scrambled back to say thanks. I am sure the other nine had an attitude of thanksgiving but never applied their gratitude. The power of saying thanks is a simple thing but hard to do. A friend of mine says that unexpressed gratitude can often be interpreted as being unthankful.

We should have thanksgiving flowing from our lips daily. The people we connect with should be soaked with thanks because we are overflowing with gratitude. I often fail to overflow with words of thanksgiving to others. My attitude is good, but my action is lacking. Let's make sure we say it! No more withholding blessing from those who deserve it. What are you waiting for? Tell others how grateful you are for them because the power is in the action.

*Father, move me to action to express my thankfulness for those in my life.
Amen.*

ARMOR UP

Be strong in the Lord and in his mighty power. Put on the full armor of God, so that you can take your stand against the devil's schemes.

EPHESIANS 6:10–11

When I was a young boy, my mom refused to let me play tackle football. She was trying to protect me because I was small for my age, but I had a fierce, competitive spirit. So I got creative in the ways I would explain to my mom where I was going and what I was doing after school. A bunch of my buddies and I met at an open backyard in the neighborhood for a game of "kill the guy with the ball." One of us would throw the football into the sky, and we'd all fight for possession. Whoever got the ball would run for his life as the others chased him down and tackled him. It was a blast. Many times I had to clean and cover up scrapes and bruises, but Mom never knew.

As I got older, our neighborhood challenged boys from another neighborhood to a legit game of tackle football. I had received football pads and a helmet at Christmas, but my mom never expected me to wear them in a real game. Needless to say, I wore the armor and played the game, and our neighborhood's boys left with bragging rights.

Spiritual armor is as important as physical armor, and it gives us the power we need to live a righteous life. Without it, we are powerless against the schemes the devil uses to try to discourage and defeat us. But our armor has the power to demolish strongholds. Don't hit the field without it.

Father, give me the armor with the power to defeat every lie of the Enemy. Amen.

THANKSGENEROUS

As you have received Christ Jesus the Lord, walk in Him, rooted and built up in Him and established in the faith, just as you were taught, overflowing with gratitude.

COLOSSIANS 2:6–7 HCSB

New words get introduced into the English language all the time. The *Oxford English Dictionary* adds hundreds of words each year, including additions like *fam, prepper, swole, nothingburger,* and *hangry.* People have been inventing new words forever. Shakespeare invented or has the first recorded English use of over two thousand words like *zany, swagger,* and *lackluster.*

I'm no Shakespeare, but I would like to introduce a new word to the English language: *thanksgenerous.*

Thanksgenerous [thangks-je-nə-rəs] (noun)

1. a strategic act of abundant generosity that is unexpected, bringing wonder and blessing
2. an extravagant outpouring of thanks to God and others

I don't want to be a man who is just giving thanks. I want to be someone who is generous in thanks because people don't expect you to be abundant in generosity. There is a big difference between giving and being generous.

- Giving is good. Generous is best.
- Giving is duty. Generous is delight.
- Giving is the first mile. Generous is the second mile.
- Giving is predictable. Generous is unexpected.
- Giving is spontaneous. Gencrous is strategic.
- Giving is ordinary. Generous is extraordinary.

In Colossians 2:6–7, we learn that if we grow deep roots in Jesus Christ and build, then we overflow with thanksgiving. Is it any wonder why thankfulness is in short supply? If we are overfull with God, then we overflow with thanks. If we are not full of God, we are selfish and stingy. Let's move from thanksgiving to thanksgenerous.

Father, I want to be generous in my thanks. Change me into the man You have designed me to be—overflowing with thanks. Amen.

HAPPY HEART, HAPPY FACE

A happy heart makes the face cheerful.

PROVERBS 15:13

Have you ever noticed how a genuinely happy person can light up a room with their presence? They are like magnets: you just want to be around them. It's not a coincidence. Our inner condition impacts how others experience us.

Do you wear your emotions on your face? A happy heart is not only an internal blessing but also a visible one. When our hearts are filled with joy, it radiates through our expressions and demeanor, making our faces cheerful. This joy isn't superficial; it's rooted in our relationship with God.

One of the most effective ways to cultivate a happy heart is by practicing gratitude. A thankful heart shifts our perspective from what's wrong to what's right, what we lack to what we have, and what we can't do to what we can. Start each day with a moment of gratitude, counting your blessings no matter how small they seem.

Spending time in joyful worship and prayer can be a source of immense happiness. When we connect with God through worship and pour out our hearts in prayer, we experience His presence, which is fullness of joy (Psalm 16:11). Let your heart sing with praise, and in the quiet moments of prayer, share your joys, worries, and desires with the one who cares deeply for you. Happiness isn't just an internal state; it's also a by-product of our actions. Engaging in acts of kindness and service to others can bring tremendous joy. Whether it's helping a neighbor, volunteering, or simply being a good friend, these actions not only bring happiness to others but also fill your heart with joy.

Father, grow in me a happy heart that shows up as a happy face. Amen.

BALANCE AND BLESSING

Just as our bodies have many parts and each part has a special function.
ROMANS 12:4 NLT

Harvard Business Review research showed that 97 percent of us can quickly identify a weakness in ourselves like being unreliable, avoiding conflict, or fearing risk. However, very few of us succeed in converting our weaknesses into strengths. The study revealed fewer than 10 percent of employees make any progress one year after they receive feedback during a performance review.[59]

Many of us spend a ton of time trying to turn our weaknesses into strengths. However, I have never met anyone who spends time intentionally turning a strength into a weakness. But strengths become weaknesses all the time, and I believe it is even more costly. When we are confident in our strengths, we lose dependence on God. We start to believe we don't really need Him, and we try to do everything on our own. We begin trusting in ourselves instead of trusting God to work in and through us. There are two keys to making sure a strength remains a strength: balance and blessing.

First, our strengths must have balance. Every good and perfect gift comes from God. We must find something that balances, stabilizes, and maximizes our gifts. With awareness and accountability, our strengths will be a blessing. Without these, they become a burden.

Second, we must use our strengths to bless others. The gifts and strengths God gives to us are designed to be given away. God pours gifts into us; our job is to pour out what He has poured in. We must use these strengths for the benefit and blessing of others.

Men, let's use our strengths in balance to bless others.

Father, I ask You to ground each strength You've given me. I pray for wisdom to use them to bless others. Amen.

---

59   Joseph Grenny, "A 3-Step Plan for Turning Weaknesses into Strengths," *Harvard Business Review*, January 26, 2017, https://hbr.org.

CLEAR VISION

The LORD replied: "Write down the revelation and make it plain on tablets
so that a herald may run with it."

HABAKKUK 2:2

Vision is a clear picture of a desired future reality. And it is a powerful tool when it's written, simple, clear, and inspiring. God often places within us the visions that stir us, aligning them with His purposes. In the context of Habakkuk 2:2, the emphasis on making the vision so clear that "a herald may run with it" carries important implications:

- Vision must be easy to understand. Complexity kills even the best ideas, but when we communicate a powerful message in an easy-to-understand way, it takes root. When a vision is clear and unambiguous, there is less risk of it being distorted or miscommunicated as it passes from person to person.
- Vision must be easy to share. The phrase "a herald may run with it" suggests the vision should be so clear, it can be quickly and easily shared with others. In ancient times, heralds were messengers who carried important news or proclamations that needed to be delivered fast to various locations.
- Vision must be easy to implement. The idea of someone running with the vision implies an eagerness to put it into action. Clarity in the vision minimizes delays caused by confusion or uncertainty. It motivates people to act decisively toward the vision's fulfillment.

A clear vision has the power to inspire and mobilize individuals and communities to action. When people can see a compelling and straightforward picture of the desired future, they are more likely to rally behind it, work together, and take ownership of its realization.

Father, give me a clear vision for every area of my life. Amen.

WHAT DID YOU CALL ME?

When the king was told, "The man of God has come all the way up here,"
he said to Hazael, "Take a gift with you and go to meet the man of God.
Consult the LORD through him."

2 KINGS 8:7–8

After playing and coaching sports for over fifty years, I have picked up a bunch of nicknames. They're all over the map: cute, funny, short, rude, defining, and even obvious. I love some and hate others. The nickname I love the most came from when I played professional lacrosse. My teammates called me "Minister of Defense."

In 2 Kings, Elisha had an awesome nickname: "Man of God." Do we live in such a way that what we believe defines us? Do we serve in such a way that people know we serve God? Do others know us by our faith? It would be incredible to start giving each other God-honoring nicknames. When something significant happened in the life of an individual in the Bible, God often marked that event by changing the name of that person, like Saul into Paul, Simon to Peter, and Jacob to Israel.

Men, give nicknames that are encouraging and refreshing. Every time you call your friends by God-honoring nicknames, you build them up. Name-calling is usually bad, but in this case, name-call as much as you want.

Father, may I be defined by my faith. Also, reveal to me God-honoring names for my friends. Amen.

DECEMBER

THE POWER OF POSITION

The lions may grow weak and hungry,
but those who seek the LORD lack no good thing.

PSALM 34:10

Growing up with two older brothers, I quickly learned I needed an advantage when competing against them. My secret advantage was playing smarter, not just harder. Usually, we approached our basketball games as life or death. Since I usually lost, I tried to gain more knowledge about how to get a position on the court. As a young, aspiring athlete, I had some great coaches who taught me the power of position.

As I grew older, I realized the things I learned on the court could apply to my spiritual life. When it comes to getting in a spiritual position, I've learned three helpful tips to living with purpose and intentionality:

1. Establish position. Many people have never gained position over the competition—the flesh, the devil, and the world. We must have a strong stance and not be rocked.
2. Call for the ball. You don't post up for the fun of it. It's to get the ball. Are you calling out to the Lord and asking Him to show up and speak to you? He desires to pass His Word to you daily, but you need to ask for it.
3. Make a play and score. Once you get the ball, you are in the position to make an impact. Each day, when you fill up with God's Word, you are ready to serve, minister, love, and invest in others.

The Lord wants to bless you each day as you get in position. It's an all-out war for our souls. Know that He is waiting for you.

Father, I desire to have a strong spiritual position with You. I call upon You today. Amen.

OUTSIDE THE BOX

In the beginning God created the heavens and the earth.

GENESIS 1:1

In college, I got to design the halftime contests for the women's basketball games. One game, I sold pieces of paper and had everyone make their very best paper airplane and toss it onto circles on the court to win prizes. The best prize was a round-trip airline ticket, which was a very big deal for a college student. At halftime, paper airplanes flew from different seats in the arena. Some got close to their target while others never made it to the court. But one creative fan went down to the front, wadded up the paper into a ball, and tossed it right onto the airline ticket logo! Talk about thinking outside the box.

When God created, He made something out of nothing. That's the ultimate creativity. Each one of us is made in the image of God, so you must realize you have creative capacity. So much of life is about finding solutions to problems and challenges. It's about finding creative ways to overcome obstacles. Our ability to tap into the wisdom of God, to ask Him for insight, will often help us find solutions faster.

Plus, the wisdom of God in our lives sets our minds and hearts on things above. We have heavenly access to knowledge and the wisdom to apply it in every circumstance—friendships, marriage, family, work, and even our neighborhoods. Coming together in community to help meet the needs of others is a very satisfying endeavor. Let's continue to go to the source of all wisdom and find creative ways to apply that wisdom to our lives.

Father, give me creativity to think outside the box and apply Your supernatural wisdom to life. Amen.

THE SNOWBALL EFFECT

"You have been faithful with a few things; I will put you in charge of many things. Come and share your Master's happiness!"
MATTHEW 25:21

Just before a recent winter storm hit, I was on the radio giving tips for how to survive the storm. One of my tips was to clear the snow a little at a time—not to wait until a foot has accumulated to try to clear it. I even suggested that my boys and I would be out every two hours to clear the snow. We'd do the little things along the way so we would avoid the heavy work of removing over two feet all at once. Well, our intentions were good, but the accumulation was over twenty inches by morning. So instead of getting right on it before it got worse, we felt overwhelmed and let it snow for another five hours before grabbing the shovels.

The snowball effect is simple: little things lead to big things. Every decision, action, thought, and word counts. The little things we do, or don't do, snowball. People suffer heart attacks because of small decisions to neglect their health over many years. Marriages seem to suddenly fail, but little things over the years led to insurmountable problems. People of modest income retire with great wealth because they had the discipline to give generously and save wisely. But what we see happen didn't happen overnight. We can be sure that what we do today will eventually show up. The little decisions we make day in and day out add up. They accumulate like the snow in a blizzard.

Father, help me be disciplined in the little things, consistently doing the work behind the scenes that will lead to life and good things. Amen.

TEN TOUGH QUESTIONS

Test me, LORD, and try me; examine my heart and mind.
PSALM 26:2 HCSB

One of my favorite parts of my job is the opportunity to rub shoulders with incredible leaders from around the world and from every background (business, sports, nonprofit, ministry). When spending time with them, I always ask tough questions, and their answers often produce powerful insights and principles. The key to becoming a great leader isn't only asking others tough questions but asking ourselves tough questions.

It is hard to ask yourself tough questions—to dig into your heart and discover what lurks beneath the surface. Benjamin Franklin wrote, "There are three things extremely hard: steel, a diamond, and to know one's self."[60] Here are ten tough questions that will expose the truth about you:

1. Do I realize it is impossible to glorify Christ and myself at the same time?
2. Do I lead to win people's approval or to win souls?
3. Am I doing the things I am asking others to do?
4. Do I pray as if nothing of eternal value will happen in the lives of others unless God does it?
5. Am I touching the hearts of those I lead?
6. What's it like to be on the other side of me?
7. Do others experience God's love through me?
8. Am I making others around me better?
9. Do I seek personal gain through people I lead or serve them like Christ served the church?
10. Am I allowing my leadership to produce the fruit of the Spirit in others?

Let God have complete access to your heart and allow Him to ask you tough questions.

Father, show me the answers to my tough questions and help me be brutally honest. Amen.

---

60 "Poor Richard Improved, 1750," National Archives, accessed December 14, 2023, https://founders.archives.gov. Quote edited for readability.

POSITIVE EXPECTATIONS

The hopes of the godly result in happiness,
but the expectations of the wicked come to nothing.
PROVERBS 10:28 NLT

I spent the first several years of my professional life in sales and sales management. After some years of learning what worked and what didn't, I enjoyed some success. And then I started to train teams of salespeople in the systems and best practices I and others had discovered.

One of the most important steps to success was to have a positive expectation for every sales call, even the ones you knew might be difficult. You had to begin with the end in mind and visualize the outcome of each call. The less successful salespeople dreaded the phone. They procrastinated and put off making calls. They were projecting all the objections they were likely to get.

A negative expectation never improves the result. But a positive expectation not only changes your tone and demeanor but also, very often, produces a great result. That's because when you have a positive expectation about the future, you approach it with greater energy and enthusiasm.

Some would call our expectations a self-fulfilling prophecy. In other words, whatever you believe will happen generally does. But when our expectations are rooted in the truth that God has plans for us, plans to prosper us and not to harm us, then we can live with a sense of assurance and confidence. Life doesn't always go our way. It's not all home runs and touchdowns. But God is good and can be trusted to work all things together for our good because we love Him and He loves us.

Father, help me have positive expectations for life knowing You have good plans for me. Amen.

WHAT DO YOU STAND FOR?

Thanks be to God, who gives us the victory through our Lord Jesus Christ!

1 CORINTHIANS 15:57 HCSB

When we formed our first Fellowship of Christian Athlete lacrosse team in 1992 to compete in the largest summer lacrosse tournament, we were amazed how God used a last-second, thrown-together team to make a huge impact on the lacrosse community. At that time, the lacrosse culture was not open to a strong Christian influence. As a result of our tournament appearance, we were nicknamed the "God Squad." God granted us success that summer, and we advanced to the championship game by knocking off three powerful teams. Even though we lost a close game in the championship, God used our ragtag team to begin a great work in the lacrosse world and eventually establish the FCA Lacrosse Ministry, which is impacting thousands of coaches and athletes every year.

During the tournament, it was interesting to hear the chatter about our team. It was mostly centered on things we chose not to do: Those guys don't drink. They don't party. They don't curse. They don't…don't…don't. However, I wish people would have talked about what we stood for rather than what we were against. The world is very aware of what followers of Christ are against, but I'm not sure they understand what we stand for. Walking and acting with God's wisdom will show others how to know and experience it.

When we stand for the things of God, we need to remember Paul's words in 1 Corinthians 15:57 that God "gives us the victory through our Lord Jesus Christ" (HCSB). Not us!

Men, we need to be different. We need to know what to stand for and how to take that stand with wisdom, discernment, and understanding.

Father, help me be known for You and what You stand for, not against. Amen.

CONTENT, NOT COMPLACENT

I am not saying this because I am in need,
for I have learned to be content whatever the circumstances.

PHILIPPIANS 4:11

There's a big difference between being content and being complacent. Contentment is a sign of spiritual maturity and confidence in Christ. You can gain a sense of satisfaction because you know that no matter the circumstance, Jesus is with you and still in control. Having much or little, success or struggle, does not change your internal condition of joy in Christ. It's a surrendered position of trust. Contentment allows you to enjoy life even when it's not going as you hoped. It allows you to give thanks in all circumstances. Contentment brings joy.

Complacency, on the other hand, is a lack of desire to improve or change. Your satisfaction with your circumstances can lead to a going-through-the-motions mindset and produce an I-don't-care mentality. Or you may have a spirit of resignation that nothing will change or get better. None of these mindsets are healthy.

Paul knew tremendous hardship and ease; he knew persecution and pleasure. And through it all, as he abided in Christ, he weathered the highs and lows with strength and confidence. He knew he could trust Jesus no matter what.

Life has a way of testing our faith and resolve. External pressures can unsettle us and create fear and anxiety, but God wants us to be unshakable. Even when the world seems to be unraveling around us, we can be content. But that contentment should never result in complacency. Let's continually strive to be our best, be a blessing to others, and bring glory to God.

Father, give me a spirit of contentment as I encounter the ups and downs of life. Amen.

ARE YOU A SLACKER?

He returned to the disciples and found them asleep.
He said to Peter, "Couldn't you watch with me even one hour?
Keep watch and pray, so that you will not give in to temptation.
For the spirit is willing, but the body is weak!"

MATTHEW 26:40–41 NLT

In a *BusinessWeek* poll, employees were asked, "Are you one of the top 10% of performers in your company?" No subgroup in the survey had fewer than 80 percent of employees say yes, including 97 percent of the executives responding yes.[61] But the math does not add up. Ninety percent of us can't be in the top 10 percent.

We all have times when we think we are the hardest workers and others are the slackers. We believe other people aren't as committed as we are; they avoid their responsibilities and take shortcuts. But that's not us. Slackers can be our friends, family members, coworkers, and maybe even our bosses. But one thing is for sure: we never see a slacker in the mirror. Slackers are always on the other side of the table.

Maybe you're not a slacker at work, but are you a slacker toward God? Theologian E. M. Bounds cut to the quick when he said, "Our laziness after God is our crying sin."[62] Many times, we say we love God, but is there any evidence? Are we consumed with Jesus? Does our schedule reflect it? Our priorities? Are we pursuing God opportunities? We have good intentions. But good intentions without consistent actions are worthless. Instead of good intentions, we should have God intentions. God intentions stick! Good intentions are centered on our own plans.

Let's become men who seek God first with all our hearts, giving our passions and desires to Him. Let's not be slackers.

Father, I'm sorry for being a slacker. Help me be in Your presence daily. Amen.

61   Dick Grote, "Let's Abolish Self-Appraisal," *Harvard Business Review*, July 11, 2011, https://hbr.org.

62   E. M. Bounds, *Power through Prayer*, rev. ed. (Grand Rapids, MI: Zondervan, 1962), 44.

CLUTTER

"Watch out! Be on your guard against all kinds of greed;
life does not consist in an abundance of possessions."

LUKE 12:15

If you've ever relocated from one town to another, you know how daunting that can be. Most people dread moving because it forces them to deal with all the things they've accumulated over many years. When we moved from the East Coast to Colorado, we were confronted with the reality of twenty years of stuff. And while much of what we had saved had sentimental value tied to raising our four kids, some of the stuff we'd been storing was just junk. We ended up throwing out a full roll-off dumpster of stuff, giving away at least that much to Goodwill, and yet we still brought a ton of stuff with us. Now, several years later, we discovered we haven't even touched much of what we brought and stored in our new basement.

Clutter and the accumulation of things is a monumental distraction. After recently moving from my office and setting up in my basement again, I have found myself surrounded by the clutter, and it is killing creativity and productivity. Less is truly more. Clutter sucks the mental and emotional energy out of you. The process of decluttering brings freedom and joy. God does not desire for us to be weighed down by possessions, to pursue the accumulation of stuff. Whether it's knickknacks, a desk with piles of papers, or a garage that's bursting at the seams, it's time to get rid of the clutter and free up space in your mind, heart, and soul.

Father, give me the discipline to get rid of clutter to set me free. Amen.

RUT, ROUTINE, OR RHYTHM?

*Very early in the morning, while it was still dark, He got up, went out,
and made His way to a deserted place; and there He was praying.*

MARK 1:35 CSB

Many years ago, I decided that if I could do one thing well, I wanted it to be
spending time with Jesus daily. I realized this single decision could impact
every area of my life. If this one thing could have such a catalytic impact, I
knew worshiping every day had to become a priority.

Jesus knew the most important thing He could do every morning was
connect with His Father. He gave us a clear game plan in Mark 1:35. This verse
drips with intentionality. Jesus did whatever it took to be with the Father. It
was early. It was dark. It was inconvenient. It took effort.

For me, worshiping God has gone from being a rut to a routine to a
rhythm. Our daily rhythm should be to engage God before we encounter
people. Meeting with Him needs to be our top priority. It needs to be the way
we do life. Let's eliminate others asking us, "Did you have your time with Jesus
today?" Instead, let's have them ask, "How was your time with Jesus?"

Our hunger and thirst after God will define us. When we seek His
presence, nothing else matters. If we decide to seek His presence every day,
it will be the single best decision that will impact every area of our lives.
Guaranteed.

*Father, I long to be in Your presence. No ruts. Not even routines. May I delight
in You and experience a new rhythm. Amen.*

BUILD AND DEFEND

Those who carried materials did their work with one hand and held a weapon in the other, and each of the builders wore his sword at his side as he worked.

NEHEMIAH 4:17–18

Nehemiah and his workers faced significant opposition and threats as they rebuilt the city walls. They built with one hand and held a sword in the other for defense; they were ready for attacks by enemies who opposed the reconstruction efforts. They understood the importance of being diligent and vigilant. They carried weapons while laboring, ready to defend themselves, their families, and their neighbors.

Our responsibility is also to build the kingdom and protect our loved ones, knowing we will face both spiritual and physical enemies. As men, we are called to be protectors not just of our own interests but also of those who rely on us for safety and security. We must also balance our work with readiness, holding both tools for construction and weapons for defense. This illustrates the need to be vigilant in our responsibilities, recognizing that threats can arise unexpectedly.

In times of adversity, the builders in Jerusalem prioritized the welfare of their families and neighbors. Most of us feel safe in our homes and neighborhoods, but that doesn't mean we don't have an enemy who is looking for someone to devour. And the Enemy goes after our marriages and kids too. So while it's important that we work, build, and provide, it's equally important that we protect and defend against enemies seen and unseen. While being prepared is essential, Nehemiah's success ultimately depended on God's guidance and protection. Likewise, as men, we must recognize our dependence on God for wisdom, strength, and discernment.

Father, give me the diligence and vigilance to both build and protect. Amen.

PAY ATTENTION

Make the most of every chance you get.
These are desperate times!

EPHESIANS 5:11–16 MSG

My high school football coach would always say to me, "Are you listening or hearing?" He knew I wasn't tuning in, and he was basically saying, "Pay attention!" Paul was saying the same thing to the church of Ephesus in Ephesians 5. I imagine he was probably standing on his chair and saying, "Pay attention!" as he communicated three key points in this verse:

1. Be alert and aware. My coaches always reminded me, "Put your head on a swivel!" We need to keep our heads up to be alert and aware of what is happening, and we need to pay careful attention to Satan's tactics and schemes. We need to understand the times and know what to do.
2. Walk in wisdom. Wisdom is simply seeing the way God sees. When we walk in wisdom, we live lives of integrity, humility, and transparency. Wisdom allows our lives to shine in the darkness. When the dark gets darker, the light gets brighter.
3. Maximize every opportunity. Let's make the most of every opportunity God puts in front of us. God's job is to bring the opportunities; our job is to obey. We need to be intentional, strategic, and available when it comes to kingdom work. Let's live each day like it is our last and bring all we have to every opportunity.

Men, let's pay attention and always be alert and aware, not just hearing but listening.

Father, I long to make the most of every second You give me. My time is limited, so I desire to use every moment for Your glory. Help me pay attention. Amen.

YEAST

He told them still another parable: "The kingdom of heaven is like yeast
that a woman took and mixed into about sixty pounds of flour until it
worked all through the dough."

MATTHEW 13:33

If you've ever baked bread from scratch, you know that every single ingredient
is important. But perhaps none is more important than yeast because without
it, the bread won't rise, and you'll be left with a brick.

Jesus compares the kingdom of heaven to yeast, highlighting how its
influence subtly transforms and permeates everything it touches. We are called
to bring the kingdom of heaven here, now. When Jesus taught His disciples
to pray, He said, "Thy kingdom come, Thy will be done in earth, as it is in
heaven" (Matthew 6:10 KJV). This was a direct reminder that we are to bring
transformation to the world around us.

When Jesus refers to the kingdom of heaven, He's referring to everything
under His authority—that includes everything in heaven and on earth. In this
parable, yeast symbolizes the transformative power of the kingdom of heaven.
Like yeast that works through the entire batch of dough, the kingdom has the
potential to permeate every aspect of our lives, families, and communities.

Yeast works quietly, yet its impact is profound. A small amount of yeast can
leaven a large quantity of dough. Likewise, even the smallest acts of kindness,
love, and faithfulness rooted in the kingdom can have a far-reaching impact.

To bring the kingdom of heaven here and now means living according to
its principles. It means showing love, extending forgiveness, seeking justice,
and serving others selflessly. It means being agents of reconciliation and
peacemakers in a world filled with discord.

*Father, make me a force for the kingdom as You transform me from the inside
out. Amen.*

HISTORY FAVORS THE BRAVE

"Do not be afraid. Stand firm and you will see the deliverance the LORD will bring you today."

EXODUS 14:13

History favors the brave. And while the goal isn't to be famous in a worldly sense, it is to make God's name famous. Bravery and bold faith are markers of courageous Christians. In our current culture, not only is it unpopular to hold to a biblical worldview, but it can also lead to you being censored, being silenced, and even losing your job for expressing your beliefs publicly. Thankfully, the Bible gives us great examples to follow as we stay brave.

Moses, called by God to lead the Israelites out of Egypt, faced unimaginable challenges. As the Egyptian army closed in on the Israelites at the Red Sea, it was a moment of crisis. Moses could have given in to fear and doubt, but instead, he boldly declared that God would deliver His people. Moses' faith in God's power and his courage to stand firm resulted in one of the most remarkable events in history.

David, while just a teenager, showed incredible bravery when he faced the giant Goliath. While the entire army of Israel trembled in fear, David stepped forward, declaring, "You come against me with sword and spear and javelin, but I come against you in the name of the LORD Almighty, the God of the armies of Israel" (1 Samuel 17:45). His bravery secured victory and established him as a man after God's own heart.

History favors the brave because bravery and bold faith are qualities that lead to transformational moments in our lives and in history itself.

Father, help me be bold and brave as I represent You and Your kingdom. Amen.

DIGGING HOLES

"This is what the LORD says:
I will fill this valley with pools of water."

2 KINGS 3:16

Has God ever told you to do something that didn't make sense? Have you ever had that feeling that you needed to do something but didn't understand why in that moment? Well, God told the kings of Israel, Judah, and Edom to dig holes in the dry wilderness. It must have seemed like a complete waste of time, especially since their enemies surrounded them.

At first glance, the command to dig holes in a dry wilderness might seem confusing. However, these holes were a means to an end, a divine strategy to provide water for the armies and animals. God's ways are not always our ways. It takes a step of obedience and faith to take action that doesn't make sense to realize His plan. The kings and their armies obeyed God's seemingly unconventional command to dig holes. They acted in faith. God may guide us in ways that seem unconventional or challenging. Trusting that His wisdom surpasses our understanding is an act of surrender.

Digging holes in a parched wilderness teaches us about God's provision in our desert seasons. Just as He provided water through the holes in the desert, God will meet our needs even in the most challenging circumstances. God faithfully filled the valley with water to refresh His armies.

The kings came together to dig the holes. When facing a common challenge, they set aside their differences and worked together for a shared goal. We must strive for unity within our families, churches, and communities, especially during challenging times. Unity in adversity is our strength.

Father, help me be obedient and faithful to do what You ask, knowing You will keep Your promises. Amen.

NEVER SAY THESE TWO WORDS

He makes me lie down in green pastures,
he leads me beside quiet waters, he refreshes my soul.
He guides me along the right paths for his name's sake.

PSALM 23:2–3

Every morning when I run with my dog, Huxley, I feel like I'm dragging him the entire time. He lags behind me on the leash. One morning, as I tugged on his leash and encouraged him to pick up the pace, God revealed a profound truth: *Your soul is Huxley, and you keep dragging it behind you. You need to stop this crazy pace. Be still. Let your soul catch up.* As I reflected upon what the Lord told me, I realized my problem was two little words I've since deleted from my vocabulary: "I'm busy."

I've heard *busy* can be an acronym that stands for "being under Satan's yoke." Nobody wants to admit they're under Satan's control. When we say we're busy, we think we're in control, but the truth is we're out of control.

Unfortunately, when we are busy, the people whom we love the most suffer the most. Pastor Mark Buchanan said, "Busyness makes us stop caring about the things we care about."[63] Busyness sucks the life out of us.

In the Chinese language, *busyness* is the single pictograph of two characters—heart and killing! Busyness is the undiagnosed disease of our day, and it's robbing us of life. Is it possible to take a step back and embrace the quietness of life? The Lord makes it clear in His Word how to avoid busyness: Waiting. Resting. Stillness. Solitude. The will must be still.

Solitude is the cure for busyness; it will bring health and create space for Jesus to fill. Consistent, constant, and consuming solitude fuels worship and prayer.

Father, may my life be marked with stillness, not busyness. Lead me into a quiet place so You can refresh my soul. Amen.

---

63   Mark Buchanan, *The Rest of God: Restoring Your Soul by Restoring Sabbath* (Nashville, TN: Thomas Nelson, 2006), 48.

THE FAMILY

That is why a man leaves his father and mother and is united to his wife, and they become one flesh.

GENESIS 2:24

As we started to build our family, we worked hard to create a strong sense of identity and belonging. To this day, our group chat is named "We Are Pages." But the biblical family has been under attack for over sixty years. The idea of an intact family—having a father and mother raising kids together—has become the exception, not the norm. And all society is suffering for it.

The family is not a human invention but a divine design; it's the most important structure for human flourishing ever created. And it's critical for the well-being of individuals and society as a whole. The family, with its structure of parents and children, was God's plan for nurturing and raising the next generation in the way of the Lord. It establishes the primary environment where values, morals, and faith are instilled and passed on.

The presence of the father is the single greatest determinant of well-being. The family is considered the cornerstone of a strong, virtuous, and prosperous society. It serves as a training ground for responsible citizenship and contribution.

When both a mom and dad are present, almost every single measurement of human flourishing improves. The family often provides love, acceptance, and belonging. It also creates economic stability, safety, security, and a moral standard of behavior. And families ensure generational connection, passing down traditions and cultural heritage. This continuity maintains a sense of identity and accountability. The family is the primary environment for discipleship and spiritual growth.

Father, help me be a strong and loving presence in my family. Amen.

ARE WE THERE YET?

I'm not saying that I have this all together, that I have it made.
But I am well on my way, reaching out for Christ,
who has so wondrously reached out for me.

PHILIPPIANS 3:12–14 MSG

It happens all the time. The person we think would never blow up their life suddenly does. The businessman who is known for his integrity is embezzling money from his company. A pastor who leads a large church leaves his wife and children to run off with his assistant. Welcome to the sin of maturity. This sin is so subtle people don't realize they are entangled in it until they fall. That is how it is revealed: followers of Christ have great testimonies of faith that others admire; then, suddenly, they do the unthinkable. Others look to them as spiritual leaders, but somewhere on their journey, they stopped growing spiritually.

Maturity implies a finish line, ending point, or destination. But maturity is a process, not a destination. When it comes to spiritual maturity, we so greatly desire it and yet so mistakenly define it. The goal is not to be a professional Christian but an authentic Christian.

What begins as a pure desire to grow in Christ can subtly change into self-reliance and destructive arrogance. Fresh spiritual insight through fervent prayer and Bible study disappears. There is no fresh manna for the day. The sin of maturity manifests itself when someone drives the maturity stake in the ground and screams, "I have arrived!" As a kid, I asked my parents hundreds of times on long car rides, "Are we there yet?" No, we have not arrived yet. Men, keep growing daily.

Father, I recognize I have not arrived. Forgive me for when I've committed the sin of maturity. Amen.

ROWS, CIRCLES, FACES, AND SHOULDERS

Rejoice with those who rejoice; mourn with those who mourn.

ROMANS 12:15

Are you willing to do whatever it takes to finish faithfully? The "win" is to live well, finish well, and die well—to be faithful to the very end. That's why personal connections are key. We need to invest our time in personal relationships and build trust. We need to move from sitting and listing to walking and growing. The four levels of walking and growing are rows, circles, faces, and shoulders. Circles are better than rows. Faces are better than circles. Shoulders are better than faces.

1. Teaching Rows: Going to church and sitting in rows in a sanctuary provides a strong foundation. Teaching and corporate worship is essential for every man. Being part of a local church provides instruction and encouragement. However, this is the start, not the end.
2. Community Circles: There has been a huge swing toward getting people in circles or small groups. This is where open sharing and listening can take place. Circles offer opportunities to connect personally with others and take comfort that we are not alone.
3. Training Faces: Meeting face-to-face with someone who is committed to investing in your life provides great insight and direction. A mentor wants to see you become the person God made you to be and help you navigate life with impact and significance.
4. Powerful Shoulders: When we have someone who will go with us, we have shoulders to lean on through trials, tests, blessings, and victories. God desires for us to experience life together. Walking shoulder-to-shoulder with a trusted friend changes everything.

Father, I desire rows for teaching, circles for community, faces for training, and shoulders for power. Amen.

THE SIGNIFICANCE OF LEGACY

One generation commends your works to another;
they tell of your mighty acts.

PSALM 145:4

Deep within the heart of every person is a passion and desire to live a life that truly matters. We want to make a contribution for Christ and make a difference in the lives of others; we want to leave the world a better place because we lived well and finished well.

Choosing a Life Word helps you leave a legacy that truly makes a difference in this world and lives on long after you're gone. Your Life Word defines you and drives you to live for Christ. It's a one-word vision for your life that inspires you to live your best life and make your greatest impact for the glory of God.

In James 4:14, James said life is short. It's like a vapor that appears and is gone. And because it's short, we are compelled to make the most of it. Ordinary men and women over the years who have lived with conviction left enduring legacies and changed the world. It's fun to consider what their possible Life Words could have been:

The apostle Paul's might have been *grace*.

Mother Theresa's was undoubtedly *compassion*.

William Wallace's was *freedom*.

And perhaps the greatest Life Word was Jesus' *love*.

The journey to find your Life Word will ultimately help shape your destiny and maybe even history.

God has given you only one life, so make every day count. Remember that the power of legacy is all about what you give, not what you get; it's not about you but others. Everyone leaves a legacy, so make your legacy matter.

Father, will You reveal my Life Word to me? I want to leave a lasting legacy. Amen.

DEFINE YOUR POWER

There are different kinds of gifts, but the same Spirit distributes them.
1 CORINTHIANS 12:4

Everybody loves superheroes. When I ask leaders at my events, "If you were a superhero, what would your superpower be?" the number one answer is flying. It's fun to hear them use their imaginations and dream that they could be superhuman.

Although none of us have experienced superpowers, we've all been blessed as Christians with spiritual gifts and strengths. In our book *Life Word* with Jon Gordon, defining your power is the process of identifying your spiritual gifts and strengths, and it is the first part of finding your Life Word, a one-word vision for your life. It's up to us to discover and develop those gifts and use them for God's glory.

Some qualities we receive at salvation—we call these spiritual gifts. There are several passages that list the spiritual gifts, like Romans 12 and 1 Corinthians 12. Taking a spiritual gifts assessment helps you discover your God-given gifts.

In addition to gifts, God has blessed you with strengths and skills that you can develop over time with effort and experience. It's easy to see how God has wired each one of us in unique ways, and it's a beautiful thing when we each use these blessings for the kingdom.

Several questions can help you uncover your gifts and strengths and help you define your power:

- What do you naturally excel at?
- What strengths have you developed over time?
- What gives you joy when you do it?

The gifts and strengths you identify will help you discover your life's legacy. When you combine your power with your purpose and passion, you will leave a positive mark for Christ on others.

Father, help me discover and use the spiritual gifts and strengths You've given me. Amen.

DETERMINE YOUR PURPOSE

"I know the plans I have for you."
JEREMIAH 29:11

Everything in life is designed and made with purpose. You are not an accident. Psalm 139 says we are fearfully and wonderfully made. When you define your power and discover your purpose, your life takes on new meaning and direction.

Most people wrestle with this question: "Why am I here?" Put another way, "What am I made to do?" When we talk about purpose, we're talking about how you can make an impact on others around you. It's a sense of calling and investing in a cause. A calling is when you have a sense that "I'm made for this!" It's when you find the thing to do that makes you feel most alive. You've found your cause when you're able to say, "I'm moved to do something about this!"

Living on purpose is about investing your life in the things that matter most so you live a life of mission and meaning. Determining your purpose is the second part of discovering your Life Word. Purpose gives you a sense of direction and meaning. God reveals your purposes. Here are questions to help you:

- What does the world need?
- What am I made to do to help fill this need?
- What can I do to make a difference?
- What's at risk if I don't do what I am called to do?

Acts 13:36 says after David served God's purposes, David died. God has made you for a reason. He has anointed you to do marvelous and wonderful things. Let Him reveal those things so the legacy you leave will be about Him and not you.

Father, help me discover and live out Your purposes for my life. Amen.

DISCOVER YOUR PASSION

Whatever you do, work at it with all your heart, as working for the Lord.

COLOSSIANS 3:23

Passion is oxygen for the soul. It's also fuel for a well-lived life. No one can accomplish anything great without passion and enthusiasm. Passion is simply what drives and energizes you. It's what motivates you to act. It's the force that gets you out of bed in the morning and keeps you focused to do your best. When you productively direct your passion for the benefit of others, it can change the world for the better. It can fuel you to overcome obstacles and challenges, rebound from disappointment or failure, and fulfill your God-given purposes.

Remember that your ultimate passion should be for the Lord. Psalm 63:1 shows how David pursued God with everything he had; he was a man of God who followed hard after Him.

Discovering your passion is the third and final part of uncovering your Life Word. When you tap into your passion, it gives you the energy you need to live on purpose and maximize your power. Here are questions to help you discover your passion:

- Where do I invest most of my time and energy?
- What matters to me deeply?
- What energizes me to act and motivates me to make a difference?

Passion reminds you that what you're doing is important. God plants seeds of greatness in each of us and waters them with passion.

You will find your Life Word when you define your power, determine your purpose, and discover your passion. And when you have discovered your Life Word, don't let fear or apathy keep you from your destiny.

Father, help me use my passion for Your glory and the good of others. Amen.

YOU FIRST

Don't look out only for your own interests,
but take an interest in others, too.
PHILIPPIANS 2:4 NLT

My friend was watching his two grandkids playing at his house. Six-year-old Sophie turned to her brother, who wanted to play the game first, and explained, "You can go first…after me!" She almost got it right. My friend's heart swelled with pride for half a second. It's a funny story, but a story that highlights the disease of *me*. We are all infected with this hideous disease that others can often diagnose quickly, but we can't see it. I fight this daily, and I desire to switch my battle cry from "Me first!" to "You first!" When we make this switch, we become others focused.

General William Booth, founder of the Salvation Army, understood the importance of putting others first. On December 24, 1910, the Salvation Army was holding their annual staff conference, and he was scheduled to deliver the opening keynote, but failing health prevented him from attending. His assistant suggested that he send a telegram to encourage the staff to continue on. Booth agreed. At the opening session, the moderator announced to the thousands gathered that Booth had sent a telegram. He opened it and read one word: "Others!"

The you-first attitude crushes the selfish, ugly, draining me-first attitude. We become empty vessels for God to do His work. This is the way of the cross. Others are impacted. Others are blessed. Others see the hands and feet of Jesus. We put the love of God in action. Men, we must do this. Others!

Father, I confess I have the disease of me. Convict me when I take on a me-first attitude. Help me be focused on others, not self. Amen.

AFFECTION

Make every effort to add to your faith goodness; and to goodness,
knowledge; and to knowledge, self-control; and to self-control,
perseverance; and to perseverance, godliness; and to godliness, mutual
affection; and to mutual affection, love.

2 PETER 1:5–7

One of the most powerful actions we can take to build close relationships
is expressing affection. Expressing our love and care for another creates a
closeness and trust in relationships. Our culture celebrates toughness and
stoicism, but it's crucial to remember that genuine affection toward others is
not a sign of weakness but a mark of true manhood. Demonstrating affection
to one another draws hearts together and unites.

Genuine affection is a powerful expression that does three key things:

1. Affection strengthens connection. Genuine affection strengthens
   the bonds of brotherhood. When we express love and affection to
   those around us, we deepen our connections and foster a sense of
   unity. Showing affection reminds us we are not alone but part of a
   community that cares for one another.
2. Affection communicates approval. Affectionate gestures, whether
   through words, actions, gifts, or simple acts of kindness, are powerful
   tools for approval. They convey that we value and appreciate one
   another.
3. Affection reflects Christ's love. Our capacity to show genuine affection
   to others reflects the love of Christ in our lives. Christ's love was
   characterized by compassion, kindness, and tenderness. When we
   emulate these qualities by showing affection, our actions speak loudly
   to a world in need of love and compassion.

Toughness and self-reliance are important, but our call to show genuine
affection stands as a countercultural reminder of our calling as men of faith.
Affection is a sign of strength and grows lasting relationships.

Father, help me express genuine affection to those I encounter today. Amen.

ARE YOU READY?

Keep your eyes open, hold tight to your convictions,
give it all you've got, be resolute, and love without stopping.
1 CORINTHIANS 16:13–14 MSG

One of my coaches got the attention of his players by saying, "Ready! Ready! Ready!" It was his way of saying, "Let's go!" I believe, in the same way, God is calling each of us to be ready. We're not just to get ready but to be ready. *Ready* means "prepared for immediate use."

In 1 Corinthians 16:13–14, Paul was commanding us to be ready by doing these five things:

1. Keep your eyes open. Stay alert and ready because the devil prowls around to kill and destroy (1 Peter 5:8).
2. Hold tight to your convictions. Be willing to stand for what you believe (Jude v. 3).
3. Give it all you've got. Give 100 percent all the time—working at it with all your heart (Colossians 3:23).
4. Be resolute. Do not quit because at the proper time, God will bring a harvest (Galatians 6:9).
5. Love without stopping. Smother others in love so they experience the joy of Jesus (1 Peter 4:8).

If we want to be ready, it will take more days of maintenance than days of magnificence. Too many of us skim and go through the motions without making any spiritual investments for long-term impact. This will have us running on spiritual fumes.

Ready is prepared.

Ready is urgent.

Ready is obedient.

Ready is today.

Have you put in the time to be ready? Make an investment. Go deeper. It might be the single most important decision you make. Tomorrow depends on it.

Father, I'm ready to be used by You. Take me deeper and prepare me. Amen.

STOP, DROP, AND REMEMBER

"These stones will always be a memorial for the Israelites."
JOSHUA 4:7 HCSB

Would you rather spend time thinking about the past or the future? For me, I love thinking about the future because I love to talk about what could be and what should be. Who wants to be stuck in the past? Spending time on vision is where I camp out. Yes, evaluating the past can help us get better but only so we can improve the future.

God knows we have trouble remembering His power, promises, and provisions. It has been a problem for us since the beginning. Throughout the Old Testament, God is always reminding His people to stop, drop, and remember. Many times, He reprimanded the Israelites for not remembering.

In Joshua 4, God instructed the Israelites to build two altars of twelve stones after crossing the Jordan. *Memorial* in Hebrew means "to remember." He commanded them to build altars as signs of remembrance. He wanted them to hope in His future promises, but He also wanted them to fully grasp the power of remembering.

God always wants us to remember His faithfulness. It takes discipline to stop, unplug, and step away from the rat race and then to drop to our knees and ask the Lord to reveal His mighty work through prayer. Taking time to remember His goodness, greatness, and graciousness only happens if we stop and pray. It is too easy to keep moving through life looking for God's next blessing.

Before the New Year arrives, stop, drop, and remember. You might be surprised what God reveals to you.

Father, I want to remember Your power, promises, and provisions. Help me remember Your goodness and faithfulness in my life. Amen.

75 HARD

"They all alike began to make excuses."

LUKE 14:18

One year on January 1, I started a program called 75 Hard. It had five daily nonnegotiables: pick a diet and stick to it, do two forty-five-minute workouts (one must be outside), drink a gallon of water, read ten pages, and take a progress picture. If you fail any of these daily disciplines, you start back at day one. It may not sound too hard, but trust me, outside workouts in Colorado with negative temps, snow, sleet, and wind are no picnic.

I failed on day one because I didn't know a gallon of water was 128 ounces. Lesson learned. And I failed again on day thirteen by choice. It was more important to honor a coach who went out of his way to bring me food. (I didn't have the heart to tell him I couldn't eat it; showing appreciation was more important.)

And while the food was a challenge and the workouts were intense, the biggest obstacle was the battle raging in my mind. My warrior voice was loud when I felt rested and had time. But the whiner voice became relentless when I got tired or hungry.

There came a point when training in the snowstorm was empowering. I kept thinking to myself, *No one else is willing to do this.* It became a rallying cry for getting mentally tougher. Seventy-five days later, I knew the sacrifices were worth it. My mental game was forever changed.

Once you start making excuses, it's hard to stop. Excuses grow over time until they become a pattern of how you do life. Excuses lead to mediocrity. But commitment leads to excellence.

Father, help me stop making excuses and follow through on my commitments. Amen.

MY TOP TEN

I always thank my God for you
because of his grace given you in Christ Jesus.

1 CORINTHIANS 1:4

I love ESPN's *SportsCenter Top 10 Plays*. There is something about watching a few minutes of sports highlights that makes me want to lace up the shoes and put on the jersey again. Even though ESPN's top ten list is my favorite, there are many others out there.

At the end of each year, I see lots of top ten lists recapping various things from the past year. This prompted me to start my own list called "Top Ten to Thank This Year." My list focuses on meaningful relationships that have made a significant impact on my life. My list contains friends, coworkers, and some people whom I've never met. Realizing how powerful others' influence has been on my life, I want to let each person know and thank them if I can. "Let me say first that I thank my God through Jesus Christ for all of you, because your faith in him is being talked about all over the world" (Romans 1:8 NLT).

Men, each of us has great capacity to impact and influence others by expressing gratitude. You never know just how much someone might need to hear from you. Your thankful word might restore purpose and passion when someone needs it most. So what are you waiting for? Go and be used by God to be a difference maker. Thank those who have invested in you this year.

Father, thank You for placing others in my path to bless, encourage, and guide me. Help me find the words to thank them. Amen.

WHAT STORY DO YOU WANT TO TELL?

We can make our plans, but the Lord determines our steps.

PROVERBS 16:9 NLT

Are you sad or glad the year is ending? Your answer could be the result of the choices and decisions you made, or circumstances out of your control could determine why it was a good or bad year. As we look back, for most of us, it comes down to the daily choices and decisions we made. We find ourselves on the "Road to Reward" or the "Road to Regret."

The Road to Reward is a satisfying place where you know you've made a difference, built a legacy, developed strong relationships, and established a lasting influence. The Road to Reward is filled with impact, significance, and transformation.

Alternatively, the Road to Regret is the opposite. It's an unsettling place where you wish you had done things differently. You see unrealized potential, missed opportunities, and broken relationships. The Road to Regret is paved with complacency, selfishness, and excuses.

The decisions we make today will determine the stories we tell tomorrow. Proverbs 16:9 reminds us that we have our part and God has His part. We need to press forward, plan, strategize, and set goals, but ultimately, the Lord is going to write our story. Each year is a chapter, and the choices and decisions we make will determine whether the stories are full of reward or regret.

What story do you want to tell at the end of next year? We must be willing to embrace the circumstances God puts us in. I want to tell a God story this time next year. How about you?

Father, I ask for a life-changing breakthrough year. May this upcoming year be the best year ever! Amen.

ONE WORD WILL CHANGE YOUR LIFE

I'm asking GOD for one thing, only one thing.

PSALM 27:4 MSG

Since 1999, I have chosen one word for the upcoming year. That is right—one word. Not a phrase, not a statement, not a resolution, I choose just a single word, a theme.

In life, we tend to drift toward complexity, but we should drive toward simplicity. The one-word exercise has become a focal point throughout the year that brings clarity into a very complex world. The discipline of developing a one-word theme has stretched me in all areas: spiritually, physically, mentally, emotionally, relationally, and financially.

Your one word can be a discipline, fruit of the Spirit, character trait, attribute of God, or even a person. It becomes your filter for the year and will change the way you think, act, and live. Discover your one word in three simple steps:

1. Look In: Prepare your heart. Take action by strategically disengaging from the hectic pace of life to look inside. Eliminating noise and clutter properly prepares the heart.
2. Look Up: Discover your word. Now you are ready to receive your word. Plug in and listen up. Let your word come to you.
3. Look Out: Live your word. Keep your one word front and center throughout the year. Share it with your inner circle of friends and family. Live your word to its fullest.

Pray that God will allow you to be focused on what He has for you. Get fired up to see what the Lord will do in and through you next year.

Father, I ask for a life-changing year. I want to live for You alone. Fill me with Your Holy Spirit. Strengthen me every day next year. Show me one word to guide me. Amen.

ACKNOWLEDGMENTS

Since 1990, we, Dan and Jimmy, have been doing life together. We have truly lived out Proverbs 27:17, sharpening one another, and make no mistake, sometimes that process has been hard, and sparks have flown. But that's the point of the process. You simply cannot become your best without friction and the clashing of swords. Through the valleys and mountaintops, God has always blessed our relationship because we have both committed from the beginning to pursue God together. Thanks to all the hundreds of men who have shaped and molded us through the years. We pray that this book will be a powerful resource to help men love Jesus deeply, to honor God always, and to finish well.

Special thanks to Carlton Garborg, Tim Payne, and so many others at BroadStreet Publishing. Deep, deep appreciation to our editor Danielle Ripley-Burgess for joining us and skillfully organizing and refining our content into a masterpiece.

I, Dan, would like to thank all the men who all have loved, cared, and served me by living out God's wisdom daily: Ed Britton, Elijah Britton, Austin Muck, Garrett Shondelmyer, Steve Britton, Dave Britton, Barry Spofford, John Patton, Scott Steiner, Ward Kinne, Jon Gordon, Kellen Cox, Silas Mullis, Steve Beckerle, Andrew Evans, Holt Condren, Les Steckel, Shane Williamson, Sean McNamara, Mark Stephens, Andriy Kravstov, Jin Kang, Jud Martin, Frank Kelly, Jeff Sutherland, Todd Lalich, and many others!

I, Jimmy, would like to thank all the men who have inspired and guided me to be a strong, loving, authentic man of God: Grandpa Page, my dad, my brother John, my three sons, my wise sage Dan Webster, Lou Santoni, Wade Harman, Steve Erlemeier, Jon Gordon, John Patton, Scott Steiner, Mark Snyder, Dave Mascio, Jason Swain, Mark Walker, Trent Scott, Troy Tate, Kevin Mark, Bryan Kelly, Richie Huffman, Dale Waters, Pete Dixon, Joe Knotts, Wes Mace, Les Steckel, Joe Duke, and many more. And a special thanks to my wife, Ivelisse, for believing I have what it takes, and my daughter, Gracie, for making me want to set the standard for her future husband.

To our heavenly Father who is the creator of wisdom and provides it generously when we ask.

ABOUT THE AUTHORS

DAN BRITTON is a speaker, writer, and coach whose mission is to help people pursue their passion. He serves with the Fellowship of Christian Athletes where he has been on staff since 1990. Dan travels extensively around the world training thousands of leaders and works with over one hundred countries. Dan played professional lacrosse with the Baltimore Thunder, and he still plays and coaches lacrosse and enjoys running marathons, even doing the Boston Marathon twice.

He has coauthored nine books, including *One Word, Life Word, True Competitor, Called to Greatness, WisdomWalks*, and *The Wisdom Challenge*. He is a frequent speaker for companies, nonprofits, sports teams, schools, and churches. Dan has been interviewed by national outlets like Fox News, CBS News, and *Fast Company*. Dan and his wife, Dawn, reside in Overland Park, Kansas, and have three married children and two grandchildren. Follow him on social media @fcadan and email him at dan@fca.org.

JIMMY PAGE is the founder of Be Unstoppable Elite Leadership and the Unstoppable Freedom Alliance. He's a health and wellness expert, freedom warrior, Spartan athlete, podcaster, and former seventeen-year executive with the Fellowship of Christian Athletes. Jimmy is the author of ten books, including *One Word, Life Word, True Competitor, WisdomWalks, Called to Greatness, Strong Girls*, and more. He's an in-demand speaker on leadership, culture, and human performance for conferences, schools, sports teams, churches, and businesses, including the NFL, NCAA, YMCA, Intel, Salvation Army, State Farm, US Naval Academy, OtterBox, Hendrick Motorsports, and many more.

Jimmy is a husband and proud father of four grown kids and resides in Fort Collins, Colorado. He and his wife started a cancer foundation called Believe Big following her victory over cancer. His mission is to inspire you to live the unstoppable life. Visit his website at beunstoppable.live and email him at Jimmy@beunstoppable.live.

BOOKS BY DAN BRITTON
AND JIMMY PAGE

True Competitor: 52 Devotions for Athletes, Coaches, and Parents

Called to Greatness: 31 Devotions to Ignite the Faith of Fathers and Sons

Wisdom Walks: 52 Life Principles for a Significant and Meaningful Journey